Nytewind's Wiccan Way

And the Summerfest Events

Charlyn Scheffelman
(Lady Nytewind)

BALBOA.
PRESS

A DIVISION OF HAY HOUSE

Balboa Press books may be ordered through booksellers or by contacting:

Balboa Press
A Division of Hay House
1663 Liberty Drive
Bloomington, IN 47403
www.balboapress.com
1 (877) 407-4847

Because of the dynamic nature of the Internet, any web addresses or links contained in this book may have changed since publication and may no longer be valid. The views expressed in this work are solely those of the author and do not necessarily reflect the views of the publisher, and the publisher hereby disclaims any responsibility for them.

The author of this book does not dispense medical advice or prescribe the use of any technique as a form of treatment for physical, emotional, or medical problems without the advice of a physician, either directly or indirectly. The intent of the author is only to offer information of a general nature to help you in your quest for emotional and spiritual well-being. In the event you use any of the information in this book for yourself, which is your constitutional right, the author and the publisher assume no responsibility for your actions.

Any people depicted in stock imagery provided by Getty Images are models, and such images are being used for illustrative purposes only.
Certain stock imagery © Getty Images.

Print information available on the last page.

ISBN: 978-1-9822-1509-5 (sc)
ISBN: 978-1-9822-1512-5 (e)

Balboa Press rev. date: 11/06/2018

Here you will find rituals, ideas and events that can enhance your group and your guests' understanding of the practice of Wicca in new ways. Our group combined aspects of astrology and alchemy, drama and "hands on" experiences which we used in nine four-day camp events held in the mountains of Montana. These events were to enhance and further the understanding of the beautiful pagan religion of Wicca and share all with the public. I now invite you to take what you can and use it for your own group or public event.

Religiousness

What would you say to a witch such as me?
Would you just say "Well, that couldn't be?"
Would you say I must be delusional at best?
Or that I must be speaking in jest?

Do you believe in magick, I'd say?
(real magick always ends with a "k")
Do you believe that prayers can come true?
Perhaps that's the same as magick to you.

Spells of magick are prayers too, you know,
(Perhaps including a good bit of show.)
For prayers to work, and magick, too
The emotional impetus must come from _you_.

We both might light a candle, it's true,
But yours might be white and my candle blue.
You might gaze upon an icon of Christ,
And I at a five-pointed star incised.

You might inhale incense in a holy place,
And I burn my own, in my sacred space.
We chant and sing, sometimes even dance,
(I'll bet you'd enjoy it if you had the chance.)

Whatever we do, it must be for good
Never for ill; neither of us would.
For though I don't fear burning in Hell,
I mind the three-fold law in each spell,

Which states that whatever you send or you do
Will then be returned three-fold to you.
So no true witch would send any harm,
Nor influence another by speaking a charm.

Both of us cherish and love the Divine,
Whatever you call it; yours, or mine.
For though we might on some things disagree,
I say we agree on much more than you see.

— Charlyn Scheffelman

CONTENTS

Appendices: SummerFest

INTRODUCTION

It took me a long time to find Wicca, but when I did, I knew it was, for me, my true Religion: the spiritual path that felt just right for me. I felt compelled to write about that journey, and wrote a book called *My Strange Life: Diary of a Witch,* and I thought I was done.

Then one day my daughter said to me "you need to write another book." I looked at her and said, "I don't have anything more to say."

But the Universe seemed to have different ideas about that, and soon I received a "download" of the chapter headings you will find in this book. I learned so much the ten years that I spent in Las Vegas as a school teacher, because I found Wicca and two wonderful groups of people; one offering classes in Wicca held by a wonderful Priestess and sincere teacher, and another whose group wrote and performed the most beautiful rituals I could ever imagine. Their Priests and Priestesses were seriously committed to the path and were a blessing to find. I attended both for several years.

I wanted to share with people in Montana after I retired from teaching. My husband and I didn't want to retire in Vegas, so we moved back to Montana. I established Mountain Moon Circle and began teaching Wicca, Astrology, and a little Alchemy for the next fifteen years.

Okay, I thought, I do have a somewhat different perspective on Wicca because, for me, it dovetails perfectly with what I know about Astrology and Alchemy. Also, Mountain Moon Circle had established SummerFest, a 3-day camp in the mountains of Montana that incorporated the principles and practices of Jeff McBride's *Alchemical Fire Circles.* These were so healing, so life-changing and amazing, that I just had to bring them to Montana for my group as well. They were the basis for the camp, but the theme for each camp was one of the five elements and the goal was also to promote more understanding of Wicca.

As I am well into my Crone years, it seems it is time to share, so the appendices in this book contain all nine years of rituals, installations, and workshops we (Mountain Moon Circle) created for those camps. I could not have done this without my daughter, the one that comes up with a solution when I am stuck – that supports all that I do, and that loves me even when I'm a little crazy. Also, I could not have done it without the help and support of my circle members, who learned to dance, spin fire, drum, and apply their dramatic and musical skills with sincere devotion to this work.

And none of this could have happened without the amazing, incredibly healing Alchemical Fire Circles created by good friend Jeff McBride, who wears two hats: the professional magician, "The Earning Man," and the true magician, "The Burning Man," who developed this process that has helped so many people heal and improve their lives.

Thank you, Jeff!

CHAPTER ONE
The True Witch

I hear my ancestors in the call of the drum
Say to my heart, "Come! Just come!"
The God-forms await, their magick to bring
So come to the circle; dance and sing.

Much of what I've written comes from my heart and my memories of at least one previous lifetime as a witch. Some things will not be found in other Wiccan books because I look at things a bit differently. Also, I want to relate things that I know in my soul to be true – my truth, which may, or may not, resonate with you.

What does it mean to be a witch in these more modern times? It means you have found the belief system that speaks to your heart – what you know, and feel, to be true; for which you may have searched for a long, long time. Being a witch takes a commitment; of time, of energy, and of service, for witches are not Halloween characters that have nothing but ill will in their hearts; nor are they worshipers of any kind of devil or negative deity.

What are we then, or what should we strive to be? Many of us have been part of the old religion in past lives, for the Wiccan belief includes reincarnation. Many of us remember, and many of us are called by the love of this planet and all its beings. Many of us hold this blue and green world, its plants and its creatures, to be holy; a marvel of life, of cycles, and of love.

We stand in a circle as did our ancestors all around the world. We clap, sing, dance, and drum to call in joy and positive energy. We call to our deities, all those included in the archetypes that Carl Jung wrote of; that exist in every culture, in every ancient (and not so ancient) land. The names vary, as do the languages used, but the archetypes are recognizable no matter what part of the world you are in.

We vow to meet "in love and trust," as a group that supports each other. Ideally, we do not judge, though we are still only human, and must realize that we will sometimes make stupid human mistakes. If you have ever been part of any kind of group, you know what I mean – that humans have an extreme problem getting along with each other! I fear that until we outgrow the need to judge each other, we will not advance spiritually on this planet.

Wars are still being fought over religion, and though the witch-burning days are (mostly) over, I would not be surprised if they resurfaced. Many today will believe that if disaster comes to our planet, it will be a Christian God taking revenge on those who did not follow him that are the cause, and his servants will carry out the hate, torture and execution we have endured in the past. Still even today in countries such as Africa, people are accused of being Witches and are killed.

Too often, enemies are defined by their religious beliefs, and groups of people, including men, women, and children, are obliterated. This is or has happened in many parts of the world, and it could happen again in these United States. I hope that I don't live to see it. And at seventy-five years of age, I might not.

The Wiccan way is a way of transformation; of moving beyond petty concerns, of purifying our souls, learning to love when hate would be easier. It is also a path of improving our soul's growth; not through fear of some punishment in the world or in the afterlife, but through a genuine need to be the best we can be in this life, under the circumstances of this life in which we find ourselves this present incarnation.

This is not a new philosophy. If you've ever become acquainted with the work of the Alchemists, you will find even their goals to be the same. For hundreds of years (at least), some people have realized that you cannot change matter unless you first change yourself. Each phase of the alchemical cycle is meant to purify and improve one's character and way of being. So is, for the witch, the opportunity given through each cycle of the earth's year to improve oneself.

CHAPTER TWO

The Circle of 8

Wheel of the Year
Behold, the Wheel!
Ever changing, never ending
Eight portals of the year attending!
Marking days and passing time
To honor the Lord and Lady sublime

The Wiccan calendar includes eight holidays, or Sabbats – one every six weeks. In an era when people were living off of the land, these occasions would be welcome reliefs from daily toil that gave people opportunities to socialize and celebrate.

This would also mark the periods of time that signified a change in attitude and season; two of them mark the Solstices and two others the Equinoxes. These were very important to the Germanic people. The other four, falling halfway between those dates, were important dates to the Celtic people. During the mixing or conquering of countries and people, I think that the two dovetailed perfectly into the eight.

Whether or not all eight were celebrated by any ethnic group, today the Pagan Wheel of the Year consists of both calendar systems. Some dates have been changed slightly in modern times, probably to be more convenient for work and religious reasons.

These cycles can be interpreted and used in three different ways; the cycle of the Earth, the cyclic life of the Gods and Goddesses, and as a guide for our human cycle; or how we can live in accord with the natural world.

(I know that this interpretation may not be consistent with most books, but I am relating to you what makes the most sense to me and which aligns with Astrology.)

The Cycle of the Earth: Samhain (sow-in) – October 31- November 1: **Death**

Begins the year at Hallows Eve
Departed ones we meet and grieve
Looking deep within our hearts
As the Sun King thus departs.

Samhain, (Halloween, Day of the Dead, Shadowfest) is the beginning of the Wiccan calendar – our New Year. At this time, the crops are gathered in and, in northern climates, wintertime is cold and vegetation is mainly dormant. It is the time of rest for the Earth and for some of its creatures. The ones that remain awake through the winter face surviving the hardships of snow, storms, winds, and ice.

In the tradition in which I was trained, before all the popular books became available, I was taught that this was about death. I have most often seen it called a harvest festival, but by this time, the crops have already been gathered in or would be lost. This was, however, the time when the animals needed for winter food were slaughtered. To me though, this is not harvest; it is defiantly death.

Of the Gods:

The Sun God has returned to the underworld to await his resurrection at Yule. The Goddess has taken the form of the Crone, the Wise One, and the Keeper of the Mysteries. She is not evil, she is not cruel, but she does represent the end of the cycle. She is the bringer of death, whether it be the death of a plant, animal, or human. Without death, the cycle could not renew.

Death, however, is what humans' fear, so many have made of her an evil hag. This is also the time when the veil between the spirit world and our physical world is thin, and it is from this tradition that the present day holiday includes ghostly images and creatures from the "otherworld" beyond the physical realm.

Of Humans:

For Wiccans, this is the time to remember the ancestors and those family members and friends that have completed their lives on this planet. We honor and commune with them now, as the "veil" between our dimension and the spirit world is thinnest and we feel particularly close to the spirit world.

Often our Wiccan celebrations include a "dumb supper." This is a feast given for departed loved ones who have been invited by the High Priestess at the request of the guests. She invites the spirits through a thirteen-day meditation on their picture or name previous to the Dumb Supper.

The table is set with a place for each attendee and an unoccupied place across the table for their spirit guest. Once the sacred space has been made impenetrable to unwanted guests, the invited spirits are called in. The supper is observed as a silent communication between each guest and the spirit called for them. Food is offered that appeals to the spirit world, but emotions run so deep, that little or no food is actually consumed by the participants.

From Samhain to Yule, we enter a time of contemplation, though we also have to show up at our jobs and maintain our everyday lives. We use various methods of divination to help us plan for the next cycle. Whether the answers come from divine beings or from our own subconscious, it makes no difference. The task is to find the path that is best for us and the growth of our souls in the coming new cycle.

We are also called upon to forget the plans made in the past; the hopes and wishes that did not come to fruition in the past year, and to let them go without regret or unease.

The Cycle of the Earth: Yule – December 21-22: **Birth**

Until the Yule, when He returns
As light within to flicker and burn.
We search our souls through darkest night
And seek the answers to our plight.

Generally, the top spoke of the wheel represents Yule, (Winter Solstice, and Solstice Night), which occurs around the 21st of December. This point in time has always been referred to as the darkest night, as it is the longest night of the year. The Sun has completed its journey south (if you are in the Northern hemisphere), then slowly begins to retrace that journey, increasing the hours of daylight by 4 minutes of arc each day. Though the weather may still be very cold, the world is moving toward warmth, which precedes the birthing of new life in the plant and animal world.

Of the Gods:

In the mythology of the Gods, this significant change is interpreted as the Birth of the Sun King, or Sun God. The physical Sun seems to pause for three days under the "Grand Cross" constellation in the sky, where its movement is imperceptible. But by December 25th, its movement, now northward, becomes observable again, and so the previously sacrificed God is reborn. Many pagans stay awake on the longest night to greet the sunrise in the morning to celebrate this event. The birth of the Sun God is the beginning of the cycle.

Obviously, this Pagan holiday has been given a new suit of clothes, and the Sun King has become the Son of God instead of the Sun God. When introducing a new religion, such as that of Christianity and of Catholicism in particular, it is always easier to keep the observance of the important holiday celebrations more or less intact in order to appease, convert and sway the people.

Never overshadowed, though, it is the Goddess that reigns supreme in most Pagan traditions. Her role as Mother is most important as she births the new Sun each Winter Solstice. Christianity, which is obviously male oriented, downgraded the Goddess to become the rather unimportant vessel that birthed the Savior, Mother Mary. Yet they kept her statues in their churches for obliterating her completely would have upset the people.

Of the Humans:

This occasion marks the end of a period of meditation and contemplation – the quiet winter during which one plans for the spring. These plans included more than planting crop, though. They include planning one's life.

Since most of us do not farm these days, we may not be planning our field of dreams in the same way as our ancestors did, but we will be laying plans for what we want to "grow" in our lives. We need to have goals in mind for the next growth cycle.

These goals can be whatever you want or need – a new career, better health, more love, etc., but how can you achieve anything without a plan? What physical steps will you need to take to bring this plan to fruition? Hopefully, you have sought guidance and information from the divine previous to the Darkest Night.

On a more mundane level, we engage in other activates during these dark times. These include all kinds of crafts; needlework, candle making, writing and creative activities, as well as getting our "house" in order; which means anything that needs organizing or decluttering in order to move forward with a "clean slate".

The Cycle of the Earth: Imbolc – Feb 1-2; **First Fertility Festival** *(I think this was originally Jan. 31.)*

> *He strengthens and grows with Imbolg's approach*
> *This Goddess welcomes with no reproach.*
> *And hope begins to lighten the land*
> *As fertile flocks and fields are planned*

Six weeks after Yule comes the Sabbat of Imbolc (Oimelc, St. Brigit's Day, Candlemas, Imbolg). Though the Sun has been steadily moving north since Yule, it is not until about six weeks later that the morning light arrives noticeably earlier.

The fertility of the Earth becomes apparent during the next six weeks in both flocks and fields. New life makes its way into the world as new lambs and other animals are born. Oimelc translates to the fresh milk now available from sheep that have given birth.

New green plants become available for consumption, and we celebrate the fertility of the Earth as their seeds burst forth. As the green things start to show their tender leaves, the cold, though not willingly, begins to give way to warmer days.

Of the Gods:

In Wicca, the Goddess is always present, though she is triple in form (Mother, Maiden, or Crone). She gave birth as Mother at Yule, but now has regained her youth and has become the Maiden. The Maiden brings the promise of new life, fertility, love enthusiasm and joy to the Earth.

The God has quickly grown into a young adult (who says it has to take years?) and love is in the air! This tradition has been hidden in plain sight as Valentine's Day. (In old English, a V was pronounced as "G", and this date was originally "Galantine's Day", from the old term for a gallant and handsome young man who woos the young ladies).

One Goddess stands out as the primary deity of this holiday, and that is the Celtic Goddess, Bridget (Breed, Brighid). Most pagans believe that this Goddess has been appropriated by the Christian church to become <u>Saint</u> Brigit, and her reputation as the "bringer of the light" worked well for adapting this holiday; now called Candlemas.

In Jewish tradition, a woman was considered "unclean" for six weeks after the birth of her child and was not allowed in the temple during this time. Since Mary was once again pure, she was able to enter the temple with her son, Jesus.

Of the Humans:

This holiday has retained the importance of the growing light and is celebrated as such through candles and candle-making. Though recognized as Candlemas in Catholicism, it is not widely celebrated in other faiths. However to Pagans, it is time to bless the seeds, both physical and emotional, that we intend to plant. Physical seeds may be planted indoors; others blessed for planting in the garden later.

Emotionally, we continue to develop plans for our lives, using the information gleaned during the dark time. We light many candles to celebrate returning light. We might even begin to initiate some projects or ideas toward our goals.

The Cycle of the Earth: Ostara – March 21-22: Second Fertility Festival

Oestara brings the promise of life,
And dreams abound to overcome strife.
We bless the creatures and the Earth
As the cycle continues of life and birth

Someone once said to me that Pagan holidays were disgusting because they were about fertility, and she certainly didn't need to celebrate that! I didn't say anything, but if this planet were not fertile, none of the plants or animals would be here. Neither would we!

Ostara (Also known as the Vernal Equinox, Alban Eiler, Lady Day) is a celebration of spring and new life. It is, for pagans, our "Easter." Some of the pagan symbols (eggs, bunnies, etc.) that represent fertility are still seen and used on the Christian holiday of Easter, a name that originated as Eostre, or Ostara, a Goddess of spring in the Germanic lands.

As the days become longer and the weather warmer, we see signs of life everywhere. Early flowers bloom, and spring grasses and herbs show their green. Buds on trees and birds making nests are all signs that the Mother is once again in charge. The urge to procreate is strong in the animal kingdom as well.

Of the Gods:

This is the Spring Equinox and a time of burgeoning love between the Maiden and the Young Sun God. She becomes pregnant with the babe that will be born the next Yule as the new Sun God, resurrected. It is a time of light and love, of nature and its blessings.

Of the Humans:

The same urges affect the human population on the planet as those in nature. Poets echo that theme in phrases such as "in the spring, a young man's fancy turns to love." Of course, this results in many pregnancies. In earlier times, pregnancy was looked upon as fortunate, for if the woman you desired proved to be fertile, there would be offspring to take care of the fields and chores, and to take the place of aging parents. A pregnant bride was a fortunate thing.

Many of us are "mothering" the indoor seedlings or new born animals at this time. It originally was a time to show off the new clothes that had been made during the winter months, but most people now buy them "ready-made," and even Easter parades are dwindling.

> *We honor the fairies and Otherworld creatures,*
> *And welcome the Green Man with foliate features.*
> *As Beltane fires burn, we salute the Spring,*
> *The divine couple and all that they bring.*

This Sabbat (Bealtaine, May Day, Roodmass) celebrates fertility as well. The calendar date for Easter changes, supposedly because of a political compromise among Nicaea's gathered factions. According to the Encyclopedia Britannica, in 325 A.D., the emperor Constantine I, an unbaptized catechumen, presided over the opening session and discussions held to solve the problems created in the Eastern church by Arianism, a "heresy" proposed by Arius of Alexandria that affirmed that Christ was not divine but was a normally created being.

It was also to determine what works were to be included in the Bible and to resolve other issues in order to establish church policy. The Eastern Bishops injected the irregular phases of the moon into the calculations of this holiday. They wanted the lunar calendar to keep its historical (though problematic) role in determining important dates.

However, I think it more likely that the Church fathers did not want to celebrate the resurrection of Jesus while the pagans were celebrating the "resurrection" of the Sun God as the old holiday, Ostara. Hence, Easter is scheduled to fall after the first full moon after the Equinox. (Full moons are Pagan celebrations and are to be avoided as well). In that way, they could disassociate the resurrection of Jesus from the spring pagan holiday, which honors the resurrection of life on Earth.

Of the Gods:

This is the official wedding of the God and Goddess, whose child is now growing in her womb. It is a commitment to take care of the Earth and its children; to bring the sun and the rain in sufficient quantity to benefit the crops and wild things, and to nurture and bring them all to fruition. Their marriage insures their commitment to this task.

Of the Humans:

The hard work in the fields has begun, and, those of us not in the fields must take physical action toward reaching the goals we have set. One cannot expect magick to work without putting forth effort! Our efforts show the divine that we are serious and committed to do our best, to achieve the goals we have envisioned. In this way, we "tend our gardens," or work diligently to accomplish our will.

The Cycle of the Earth: Litha – June 21-22: **The First Harvest**

The Sun King is strong and energy high
The daylight long when Litha comes nigh.
Tend to your crops—whatever they be
And harvest the first of your fields merrily

The Summer Solstice marks the beginning of summer and the time of growth and abundance. This is the First Harvest, for early greens and berries; even peas are ready to eat. With the sun at its zenith, the days are warm and the earth is full of new life – baby animals, early plants, trees dressed in green: it is time to appreciate all that has been given to humanity – and to remember that we, too, are the Earth's caretakers.

We do not have "dominion" over nature. By adopting that attitude, humanity has pillaged the Earth and its resources. Plants and animal species are disappearing all over the world because of the infringement of humans and the disregard for the habitat of other life forms. Will the day come when we have nothing to eat? Most probably

Of the Gods:

On this day, the sun reaches its full potential in northern climes. The mature Sun God is free and unbounded, happy, supportive, generous, educating and illuminating, most beautiful in his purest light. But after this day, He begins to retreat southward. In the myths of the Gods, he is seen as weakening, which is often dramatized as a battle between himself and the Dark Lord, the Guardian of the Underworld.

Sometimes this is portrayed as his death, but the more appropriate theme, I think, is that in which he is wounded. From that wound on, he will weaken and die, sacrificing himself so the cycle can continue. Just as plants must die to release their seed for the next generation, the Sun God willingly dies to be reborn anew. The Goddess, on the other hand, is now Earth Mother, still full of life and abundance.

Of the Humans:

We still must pursue our goals by taking the actions needed. This is no time to give up, for the growing season has a long way yet to go. We continue to ask for guidance and assistance from the Divine Ones, and thank them for all they have already given. We may have noticed some benefits have come our way from the early harvests that have matured.

The Cycle of the Earth: Lughnassadh – July 30 - August 1: Second Harvest

The burning of Lugh and the first harvest bread
Mark Lughnasadh with joy--and the Sun King with dread
As he grows weaker, the light to wane,
He gravely foresees the end of his reign.

Some of the grain fields, particularly wheat, and many other plants and herbs are ready to harvest. Nature's bounty becomes available to all that inhabit this planet, but nature is not always kind. Storms, droughts, winds, and fire are also part of her plan.

Of the Gods:

This Sabbat is named for the God Lugh particularly. Legend says that Lugh sacrificed himself and poured his spirit into the grain so that life could continue. His mother, who died of exhaustion after clearing the plains of Ireland for agricultural use, requested a festival in Lugh's honor. There were funeral games (much like today's Olympics) during which a truce was called from whatever wars were going on; horse races, storytelling, trading, music, and games took place. Laws were proclaimed and legal disputes were settled at this time as well. Today this season is still the time for craft fairs and competitions in our modern world.

Of the Humans:

Some of the work, especially for those of us who do not farm or garden, is suspended for vacations and travel; for attending those fairs and markets, sightseeing, enjoying the summer weather and having time with family. Our work toward our goals is not finished, however, and we try to keep our eyes on the prize as well.

The Cycle of the Earth: Mabon – September 21-22: Third Harvest

We give thanks for all that has been
Knowing the wheel must turn yet again.
Now light and dark even, the ageing King fades,
The fields soon lie fallow, the darkness pervades.

This is the Autumnal Equinox, with daylight and darkness in balance. The harvest season draws to a close, and signs hint of the coming of fall. The animals that store their food for the winter have been busy, and most blooming things drop their seeds. Some days are crisp and some still warm, but winter is approaching.

Of the Gods:

This holiday is the Wiccan Thanksgiving. For the most part, the harvest has been brought in and the yields have been preserved. It is time to give thanks to the God and Goddess for all that we have reaped. But also at this time, the Sun God succumbs to the wounds he suffered on Summer Solstice. His death is mourned, but his sacrifice is necessary. He enters the underworld (or the womb of the Goddess) to await his rebirth at Yule.

The present date for this holiday was set by President Lincoln. This decision makes no sense. If the harvest isn't in before this time, it would be lost. Also, in earlier times, travel to join with others in celebration would have been difficult at best.

Of the humans:

The growing season has ended, the harvest reaped and, hopefully, you have preserved food or stocked up for the coming winter. If you have not reached your other goals by this time, they will probably not come to fruition until, perhaps, the next cycle. Physically, we ready ourselves for the coming cold of winter; buy new boots, put away summer things, and stock up our library and supplies for winter projects and food. It is time to clean the house and yard before the cold comes.

Constant through all, the Goddess is nigh,
Her symbol, the moon, marks the time in the sky.
Her influence guides us throughout the year,
Her love and her magick always are near

This concludes the Cycle of the Great Year and explanation of the major celebrations of the Wiccan faith. Of course, the moon has its' own roughly 30 day cycle, and rituals are often performed to the Goddess in accord with her waxing and waning cycle. In general, rituals (or spells) for getting rid of something are performed when the moon is waning. Rituals (or spells) to bring something into your life are performed when the moon is waxing. Rituals honoring and thanking the Goddess herself are often performed when the moon is full.

CHAPTER THREE
The Trinity

In ancient times, women were the givers of life and were held in high esteem and worshiped as Goddesses. Most historians often say that early humans did not understand the connection between sex and reproduction. Pregnancy would often result, but not consistently, and indications were not immediate. Therefore, the cause was not easily established, and birth was a miracle achieved only by women.

I strongly disagree with part of this idea. Our ancestors were not stupid. They hunted and raised animals. I'm sure they recognized the act that, for animals, only took place certain times of the year, and discerned the results. Also, archeologists are continually finding that these ancient people were capable of much more than they have been given credit for in the past.

So I'm quite sure they knew what caused pregnancy. However, monogamy was not the norm. Sex was not sinful; it was a natural act – even considered a holy act, which was even often performed in a holy ceremony with the Priestesses of the Temples. Therefore, you might not know the identity of the father, but you would always know who the mother was. Heredity was matrilineal, and (now) can be traced most effectively through matrilineal DNA. Women were obviously seen as the creators of life and were thus revered.

Statuary found all over the ancient world was generally voluptuous; possibly depicting fertile mothers. But many scientists have recently decided that these were **not** Goddesses. This assumption was made because many statuettes were broken and thrown into dumps, (so they must not have been holy). Could it be that men do not want to recognize the Supreme God as a Female Goddess?

Of course, what they do not understand is that an object made with magickal intent (prayer) is very often broken and discarded when that prayer is answered.

Some examples of these statues are:

- The Venus of Hohle Fels (also known as the Venus of Schelklingen; She is an Upper Paleolithic figurine carved from a mammoth tusk; found in 2008 near Schelklingen, Germany. It is dated to between 35,000 and 40,000 years ago and is associated with the earliest presence of Cro-Magnon people in Europe. It is the oldest undisputed example of a human yet discovered. Hundreds of them have been found. They all look alike, so are not portraits.
- The Venus of Dolní Věstonice: is a ceramic statuette (29,000–25,000 BCE) that was found at the Paleolithic site Dolni Věstonice in the Moravian basin south of Brno. This figurine, together with a few others from nearby locations, is the oldest known (recognized) ceramic article in the world.
- The Willendorf woman (used to be the called Willendorf Venus) is 25,000 years old at least. It is Paleolithic Period, also known as the "Old Stone Age" which started around 30,000 BCE.
- Why more women statuettes? Why large breasts and bellies? Why nude? The answer to these questions seems simple to me. The answer, of course, is that they were symbols of fertility. Well-fed and voluptuous females. Again, If the world (and its people) is not fertile…
- Ancient Sumerian texts, (the first known written language) reveal that women's rights were equal or superior to men; they owned property and governed. Ancient societies were often matriarchal.
- One more find I'd like to mention because it defies current ideas of evolution and history (both of which need to change) is the one inch clay statue found in Napa, Idaho during a well-drilling operation at a depth of 320 feet in 1889. This depth would appear to place its age about two million years ago; far before the traditional date for the arrival of man in this part of the world. It is sex neutral, so probably not a religious item, but very interesting.

So what changed? Around 4-5000 years ago, the stories (though not written down until 2000 years later) begin to change. Some historians (such as James DeMeo, Ph.D. and author of the book *Saharasia: The 4000 BCE Origins of Child Abuse, Sex-Repression, Warfare and Social Violence, In the Deserts of the Old World,*) say that the geographical record shows a climate change around 4000 BCE that led to famine in the Sahara, Arabian Peninsula, and what are now the Central Asian deserts.

They've deduced that tribes began warring with each other over the availability of food, which is probably true. If this is the case, armies would be very necessary, and armies are generally patriarchal structures. Strong leaders and warriors would be necessary in order to conquer others and secure food sources and territory from them.

Another theory claims that invaders, wars, and conquests produced stories stating that the God, Marduk (Babylonia) or Asur (Asserya) murdered the respective Goddess and became head deity in her place. Thus, survival, famine, starvation, and mass-migrations related to land-abandonment would severely traumatize the originally peaceful and sex-positive inhabitants of those lands. This could result in abandonment of the original matriarchies in favor or patriarchal forms of society.

Domination by men of women is found in the Ancient Near East as far back as 3,100 BCE, as are restrictions on a woman's reproductive capacity and exclusion from "the process of representing or the construction of history". With the appearance of the Hebrews, there is also "the exclusion of woman from the God-humanity covenant". Laws changed concerning the rights of women. For instance, Hebrew law stated that if a woman who was married or betrothed was raped, she must be killed.

Not everyone is aware of the story of Lilith, the first woman, which makes Eve Adams' second wife. The story, which comes to us from Ancient Samaria, claims that Lilith was created exactly the same way as Adam; from clay. She, however, did not like being subservient to him and left Eden. She bore many children, and, according to the Bible, they were demons. Eve, then, was created FROM Adam, and, I am guessing, was obedient – until she ate the apple. Hard to keep those darn women down...

Who determined that the Bible was holy – the word of God? Again, it was the council of Nica in 325 C.E. Why? To gain control of the people and settle disputes and claims that any other religion was valid.

When Christian bishops convened in Nicaea at the request of the Roman Emperor Constantine, there were several goals they wanted to accomplish: 1.

Settle the issue off the nature of the Son of God and his relationship to God the Father, 2. Construct the first part of the Creed of Nicaea, 3. Establish uniform observance of the date of Easter, and 4. Seek clarification of early canon law.

Of interest to me, since I am a member of the Unitarian Universalist Association, is the two bishops who did not agree with what was being decided by the council. One left and founded the Unitarians, and the other left to found the Universalist movement. In the 1960's these two factions still existed and combined to form one organization.

A prominent Greek General, Meno, said, in the Platonic dialogue in Classical Greece, concerning men: *"man's virtue is this—that he be competent to manage the affairs of his city, and to manage them so as to benefit his friends and harm his enemies, and to take care to avoid suffering harm himself."*

But of women, he said *"Virtue of women: the duty of ordering the house well, looking after the property indoors, and obeying her husband.*

Even the mythology changed! Zeus impregnated a human woman, Semele, but she died. He managed to rescue the fetal Dionysus from her womb, stitched him into his thigh and kept him there until he was ready to be born. His birth from Zeus conferred immortality upon him, but also suggested that women were not important or necessary; even for reproduction!

Patriarchy overtook civilization, and women were demoted and no longer divine. Female babies were killed or allowed to die in several societies even unto today! Sex was no longer a holy act, but a privilege to be taken by men whenever they wanted it.

However, as we move into the Aquarian Age, we see a growing trend toward acknowledging women as men's equals. The pendulum may swing too far, as it usually does when a change comes about, but will hopefully find balance between the sexes.

Revelation or Fantasy?

When I was young, probably in Jr. High, I was shown in the middle of the night that our solar system is very similar to an atom. Atoms are supposed to be the building blocks of matter; but they are primarily energy, with vast spaces between the charged particles. I was shown that our whole existence, our solar system, could actually be compared to electrons circling the nucleus of an atom in a molecule of something else – perhaps in some giant's leg, who was striding across HIS universe. (Today's scientists are still discovering new things about the atom.)

I think the point was, that we do not have an understanding of who or what we are, but the important thing to know is that WE are also primarily ENERGY. So how could we even attempt to accurately define the concept of God?

Regaining the Goddess: Three aspects

I think (and hope) that most Witches understand that the Gods and Goddesses of mythology are symbols of a higher power that we CAN connect with, but in order to do so, we need to give them a form we can relate to. That could be man, woman, animal or mythological creature. Through these approachable forms, we can communicate, exchange love, share emotions, and respectfully request assistance; for our physical needs, for our spiritual needs, and for emotional support and healing. We will probably never know their true forms, if they even have one.

Therefore, throughout the ages, each culture has symbolized and named beings far more powerful than our human selves by giving them basically human forms. We are defiantly not the top of the heap, folks. In fact, we humans have a long way to go.

In paganism, the Goddess was immortal – she changes form but never dies. The God, her consort, dies each year, sacrificing himself for the greater good, but is reborn each year on Winter Solstice (Yule).

The Maiden:

- Triple Goddess in Maiden form corresponds to the Waxing Moon and generally to spring and early summer.
- She is a young woman; innocent, joyful, talented, excitedly ready to discover all life has to offer.
- "Maiden" does not refer to sexual virginity. She is independent, having rights equal to men. She is in love with love. The choice for marriage, or sex, is hers.

The Mother:

- She is the eternal giver of life. Before patriarchal gods appeared, the Goddess was revered in her aspect as Creatrix. After all, if there's a Father God...wouldn't it be appropriate to have a Mother Goddess too? I've never been convinced of the "Holy Spirit's" supposed identity, whatever that is and wherever it came from, but to me, father, mother, and son/daughter gods would be more reasonable.

- The Mother is the nurturing, protective warm energy that surrounds us in love and comfort in our darkest hour. She will fight for us when we need it most.
- Older than in her Maiden form and more mature, heavy with child, or the Mother with children all around her...trailing behind her or sitting on her hips. She watches over women's' and animals' fertility, and nature in general.
- She is the Full Moon, the summer, and fall. She represents the fields ripe with grain and ready to be harvested. Every culture in the world has had some type of Mother Goddess in their belief system, even unto ancient times.

The Crone:

- The Maiden is about beginnings, the Mother, about maturity, but the Crone is about endings. This is causes fear for some because she makes us unavoidably face death.
- The Crone is revered as a regent of the Underworld, where souls went to rest between incarnations before coming back to the earthly plane.
- Later, this underworld was associated with hell, and the old woman was seen as evil, (thanks to Hollywood and other religions).
- This Goddess guides us during this last phase of our lives, old age, but also gives us wisdom and understanding of the mysteries if we are willing and able.
- She is the dark moon and the keeper of magick.
- The Goddess is always present but changing, taking the form of Maiden, Mother, or Crone at will.

The God:

- In Pagan traditions, the God is the consort of the Goddess, necessary for the creation of life, including all growing things on the Earth. He is the Father, the Protector, and the Wise Man, or Sage.

- He begins his life at Yule, grows strong to maturity and the height of his strength and power through the first half of the year. He is responsible for preparing all for harvest.
- He is not invulnerable and sustains an injury in battle at Summer Solstice.
- He dies on the Autumnal Equinox, willingly sacrificing himself, but returns to the womb of the Goddess to be born again at Yule. He is eternal but cyclical.
- Other Gods in each pantheon occupy the roles of warriors, keepers of the wild, wise sages, philosophers, protectors and more, but they are seen as separate entities than the one who is the Goddesses consort.

CHAPTER FOUR
The Mighty 4

For thousands and thousands of years, our ancestors all around the world have gathered to stand in a circle; to clap, sing, drum, and dance; to call in joy and positive energy. They called to their deities, who represented all the archetypes that Carl Jung wrote about, which was based upon; refined ideas from Immanuel Kant's categories, Plato's ideas, and Arthur Schopenhauer's prototypes.

Joseph Campbell found these to be universal in the mythic tales told in every culture and every ancient (and not so ancient) land. The names vary, as do the languages used, but the archetypes are recognizable no matter what part of the world, or what historical age you explore.

All of our ancestors honored the four directions and gave meaning to these perceived forces. As Wiccans, we do the same. To us, each direction has its associations; various god forms, plants, animals, time of year, time of day, color and other significant meanings. They guide us concerning how to live our lives and teach us to live in harmony with the natural world.

Depending on the Wiccan path, the starting place (from which the circle is cast) was slightly different for different indigenous people, though it was generally the North or the East. One circle I am familiar with chose to start in the Northeast. Perhaps they felt this was an acceptable compromise between the two.

The Wiccan Rede mentions casting the circle "thrice about." I have seen this interpreted in many different ways, but I was taught that the circle was first cast with energy (yours plus that channeled from the Gods), then blessed with Holy Water, and lastly sealed with incense.

Holy water, which earlier in life I thought it was something one had to purchase from a church, is made through a ritual that combines the powers of water, which represents the Goddess, and Salt, which represents the God. In truth, this practice was in place long before "Holy Water" was adopted and adapted by the early Catholic Church, as were many other Pagan practices, including the Pagan holidays. Since the water represents Water and salt represents Earth, when followed by incense, which represents Air and Fire, you have sealed the circle with these four main elements as well.

Once the circle is cast and sealed, no unwanted spirits or energies can enter. But each element is then called in to bring its qualities to the scene. Different deities, otherworld or worldly creatures, aspects of the element, etc. will be called to be present, depending on the needs of the particular ritual. The thing to remember is that each of these forces is powerful beyond measure. We do not take them lightly!

The "circle" is not really a circle – it is a sphere that encloses the space three dimensionally. Raising your non-dominant hand to the sky and pointing your athame, wand, or sword (or the first two fingers of your dominant hand) toward the ground, visualize a SPHERE of energy encompassing everything within the boundary you create when you cast, moving clockwise.

At each quarter altar, the Priestess will draw a large star with one continuous line using her wand/atheme/sword or hand position as above. Starting opposite the star point of the element being called (water is on your left hand, air on your right; fire your right foot and earth your left), then encompasses it with a circle. Start at the top of the star just drawn, circle it clockwise (deosil, pronounced je-shill). Step forward on the left foot, pierce the center of the circle with your tool (or fingers) and call in the deity or elemental representative. Step back, bringing the tool to your lips with a kiss, then to your heart, saying "so mote it be."

This process creates a "hole" or portal through which the deity or representative may enter. When the ritual has ended, these actions are reversed. From your starting place, move widdershins (counterclockwise). First, the star is reversed, then the circle around it. Pierce the center as you say the releasing words (see examples in the appendixes), step back, touching the tool to your lips, then the heart and say "hail and farewell". This is not the only way, of course, just what my circle did most of the time. Since we were eclectic, we did rituals from many other traditions. Doing other specific rituals might require different actions and words.

Because of my background in Astrology, I include some of that knowledge when I teach about the elements, which I am also including in this volume. I have the greatest respect for the forces of this world and the deities that are connected with it. Their powers are very, very real. Never ever underestimate them or their power, and never, ever treat them with disrespect.

Also included here are the activities from SummerFest, a 4-day camp in the mountains that focused on the elements. I've included some rituals, but due to copyright/publishing issues, I have not included them all. However, if you contact me I can enlighten you about the ones that I was not able to include.

This camp was held each summer for nine years and included Alchemical fire circles, guest speakers and workshops on various qualities of the element chosen for that year. I also created "installations" that taught about each element. Some installations contained activities and information which one explored for oneself, but others were manned with people from my circle who, in costumes and in appropriate settings, delivered their messages on the current theme. I have included as much of this information as I can remember!

PORTAL OF THE EAST – Place of Air, Youth, and the Fairy World

The Fairy World

Fairies come in various sizes
A fact that some people surprises.
Some are small, like little birds,
Others are large and speak out words.

The largest I've seen, about four feet high,
Others I've seen as bright lights in the sky.
In gardens, they flourish, but in the pond too.
Some are tricksters who just might steal your shoe.

But if you are respectful, caring, and kind,
Their help, love, and devotion you'll find.
Even then you will be <u>their</u> pet,
A fact they'll never let you forget!

First State of Matter – Air (gas)

These elements cannot be created or destroyed. They are the primal elements of this planet and are necessary for life as we know it to exist. Again, never, ever, take them for granted!

- ➢ New Beginnings: East is the place of Sunrise, therefore the beginning of each day. It is also the Spring Equinox, therefore the beginning of our earth's productive cycle. It represents birth, the beginning of life in all forms; all beings, animals, and plants.
- ➢ The human representation is the young boy, the carefree youth.
- ➢ In many cultures, speech (the power of the breath) was the initiator of all: "In the beginning there was the word," is stated in the Christian Bible. Or, in the Egyptian *Book of Thoth*; "He is the Tongue of Rā, the Herald of the Will of Rā, and the Lord of Sacred Speech."
  - o In the ancient myths it is Thoth who speaks the words of power to carry out Ra's wishes; "What emanates from the opening of his mouth, that cometh to pass; he speaks, and it is his command; he is the Source of Speech, the Vehicle of Knowledge, the Revealer of the Hidden."
- ➢ In the animal and otherworldly kingdoms, all winged things are associated with air: birds, winged fairies, and the angels (including Archangel Raphael, whose character is in alignment with air). There are many angels in addition to the archangel-in-charge for all four elements as well.
- ➢ But thought precedes spoken word, and must, therefore, be considered the beginning of speech and the written word.
- ➢ I believe that the tool of Air is the Wand for several reasons. In days of yore, the "mysteries" were for initiates only, and in order to protect that knowledge, misdirection was often used, so that only the initiates knew what the actual truth of the teachings was.
  - o I believe that the tools for fire and air were switched long ago. To me, the wand has a gentle energy; is associated with the fairy world and requests politely, while the sword is an instrument of power that demands. It is the tool of the warrior, who is represented by fire and it is forged in flame. It is aggressive and penetrating and can be used in anger or righteousness. Those qualities say "fire" to me, not the winged fairy world of Air.

(Each of the four mighty elements will be viewed through Astrology as they are three very different types.)

1. Gemini, First Air: ruled by Mercury – This first zodiac air sign's character is "swiftly moving air," which can mean anything from a gentle breeze to a hurricane! This aspect of Air represents the workings of the brain; cognition, speaking, writing, learning, wit, educational facilities, and teaching. It also represents early childhood, since most of our thoughts and feelings are formed when we are very young. If your need or request involves these attributes, calling upon the Gods/Goddess who are in alignment with your purpose is key.

Mercury is known for his ability to access any realm to deliver or receive messages. He is in contact with the spirit world and the realms of angels, so ask for his help when seeking contact with either realm. He is also known for his speed, (swiftness) and invented racing! Thoth can aide you, especially with the sciences or learning of any kind, as he invented hieroglyphs, mathematics, books, and writing. Appeal to him if you need help with your studies, (such as passing an exam or getting an education.) Brigit, the poetess, and Freyr, the mistress of writing and poetry, are two others.

The nervous system is the "messenger" of the body, so if you need help with nerves or nervousness, call Bast, Kuan Yin, or other calming influences to counter-act anxiety or jumpy nerves.

The symbol for Gemini, the twins, represents duality; perhaps you see both sides of an issue and need guidance, or continually flip-flop on an issue. Appealing to Janus, God of past wisdom and new beginnings may help.

These Gods and Goddesses can help you be more convincing when you speak to others, or more eloquent. But mind the three-fold law of return, for all can be used positively or negatively to influence other people: to inspire or to control.

In the physical body, Gemini/Mercury/Air represents pairs of things in the upper body: eyes, ears, arms, hands, and lungs. Appeal to the element of Air and its' deities for any healing help you might need in these areas.

Call upon the Gods of Air if you need information, the ability to speak and write, sing or increase your knowledge. Thoth, who spoke the words that brought matter into being, Mercury, who carries messages to and from the Gods, even into the underworld, Butterfly Maiden, who brings about transformation, or Iris, Goddess of the Rainbow who was the messenger for the Olympian Gods. There are others in every pantheon.

2. The second Air sign of the Zodiac is **Libra: ruled by Venus** – "Refined, controlled Air," reminding me of air conditioning, which balances the temperature in a confined space. Libra seeks balance and justice; wanting fairness to prevail, but also knowing that the scales can tip either way. It is usually the statue of the Greek Goddess Astraeus holding the balance scale that we see representing justice even today.

If it is justice you seek, call upon a God or Goddess of justice to aide you in your cause: Lady Justice, Maat, Ammit, Astraeus, Shamash, or Forseti. (You will find, over time, that certain pantheons are easier to work with than others, depending on your own past lives and interests.)

Venus, it has been postulated, is a newcomer to our solar system; that she either joined in as a comet captured by our sun or was misplaced during a colossal event in our solar system that rearranged the planets. Venus does have a "tail" very much like a comet, which was often portrayed as her hair streaming behind her. This event would have caused great cataclysms on our earth. We are learning much more about this planet through recent space explorations. (For further information on this subject, visit Thunderbolts. info on the web or read Immanuel Velikovsky's work).

Traditionally, Venus rules sexuality, sexual preferences, and love. Call upon a Goddess of love if you need more love in your life, (Vishnu, Hathor, Circe or Freyja) but NEVER EVER cast any kind of spell that influences another person! This is strictly forbidden in the practice of Wicca and the results (often not a pretty sight) will come back to you three-fold!

I had a call one day from a young man who had picked up a spell book and cast a spell to bring his ex-wife back to him. Instead, her anger against him seemed to increase exponentially. After he explained what he had done, I explained the three-fold law to him, and emphasized that this was something he should never have done.

A couple of weeks later, he called again, wanting to fix the negative situation he had created. I asked if he had "made" anything during the spell. He said "yes", and I told him he needed to destroy the object – in a ritual asking to release the spell and counter the damage it had caused. I haven't heard from him since, so I hope it worked out for him. And for his ex.

In air, however, Venus also refers to courts, lawyers, and seeing both sides of an issue, or being flexible enough to take either side in a debate. If you are unable to make up your mind about something, appeal to Maat, Goddess of truth and divine order for the right decision.

Venus also rules beauty, and in Air, especially, the expression of beauty through art. If you are a musician, model, vocalist or artist, work with Venus, Athene, Apollo, or Taliesin for inspiration, recognition, or improvement to name just a few.

In the physical body, Venus rules the kidneys, and, as Venus is connected with sugar and sweet things, it can indicate diabetes or other blood sugar problems. Balance is the key. (She also rules the sign of Taurus, but operates differently in an earth sign.)

3. Third air sign: Aquarius, ruled by Uranus – This is "cold, still air", which can jeopardize or even end life. In temperament, the qualities are more intellectual and the emotions cool or detached. We have entered the Age of Aquarius; thus the great leaps of advancement in technology, especially electronics and physics.

Aquarius is about looking toward the future and making forward strides in all fields of science. Aquarius is about unseen energy, and as we are at the mere beginning of the age, the future will hold new sources of energy that are, as yet, unknown to us. Even in our own electrical nature may change or open new possibilities – think of the "aps" on electronic equipment now. Where might this lead? Computers are now able to "think for themselves" which is pretty scary to me!

It is also about humanity and the human condition. However, the concern is not necessarily backed by empathetic emotion, as the Element of Air is noted more for intellect than emotions. Aquarius often becomes obsessed with new things, which is obvious in our society. When the current subject becomes old, it will be dropped as soon as something new catches people's interest.

Call upon these Gods for easing the transmission into the new age, or for change in your life; (Djin, Gwydion, Khepera, Janus or Hecate for change and transition) and for knowledge of the other-worlds, physical, scientific or ethereal (the Dagda, Brahma, or Paralda) are good choices.

The etheric energy systems of the body such as the aura and the electrical synapses in the brain are Aquarian in nature. Appeal to Gods/Goddesses of compassion (Matsu, Shiva, Saraswati) for humans and/or the planet, as they can be helpful for the changes ahead. Call Bel, Minerva or Urania for scientific projects.

To Air:
Divas, fairies, and sylphs of the air,
Daybreak and Springtime are part of your fare.
We inhale the prana of four mighty winds
And honor you too, as new things begin.

Airs Response:
From mighty gale to gentle breeze
I destroy when I will, or aim to please.
My might, when unbridled, you'll doubtlessly see
I'm essential for life; don't underestimate me.

PORTAL OF THE SOUTH – Place of Fire, Plasma, and the Dragon World

Fairie World (Cont.)

There lives a dragon in my big maple tree
He's red and winged and is there for me.
He watches the rituals taking place in the yard;
The calling of elements, the song of the bard.

He wasn't so happy when the tree was trimmed.
His favorite perch was on one great lost limb.
But resigned to fate, he relocated his perch
And continues to guard our Pagan church.

Second State of Matter – Fire (Plasma)

I always felt there was something amiss with the elements assigned to the four directions since only three of them were actual States of Matter, the definition of which is "one of the four principal conditions in which matter exists—solid, liquid, and gas." But now, finally, the forth has been recognized! It is plasma, an ionized gaseous substance; highly electrically conductive to the point that long-range electric and magnetic fields dominate the behavior of matter. It is the force we see in the nebulas as colorful clouds. It is not found naturally on Earth, but creates the "northern lights" and brings fire to earth as lightning strikes.

➢ Maturity. South is the place of High Summer and of noon each day. It is the time of Summer Solstice and represents maturity in all living things. South represents taking responsibility; for raising the young (full bloom in the plant world); for working and providing (or producing seeds) for the "family" and the height of life before the decline into death. Its human representation in the Wiccan circle is the mature young woman.

➤ Fire represents energy and power: the power to procreate or destroy; the power to harm or heal. It is passion, whether that be sexual passion or being passionate about – well, anything. In the animal and otherworldly kingdoms, it is represented by all things that exist in the desert climates or that breathe fire, as well as those highly successful predators, such as all types of felines. The Archangel of the South is Michael (very aptly portrayed by John Travolta in the movie of that name) and the other angels whose character is in alignmnet with fire.

➤ Energy is needed by all things to accomplish all things. Fire is energy; best represented by the energy of the Sun. In most, but not all traditions, the sun is seen as the King; the highest ranking male in the pantheon. He is the one who sacrifices himself in the fall when the grain is harvested and who returns to the womb of the Goddess to be reborn at Yule.

➤ As previously stated, I believe the tool of fire to be the sword.

1. Aries, the first Fire: Ruled by Mars – Aries is the first fire sign of the zodiac, and is characterized as "Uncontrolled Fire" such as a forest fire. Fire emulates the power of the Gods. It is the raw power of creation. It is said that the fire deities could create a universe out of nothing. They were frequently credited with the fertilization of the Goddess, giving life and warmth to the Earth. But fire can be destructive, a fact that we are reminded of very frequently.

The planet that rules Aries is Mars. To the Romans, Mars was the god of War and was supremely important. They believed him to be the father of Romulus and Remus, the founders of Rome.

The Campus Martius, or field of Mars, was next to the river Tiber. In ancient Rome It was used to train soldiers and hold horse races. Ancient ceremonies included cleansing and preparing the land for crops and protection for both crops and animals through animal sacrifices and dancing. Competitions, especially physical ones, are under the ruler ship of Mars in astrology.

The "red" planet has been under close scrutiny since our advent into space. It is believed to have had climate changes, and I've recently heard that scientists now believe there is (or once was) water on that planet. Other say the "canals" were carved by electrical discharges (plasma) hitting the surface. Or possibly there were huge volcanoes that left lava flow lines. It is about half the size of Earth with an elliptical orbit and two moons. It spends about two months in each zodiac sign.

Call upon a warrior god such as Mars, Ares, Horus, Sekhmet, Athena, (yes, some of them are women) or Tyr if you need protection, strength or energy. The will defend you against all evil; they are fierce protectors.

2. Second Fire: Leo, Ruled by the Sun – This is "controlled fire," the productive fire of the hearth; the fire that warms us or cooks our food. It also represents healing energy. Thus fire in the second sign, Leo, is more creative and more loving.

The Roman god, Apollo, was known as the "ripener, the nourisher, the grower of things, and the protector of crops". Romans also saw him (because of his skill at healing both body and soul) the God of healing. He was also the god of music, archery, prophecy and young growing creatures. Greek statues attribute great physical beauty to him. His love affairs were numerous, and he loved to party!

The energy of the Sun is healing energy. Human health is threatened both physically and emotionally if we are not exposed to enough sunlight. The Sun Gods and Goddesses, (Osiris, Odhinn, Bridget, Astarte, Ganesha and others) are healers. Call upon them for their healing energy.

The sun itself is essential for our world to exist and support life of all kinds. New theories suggest that the Sun is NOT burning inside, nor is it a nuclear reaction. New theories (which I think are true) make sense. Some scientists are saying that since the surface of the sun is hot, but the sun spots or holes in the surface are cooler, heat could not be generated internally.

And though the surface is hot, the further away from the Sun we measure, the hotter the atmospheric temperatures rise. It is postulated then, that the heat is coming INTO the sun, not generated outwardly by it. Scientists also say that the energy is electromagnetic and that the sun will not "burn out." They have actually been able to recreate this process in the lab. I refer to the "Electric Universe" again concerning these theories.

3. The third fire sign, Sagittarius, ruled by Jupiter – is a totally different kind of fire, a cool fire. This is the Aurora Borealis, or the aura you see around living things. It is ethereal – the result of plasma's electrical activity. Therefore, the Gods associated with this form of fire (Thor, Zeus, the Dagda, Amen, Marduk, Isis, Spider Woman for example) are the teachers and magicians, and the givers of philosophy and knowledge.

Jupiter is the largest planet in our solar system, has four moons, a big red spot (which scientists are still puzzling over) and makes one complete rotation in ten hours. It stays in each zodiac sign about one year.

Call upon the aforementioned Gods and Goddesses to help you learn, expand your mind and thinking, explore the unknown, develop your spirituality or psychic abilities, or bring abundance into your life.

However, there is another side to Sagittarius. The symbol for Sagittarius, the Centaur, is the mythic example. Some people will exhibit both the human and animal side, some lean more toward the human intellectual, and some more to the natural world represented by the horse. Those people will be more inclined to enjoy being in the wilderness; explorers, hunters, archeologists, and sports enthusiasts.

For help in these endeavors, the Gods to invoke would be Pan, part human, part goat, the Green Man, part human, part plant, Mielikki, Goddess of the forest, and hunter gods/goddesses such as Artemis, Herne, or Tirawa. Always be sure to ask permission before taking anything from nature and leave an offering in its place.

To Fire:

Divas, dragons, salamanders of fire
We come to you with our heart's desire.
The planet; purified from flames within,
Let our purification and transformation begin.
Give us your energy and zest for life
Give us the courage to overcome strife.

Fire's Response:

From mountains of fire, deep underground
To the fire in the sky, my presence is found.
Warming your homes or cooking your food,
I can be gentle or I can be rude.

PORTAL OF THE WEST – *Place of all states of Water and the Mermaids World*

Fairie World (Cont.)

Mermaids live in this dimension still,
While dragons and fairies come and go at will.
I must admit, no Mermaids I know,
For where they live, I cannot go.

They've gone down deep into the sea
Hiding from man, their worst enemy.
Yet recently rediscovered and filmed for TV
A series of programs you really must see.

Third State of Matter – Water (liquid)

Water flows where it will. It is essential to all life, and as such should be treated as holy. I fear the day may come when we humans realize that we have NOT appreciated this element and find ourselves short of good, clean water. Those of us in this country (the United States) have unthinkingly taken water for granted. Even people who realize how sacred water is have polluted it. The Ganges River is one shameful example. When will we realize that if the oceans die, so does all life on our planet?

➢ The West is the place of the setting sun, and of the Elders. It is the place where all is "past its prime." It is the harvest time, the dying time, the fading of life and what lies beyond. It is the time of the Autumnal Equinox when the darkness overtakes the light as the Sun journeys southward. The West is the gate to the afterlife and has always been so in many cultures. The Celts, for instance, placed the afterlife across the western sea on the island of Anwenn.

➢ It is the place within us that reaches beyond the physical – that connects to divine spirits, especially the Goddesses, and communicates with them. Our paranormal abilities are connected to the Western gate. Here we can access the spirits of the dead as well as those of the deep.

➢ It represents our emotions, both positive and negative.

➢ Since we are 70% water ourselves, the tides of the moon most definitely affect our emotions and activities.

➢ The human representation is the Sage or elderly man.

1. Cancer, the first water: Ruled by the Moon – The type of water addressed by this first water sign is "warm, moving water," such as gentle waves lapping at the shore, or a meandering stream. This is usually seen as comforting; warm water for bathing and cooking, or a cup of tea, perhaps. And Cancer is the sign that hopes to comfort the world; taking care of the sick, feeding the hungry, raising families, and healing the world. However, too much water, and we will drown!

We know how changeable the moon is, and the moon rules emotions, instincts, and psychic abilities. Thus, moods and emotions are very volatile. That loving, caring Cancer-ruled individual you know can quickly become vengeful, hurt, angry, spiteful, hysterical or a sobbing mess.

The moon is also the symbol (in most cultures) of the Divine Feminine, who also is portrayed in all of these different moods; from charming, loving maidens (Persephone, Aphrodite, Venus) to the mother goddesses (Isis, Demeter, Gaia) to the destructive warring goddess (Athena, Kali, Pele). It all depends on her mood! Thus, the Goddess is seen as threefold, as is the physical phase of our moon.

2. Second water sign, Scorpio: Ruled by Pluto – "Hot seething water, often hidden under the surface" typifies this form of water. Geysers and hot springs are fine if you know where they are, but unexpected appearances can be disastrous.

Pluto, the ruling planet, is small but mighty, and astrologers will never doubt its place in the zodiac or its planetary status. It has a generational influence on humanity. As of this writing, Pluto is in Capricorn, and we are witnessing the disintegration of systems that have long been in place. Pluto will tear apart what we think we know and bring in new knowledge and ways of living and being on this planet.

Looking back, for instance, its recent reign in Scorpio (1984 -1995) brought us an age of sex, drugs, rock and roll; the stock market crash, the fall of Berlin Wall and the collapse of the communist system, plus an AIDs epidemic stemming from the sexual revolution that infected and killed large numbers of people.

In Sagittarius (1995-2008), we saw the outbreak of religious wars that are still going on all over the planet. Political ideas became polarized as well. The World Trade Organization shifted manufacturing to many countries outside of the US during this time, as Sagittarius rules foreign countries, people, language, and knowledge. The influx of foreigners into this country and others has vastly increased.

Pluto will move into Aquarius and stay for twenty years (2024-2044), so we can expect to see unbelievable advancements in technology; far beyond the ones we are seeing now (in 2018). Since Aquarius does have <u>some</u> concern for humanity, we will eventually see a kinder, more humanitarian world. Sadly, that will be a future time, and my hope is that it's not in response to a global tragedy.

Scorpio is a very complex sign and actually has <u>four</u> representations. The usual symbol is the scorpion. But this astrological sign is most powerful because it can be the best or the worst in the human species.

The symbol of the lowest form is the snake: unfortunate for that usually harmless creature, but it represents the ability to be deadly – and so quick about it you may not see it coming. The worst of humanity, the serial killers, torturers, power-grabbing maniacs, etc. would fall into this category.

Calling the trickster Gods (Loki, Thorr, Shiva, Pele) can be dangerous, and something I wouldn't recommend unless you already have a good relationship with them and mutual understanding. Just remember, they are called tricksters for a good reason. They are very good at it, and can lead you to places you might not want to go before you even realize where you are headed.

One step up, the symbol is the Scorpion; underhanded, deadly (but more likely kills to save oneself, rather than killing for fun) unpredictable, and cunning. For humans, it is a struggle trying to keep self-control, but many can, and do, succeed. It is the same for gods such as Ba'al, Mithra, or Sammael.

The third rung of the ladder is represented by the eagle. Those gods (or people) that have overcome their baser instincts have risen about the previously mentioned deeds. They take a higher path. They also know what they are capable of if it came to defending their loved ones or their country, but otherwise can be kind, even gentle.

The highest order is the complete opposite of the lowest and is represented by the phoenix bird. These are often healers, spiritual leaders, gifted psychics and people who are generally here to serve and lift up mankind. These people are examples of what many of us strive to become – the best humans we can be, and Scorpios can achieve these heights.

Call upon Crone Goddesses (Hecete, Kali Ma, Ereshkigal) or the mighty warrior Kings (Baal, The Dagda, Perun) if you are in dire need of help. They are very strong defenders – the army behind you in your time of need – IF you are on good terms with them and use their power and advice for good.

3. The third water sign is Pisces: Ruled by Neptune – "Deep, still water" characterizes this water aspect, which, also, can be divine or destructive. The sign of Pisces is depicted as two fish swimming in opposite directions. Each and every Pisces will be making choices in life to swim in a positive or a negative direction. Psychic abilities, the unconscious mind, self-destruction, enlightenment, and addiction are all ruled by Neptune.

Neptune is a giant, gaseous planet (17 times larger than our own) about which little is known. With the exception of Pluto, it is the farthest planet from the sun in our solar system. It is very blue in color; very appropriate for the planetary ruler of a water sign.

In a way, the same kinds of choices are given to people with strong Pisces/Neptune as with Scorpio/Pluto. The difference is that Pisces will destroy themselves, whereas Scorpio will destroy others. But EITHER could be a spiritual leader! There is as much hidden in the deep ocean, as there is in the human subconscious! Pain is synonymous with the human condition, but denying pain or stuffing it down inside is harmful. Meditation, contemplation and prayer can help.

Call on Gods/Goddesses of compassion (Matsu, Quan Yin) if you seek to heighten your spirituality or your psychic abilities. Also, ask their assistance if you are trying to overcome and addiction or are dealing with a mental or emotional problem.

To Water:

Divas and merfolk of the sea
Thee we approach most humbly.
Heal our emotions, banish our pain
That we may be loving and whole again.

Water's Response:

Life and death I hold in my hand
The waters you drink and that nurture the land.
Joys and sorrows are mine as well
And mysteries and secrets I cannot tell.

PORTAL OF THE NORTH – Place of Earth and the Gnomes World

Fairie World (Cont.)

Gnomes are the most left-out specie,
Not nearly as popular as the other three.
But I have met gnomes, and learned right off,
That if you acknowledge them, their hats they will doff

For, like any other living thing

> *The importance is the love that you bring.*
> *And all creation from flea to man*
> *Wants all the attention and love that it can.*

Fourth State of Matter – Earth

Until rather lately, we would have said we knew what matter was. It is something you can see and touch, smell, and taste. It is things we can handle, manipulate and use. But we are finding out that matter is not what we thought it was. It is composed of tiny particles of energy!

➢ North is the afterlife (or the in-between life since we believe in reincarnation.)

➢ The harvest time is over, and the crops rest, just as we rest in the otherworld after death.

➢ For most climates, it is the season of cold, ice and snow, when the Winter King and Queen preside.

➢ Some animals hibernate while others, including humans, try to survive.

➢ The North represents material things – those we need for survival, and those we value.

➢ The human representative is that of the Old Crone, who knows the deepest mysteries and wields the most powerful magick.

➢ Mythology gives the Crone power over life and death. It is she who decides when life dies, including human life, and when it is reborn.

➢ It is Earth, the planet we call our home: beautiful and fragile, yet unpredictable and dangerous.

1. The first Earth sign is Taurus, Ruled by Venus – "solid, fertile earth". We call this planet home, though we may not have originated here. We see it as dependable (though threatened by the other elements) and want to believe it will remain as it is forever, though this also is improbable as the history of this planet shows it also evolves and changes. There is no doubt that it is beautiful, however, and we must honor that beauty, not defile it nor take it for granted!

Taurus/Venus represents the fertility needed to grow plants - the food we humans eat and that nourishes the huge variety of animals found upon and within this planet, and the incredible natural beauty we find all around us.

Rituals for the earth and its creatures and caring for and about this planet fall into this category. Call upon the Gods and Goddesses of Earth (Archangel Uriel, Gohb, or Gia) for help in caring for our spaceship home. Call upon them to help take care of the plants and animals, and to aid the growth and abundance needed to sustain life here.

Call on the Gods and Goddess of Earth (Tonantzin, Cernuous, Brahma) if you are lacking what you need to survive, or to ask for help healing the planet.

2. The second Earth sign is Virgo, currently ruled by Mercury and is "productive Earth". I say it is "currently" ruled because Astrologers believe that each sign should have its own ruler, and if not, the other planet has not been found or has already been destroyed. Yet there are ways that stable Earth and mercurial Mercury can work together.

Writing, designing earthly structures such as buildings, bridges, gardens, and parks are all works of Mercury in Earth, so if you are seeking inspiration for planning a community garden, ask for help from Hegemone or the Green Man. If you are working in a forest, Pan will help, as will the nymphs of the forest.

The physical body is of earth, and the healing arts are the prevue of gods and goddesses such as Thoth, Ixtliltox, or Brigit, so if you are suffering health problems, appeal to them for healing. Appeal to them also if you want to develop your own ability to heal others.

Things that are mature also fall into this category – crops for the harvest, fruit ready to pick from the trees, even the animals taken for food.

Earth is our mother, and we come here so that our spirit selves can have physical experiences to further our growth and understanding. Our incarnations will be prosperous and poor, sick and healthy, productive and destructive, honorable and harmful for we must experience all for the growth of our souls.

3. Capricorn is the 3rd Earth Sign and is described as "cold, hard rock". These are things that we see as set permanently in place (though nothing truly is), or things that govern our lives, but perhaps are not under our own control. This includes the structure and the authorities that be; government, laws, socially acceptable activities and precepts, physical prosperity or lack of, and higher authorities of all kinds.

Capricorn deals with business, so if you are looking to advance your career or to help your business prosper Hermes, Osiris or Inari can help guide you. They can also help if you are dealing with governmental things or the laws of the land.

If you are working with precious gems and stones, metals and minerals, alchemy, psychics or chemistry, seek guidance from Athene, Vulcan, or Quetzalcoatl.

This phase of Earth also represents the obstacles and hardships one meets in this world. Ask Ganesha, Odhinn, or Hecate to help remove the obstacles or blocks within yourself or your life that stand in the way of your success.

To Earth:

Divas, elves, and trolls of the Earth
We enjoy your friendship and your mirth,
Through death to rebirth life's cycle, we see
The seasons, the fields, the flocks, even me.

Earth's Response:

In anger I'll shake, Intent to destroy
Or tend to my forests and bring to you joy.
Mine is the material plane of this world
I can help you grow like a leaf unfurled.

CHAPTER FIVE

The true pentagram

I've often wondered just HOW a person could stop Hollywood and its ilk from portraying an up-side-down pentagram as a sign of devil worship! Why, oh why, do they keep perpetuating this idea? As Pagans, we do not believe in the Christian Devil. We know that evil exists; we know that there are evil people and evil spirits, but we do not believe in Hell or the Master of it.

Even as a child, when they tried to teach me that if I (or anyone) was "bad" by their definition, (which consisted mostly of either silly or obvious rules) I would burn forever in Hell. This made no sense to me since they were also telling me that God loved me. Perhaps he needed to learn better parenting skills if he were to be my Daddy!

Let's first address the rules, or Commandments, as they are called. If you've ever looked into the ancient records found in plain sight on walls in ancient Egypt, you would find these same concepts were written 2,000 years B.C. except they were not a list of *rules*. They were the worlds of ancient Egyptians who were recounting and justifying their lives to their Gods as they entered the afterlife.

The deceased person explained that they had led a good life. They did not write "thou shalt not," they wrote "I have not," and there were many, many more than ten "sins" on their lists; in one case, forty-two. Here are some examples from *The Egyptian Book of the Dead (Chapter 25);*

"Hail to thee, great God, Lord of the Two Truths. I have come unto thee, my Lord, that thou mayest bring me to see thy beauty. I know thee, I know thy name, I know the names of the 42 Gods who are with thee in this broad hall of the Two Truths . . . Behold, I am come unto thee. I have brought thee truth; I have done away with sin for thee. I have not sinned against anyone. I have not mistreated

people. I have not done evil instead of righteousness . . . I have not reviled the God. I have not laid violent hands on an orphan. I have not done what the God abominates . . . I have not killed; I have not turned anyone over to a killer. I have not caused anyone's suffering . . . I have not copulated (illicitly); I have not been unchaste. I have not increased nor diminished the measure, I have not diminished the palm; I have not encroached upon the fields. I have not added to the balance weights; I have not tempered with the plumb bob of the balance. I have not taken milk from a child's mouth; I have not driven small cattle from their herbage... I have not stopped (the flow of) water in its seasons; I have not built a dam against flowing water. I have not quenched a fire in its time . . . I have not kept cattle away from the God's property. I have not blocked the God at his processions."

Many, many more "confessions" similar to these can readily be found there.

Let's not forget that Moses lived in Egypt for many years. He obviously knew of this practice. Draw your own conclusions, but I'm pretty sure he picked the ones he thought were most appropriate for his purpose, which was either to set down rules of conduct for his people or to control the people through fear of God's wrath. Or both.

Secondly, the "hell" that is commonly thought to exist has pretty much been taken from *Dante's Inferno*, published in 1307. He was a poet and philosopher, and his work was considered to be a great piece of literature, but it was a work of fiction. So, you see, in order to believe in this Devil, you must be Christian, which we are not. The proper sign, therefore, of a Devil worshiper is the up-side-down crucifix or cross, not the up-side-down pentagram. Now I suppose that if Hollywood used this correct sign, Christendom would come unglued! It's so much easier to pick on a religion that is already seen as evil by most people.

(I always thought it was too bad there is no official remembrance for the hundreds of thousands of people (mostly women, but men, children and pets, too) that suffered horrible deaths during the burning times, like there is for the Jewish people, veterans, disaster victims, etc. Guess they would rather forget about it.)

Now that we have established what the pentagram is not, let's look into the history of what it has been in the past, and what it represents to Wiccans today.

In the Israeli Negev desert, archaeologists found a flint scraper decorated with a pentagram. This was dated to the Chalcolithic period (4500–3100

BCE). Also, on pottery from Mesopotamia, around 3200 BCE: a five-pointed star on a tablet from Uruk, a design on a vase dated to 3000 BCE from Jemdet Nasr, and another design on a spindle whorl from the same time, also from Jemdet Nasr. And a pentagram appears on a jar dated to 3100 BCE, which was found north of Thebes in Egypt.

The ancient Greeks considered the pentagram t sign of perfection, because it was formed of five A's, and for its relationship to the "Golden Ratio."

I was taught that to early Christians, it symbolized the five wounds of Christ: also, the first five books of the Hebrew Scriptures. Five has always been an important number, especially to the Celts. Christians later dropped the circle that surrounded the star, possibly because the Pagans kept the pentagram intact. To modern Pagans, it represents the four cardinal directions and the four elements as previously discussed, with the fifth point representing Spirit presiding over all.

A pentagram is a five-pointed star that is drawn with a single line. Since each of the points represent an element or spirit, how you draw it is important, as mentioned earlier. If you are drawing it for a particular quality, you start at the point opposite and draw your line toward it. I found it interesting that while I was teaching school, I always drew a star for exceptional student work, and I always started with the left foot (Earth), up to the peak of the star (Spirit). Later I learned that I was calling in Spirit. I often, but not always, circled the star, which made it a pentagram.

In traditional Wicca, a novice wears the sign upright, which shows they are studying the four forces or elements. Once they achieve First Degree, the pentagram is turned point down. As second degrees, they are studying the element of Spirit. Part of their "job" is now to teach others. The last degree, 3rd degree, means that you have achieved mastery and knowledge of all five elements and are eligible to become High Priestess (or Priest) and can preside over a Wiccan group or Coven. It is worn point up again to signify the new status.

Sadly, this tradition is suffering the advent of the internet and the many books and ways to study Wicca available now. In the past, one could not become a second or third degree witch without the approval of their High Priestess. This meant not only having the knowledge but having the wisdom and ethics that accompany the responsibilities of these higher degrees.

Today, one can become any degree over the internet, which can be bestowed upon them by people they have never even met. I think the ethics and honor of the degree program have suffered greatly because of this.

So – my advice, if you are looking for a group or teacher, is: Carefully assess their character and practices. If they require an excessive amount of your time, money, or person; beware. There are some that thrive on power – and I highly suggest that you avoid these people and their groups.

CHAPTER SIX

Conducting and Writing Ritual

Conducting Ritual

Perhaps I should address this, as I have seen many different ideas and interpretations concerning how things should be done. The Wiccan Rede, which is sort of like our one-page bible, leads to much confusion. I can only relate what I was taught, but remember that there is no really right or wrong way to do most things in the Wiccan religion if your heart is in the right place. Some ways, however, might make more sense to you than others.

For instance: The Rede says "Cast the circle thrice about, to keep unwanted spirits out."

Not everyone knows just what this means. I once visited a circle where that was interpreted as having everyone in the circle troupe around three times and that was all.

Here is what I was taught, which is beautiful, meaningful, and makes sense to me. The ritual space has been prepared (swept and smudged with sage or copal) and the altars and quarters have been readied. Personally, I prefer to use copal, as they do in South America for the same reasons we use Sage here (cleansing and protecting.)

The High Priestess calls in energy from the divine, then begins in the east (or north) and casts the circle clockwise, directing the energy with the first two fingers of her dominant hand or using a tool (wand, athame, sword, or cucumber – whatever feels right for that particular ritual).

She cuts a doorway (and guards it). East enters with incense and smudges the entire circle beginning from the point it was cast. This is usually a scent that will honor a particular God or Goddess, or that is in alignment with the purpose of that particular ritual.

Next she admits West who bears the holy water, if it has been prepared ahead. (The process is the same, whether done at the altar during ritual or beforehand.) West starts from wherever the circle was cast and sprinkles the water completely around the circle to bless the space.

(See chapter 7 for the preparation of Holy water.)

The circle then has been cast "thrice" about, first with energy, then with incense (fire and air) and lastly with holy water (water and earth). All four elements have then cleansed and protected the circle.

Finally, West and East stand at the gate to smudge and bless each of the participants as they enter the circle, usually admitting the High Priest first if there is one. When all are in, the High Priestess closes and seals the "doorway" and stands at the altar.

Alternatively, if it is a group that works together consistently, they might enter the holy space and be present during the casting. Each, in turn, is then smudged and blessed at the same time the circle is. This method is often used for a large gathering as well since the first method takes a long time if there are lots of participants.

Once the circle is cast and sealed, the Quarters are invited in, (the lords of the directions, deities, animals or angels) as described in the pentagram section, and the ritual has begun.

When the ritual has ended and the quarter elements have been dismissed, the High Priestess opens the circle, dismissing the energy by drawing it in counter-clockwise from the starting point.

Mountain Moon Circle was eclectic – we performed all kinds of rituals, as I felt that I wanted to honor all the Pagan religions that came before us. But many circles choose one pantheon to work with, and some even use the same standard ceremony most of the time. Choices are made by the High Priestess and High Priest, so every group has their own way of doing things. With some, the rules are hard and fast. With others, variety is the spice. All is up to the HPS & HP.

I do think it's important for people to dress in ritual garb and prepare themselves mentally before ritual in order to channel the highest energy.

Cleansing and preparing oneself to expect something special; something magickal; something holy, helps to make the ritual just that.

This did not apply to guests in our circle who were checking Wicca out for the first time, but guests were invited only to Sabbat (our holiday) ceremonies. I found early on that, because of the fear mongers out there against Wicca, if we did deeper rituals, which often would be at Full Moon or New Moon rituals, newcomers might freak out. If they are first exposed to Sabbat celebratory rituals and gain an understanding of what we do and are interested enough to learn, they are then welcomed.

The severity of the rules is up to the group. Some are more casual, some are very formal. As long as their motives, hearts, and minds are in the right place, the work will be holy, no matter how it is performed.

Writing ritual

Writing ritual used to be quite a task, when there were no books and no internet. I had a metaphysical bookstore in Montana in the early 70's, and the only book that related to Wicca at all was one about an herbalist witch, not really about being Wiccan.

Our store concentrated on psychic things, alternative healing, reincarnation, and astrology. My first encounter with Wicca was when several of us decided to attend an astrology conference in Minneapolis, Minnesota in 1974. The first week of this conference, put on by Llewellyn Publications, was for astrologers. The second week was for witches. At the time, I knew nothing about the later.

I have forever regretted that I didn't attend both weeks because I could have learned about Wicca much sooner than I did, and could have witnessed Oberon-Zell Ravenheart and Morning Glory's wedding!

Also, at our second SummerFest, Isaac Bonewit was a guest speaker. In conversation with him, I asked, in reference to the *"Principles of Belief As adopted by The Council of American Witches, 1974"* that came out of that conference, how they had managed to agree so quickly and get that tremendous job accomplished.

Isaac told me then that he authored it. He said that he just listened, wrote down what he thought they were saying and submitted it to the group for approval, which they did. If you haven't read this document, I suggest you look it up and print a copy. I thought it was very well done, and usually give a copy to each of my new students.

But the days of no books and no information have passed. There are many, many books. Of course, not all of them are good, but many are, and they discuss many forms of Wicca. Most of them contain short rituals for your use; plus there are probably millions on the internet.

I admit, as before, that I have often taken parts of other rituals but have "fleshed them out" to suit the purpose of my ritual. I think (and hope) that people put their rituals on the web so that others <u>can</u> use them. Once you have the pattern of the ritual the way you like it, you will find it gets easier. Here are some helpful steps to keep in mind:

- Most important is the *purpose* of the ritual, for that could be anything from celebrating a Sabbat to healing and animal. Try writing the purpose several ways until you feel your intention is perfectly clear.
- Now determine what pantheon; what Gods and Goddesses would best suit that intention; what deities would be best to call in for the four quarters, and begin to make a list of all items you will need.
- Write (or find) quarter calls and invocations to bring in and dismiss the quarters and any other deities. These might be Gods and Goddesses, otherworldly beings, animals, angels, or elementals.
- Make sure that the Priestess/Priests speeches clearly explain the purpose of the ritual (again, find or write) to the group so that they are ready to contribute their energy.
- What "act of magick" will physically demonstrate your purpose? This can be anything from lighting a candle (in ceremony) to jumping through a hoop (also in ceremony). Make sure that whatever it is, the whole group takes part in the experience.
- I like the altars and everything to reflect the theme, and think that costuming is important. Over the years, I've collected many, many statues, altar cloths, types of garb, and beautiful things to create an atmosphere that says "this is special." You don't have to have it all in the beginning, just find a way to make everything special, even if it's a bouquet of dandelions at each quarter. Use your creativity and your imagination.
- Determine the right time (of day, of year, of moon phase, etc.) that would be most beneficial, and where the ritual would take place (indoors? Outdoors?).
- Cleanse the space and all objects you will use.

- Decide if the holy water will be made before, or during ritual and get things ready.
- Make a list of everything you will need (herbs, cauldrons, cakes, cloths, statues, etc. etc.) to make sure that everything you need will be in its place. Nothing breaks the mood like "Oh, I forgot the firecrackers" or whatever.
- After the Quarters are called in, the main Gods and Goddesses will be invited. There can be as many or as few as you need to convey your main purpose. The deities may be invoked into the body of the Priest/Priestess/other or evoked to be present but not embodied. Always thank and dismiss them, or invite them to stay when their part is concluded.
- Will the "magickal" event occur before, after, or by the deities invoked? Plan accordingly. I like using magick tricks or some sort of surprise, or something they all do to take part so that everyone feels involved.
- Cakes and Wine can be done many ways. For all these things, I think you can find examples in the rituals I've included in this book. And – other books and, of course, the internet!
- Dismiss the quarters and open the circle.

We always followed rituals with snacks as a way for people to "ground" as a good ritual may leave them feeling spacey. For the main Sabbats, we provided dinners. Don't let anyone leave until they are again fully present in this realm. Food really helps with that!

CHAPTER SEVEN
Tools & Spells

One's personal tools are very important in Wicca. Keep in mind that their value has nothing to do with their cost. What is important, is how the tool makes you <u>feel</u>.

I was in a small town in Iowa many years ago and felt I needed to perform a ritual. I went to a "dime store" and hunted amongst their toys. I eventually found a clear plastic wand filled with some kind of liquid and different colors of glitter. It quickly became one of my favorite tools. Currently, I teach Wicca at the Women's Prison. I cannot bring in an athame, or anything metal, but everyone loves my wand! It doubles as a "talking stick" as well as a wand.

Both the athame and the wand are used to direct energy, but their energies are very different, as I mentioned before. Use whatever suits the purpose/theme of your ritual. Many prefer natural things, so wood wands are always popular. A true athame is not sharp and never used to cut anything. It should never have had contact with blood. It is solely to direct energy. A white-handled knife is traditional for cutting if you need to cut bread or whatever in ritual.

There seems to be some confusion between a pentagram and a pentacle. The pentagram is the circled star, used for jewelry, tee shirts, books of shadow, etc. A pentacle is a plate-like object, usually <u>inscribed</u> with a pentagram, used in ritual to make holy water upon and carry things. It is also known as an altar paten.

Holy Water: Ask the Goddess to bless the water by holding your receptive hand up to the sky and putting your tool or first two fingers into the water. Feel the energy flow from the heavens through your hand and body to be projected by your tool into the water. (Most rituals have a few lines consistently used for this process).

Hold it up to the Goddess and say "Mother be thou adored" or something similar. Put the water aside and place the container of salt (symbolizing the God) on the paten. Bless it the same way. Place the water on the paten again, add three pinches of blest salt and stir clockwise three times. This combines the energies of male and female. Hold up for blessing, say a few words to that effect and it's done!

It is good to keep a "Book of Shadows." This is supposed to be a record of your work; your magickal workings, rituals, recipes, even thoughts, and dreams, if you wish. And I wish I was that organized! I have stuff all over the place!

I suggest that any BOS you purchase be blank – to record your own work, not someone else's. I'm not saying you shouldn't use other people's published work – just saying that it should be in a separate place. Keep your BOS personal. If I didn't want to share with you the work I have done, I wouldn't be writing this. But this is not my BOS.

So many people are buying books with spells in them without knowing what they are doing. I get frequent calls from people who have done this – and it has gone very wrong. The final part of the Rede states "An it harm none, do as you will." I'm afraid most people don't realize the scope of these eight words.

This phrase is saying, that as a Wiccan, you are allowed to do whatever you want, magickly or otherwise, as long as it doesn't harm **anyone**. That means no harm physically, mentally, emotionally, or spiritually, and it includes YOURSELF!

In truth, that is a BIG order! So before you think about influencing anyone with a spell, think through all the consequences, then, even if you are asking for healing, ADD this phrase! "An it Harm None." This will nullify the spell if there is any harm that could transpire from your actions and will protect you from the three-fold law, which states that whatever you do will be returned to you threefold.

These phrases are not just whimsical sayings; they work! No matter what the media says, a true Witch will not cause harm or perform evil spells. OR – sacrifice animals! Every, and I mean EVERY witch I know is a devout animal lover, and would **never** hurt an animal OR another being that cannot defend itself. A True Witch is a very ethical person!

Air Her Breath, 2004

Mountain Moon Circle
~ Presents ~
Air, Her Breath ~ SummerFest 2004

Welcome to Mountain Moon Circle's sixth annual SummerFest event! We're excited you are here to share this experience with us and our very special guests, Ariel Fernandez and Draco Alexander.

Mountain Moon Circle is an eclectic Wiccan/Pagan Circle in Billings, MT, which was established in February of 2000. Lady Nytewind offers beginning and advanced classes in Wicca, a nature-based religion that honors the changing seasons, the Earth and the divine. We seek to align our personal energies with the energies of the Earth and live the philosophy "an it harm none."

Our event kicks off with the two pre-opening workshops (beginning at 5) and Opening Circle at 8:30 p.m. tonight. But first, feel free to settle in to your cabins and then take a walk over to the Faery Portal (see enclosed map) to experience the Feiry World and the Element of Air. It is at the Portal that you can let go of your worldly cares and prepare yourself for a weekend of spirit, love, laughter and fun!

While you are here, we have just a few things we ask of you:

- No motorized vehicles are allowed except in the designated parking area.

- Help keep our campground clean by picking up any garbage. We'd like to leave the campground spotless.
- Please stay after the closing circle on Sunday to help with cleanup and take-down. Your efforts will be much appreciated by MMC, and it's a great way to get grounded! We must vacate the campsite by 2 pm.
- To promote atmosphere, please leave cabin outside lights off, and interior lights off during the Bardic Circle Saturday night.

We hope that while you are here, that you make many friends, enjoy the workshops and have a spiritually uplifting experience.

"Be Healed", "Be Inspired", "Listen", "Speak Your Truth", and "Begin Anew!"

Welcome Home!

Lady Nytewind & Mountain Moon Circle

Welcome Home! Lady Nytewind & Mountain Moon Circle

Air, Her Breath: Schedule 2004

Friday, July 2, 2004

3:00 – 8:00   **Registration**—packet and check in at the Recreation Hall, unload gear into your cabin and visit the Fairy Portal.

5:00 – 6:00   **Sacred Breath**—chants taught by Karen Eddy in the Story Cabin.

6:00 – 7:30   **Dinner**—served in the Dining Hall.

7:30 – 8:30   **Arrows of Intention**—instruction by Debra Harris.

9:30 – 10:30   **Sacred Smoke**—Instruction by Barbara Merriman on creating incense

11 pm –   **Opening Circle**—listen for the call to participate (horn and chanting).

Saturday, July 3, 2004

7:00 – 8:30   **Breakfast** served in the Dining Hall

9:00 – 10:30   **The Art of Aromatherapy**—Special Guest Instructor, Ariel Fernandez.

10:45 – 12:15 **Pranayama Breathwork**—Special Guest Instructor, Elizabeth Klarich.

12:15 – 1:15   **Lunch** in the Dining Hall.

1:15 – 2:45   **Vibratory Air: Tthe Drum**—Special Guest Instructor, Chet Leach.

3:00 – 4:30   **Vibratory Air: Sounds of Your Heart Tones**—Ariel Fernandez.

4:45 – 6:15   **Bardic Storytelling:** Special Guest Instructor, Don R. Larson.

6:30 – 8:00   **Dinner** at the Dining Hall

8:30 – 900   **Arrows of Intention**—Sending your intentions into the air

9:30 – done   **Bardic Fire Circle & Journey to the five Temples of Air**

Sunday, July 4, 2004

7:30 – 9:00   **Breakfast** in the Dining Hall

9:30 – 11:00   **Peruvian Whistling Vessels;** Ariel Fernandez.

11:30 – 12:30 **Lunch** in the Dining Hall

1:00 – 1:30   **Closing Ritual**

2:00   **Goodbye** until next year!

(We needed to vacate the camp by this time.)

Mountain Moon Circle's Summerfest: rituals from "Air – 2004"

Mountain Moon Circle is an eclectic Wiccan/Pagan Circle in Billings, MT, established in February 2001. High Priestess Lady Nytewind offers classes in Alchemy, Astrology, and Beginning and Advanced Wicca (a nature-based religion that honors the changing seasons, the Earth and the divine.) We seek to align our personal energies with the energies of the Earth and live the philosophy, "an it harm none."

Our first camp was in 2004 and was a sudden decision to offer a camp in Montana. I had attended some in other states, but no one here had any experience with Fire Circles. I came home from one on the east coast and decided that I'd see if a camp was available. I found one that was perfect, but only available for two nights. I thought that would make a good start.

I decided not to try the Alchemical all-night fires at our first event. I would have a year to teach my circle the purposes and practices of the alchemical fire circles. It would be impossible to give credit to each and every piece of writing I included in my rituals, as many bits and pieces came from sources on the web long ago. At the time, I had no idea that I would ever publish this work, which is my sort of *Book of Shadows.* All of the things I used in the past for these camping events, which were held annually for nine years, I include here, but much in the rituals has been removed as I cannot determine authorship. Contact me if you have questions.

None of this could have happened without the help and cooperation of our Mountain Moon Circle members, who worked hard and put up with my bossiness and perfectionism. Also, I give many, many thanks to the great guest teachers and friends that taught the wonderful workshops throughout these days and nights!

Opening Circle – 1st Night
2004: The Four Winds

Needs: censor, incense, lighter, basket of bubbles, CD player & *Fairy Heartmagic* CD, athame, and sword, flour to mark the circle, feather fan, flower garland, book, stand, weights & light.
Gather Participants, using 'Between the Worlds' Chant. All form circle except Quarters, who stand at the gate.

Chant: Come and walk between the worlds and see what's waiting there;
Between the worlds, within the sphere, there's magick in the air!
Come and walk, and walk your talk and see who's waiting there;
The Gods are there the Goddess is there, there's magick everywhere!

Cast circle: *Cut a door and admit quarters, twirling capes to CD: Fairy Heartmagic #9 by Gary Stadler. Seal Circle w/Holy Water & incense.*

East: *(Begin by playing flute or tin whistle)*
Ancient ones of the East, Portal of Air,
With flute, we stir and summon thee
To ask and honor your presence here
Dancing winds and sylphs of air
Join with us this evening fair.
Winged ones, birds of flight,
Breaking dawn that dispels night…

South: *(Play soft strings)*
Ancient ones of the South, Portal of Fire,
With strings, we stir and summon thee.
To ask and honor your presence here!
Salamanders, spirits of fire
Join with us as we desire.
Sparks and flames feed our souls
Give us the courage to reach our goals…
Light this magick in the dark
So Mote it Be!

West: *(rain stick)*
>Ancient ones of the West, Portal of Water,
>With rain stick we stir and summon thee.
>To ask and honor your presence here!
>Merfolk and water sprites
>Join us in our magick rites.
>Mother's love and care we seek
>Since first from out the womb we peek.

North: *(drum heartbeat)*
>Ancient ones of the North, Portal of Earth,
>With the drum, we stir and summon thee.
>To ask and honor your presence here!
>Wee Folk, Elves, and Gnomes below
>Join us now and help us grow.
>Earth below, sky above,
>All that lives infused with love.
>
>With Her Body beneath our feet,
>The Wheel of magick, is now complete!
>So Mote it Be!

(I do not know if I wrote the words spoken by the High Priest (HP) and High Priestess (HPS) so I have removed most of them. I often do automatic writing, so it's too hard to tell.)

Dance w/fans: CD: *Fairy Heartmagic* by Gary Standler (Since I had been a dance teacher for many years, I formed a Belly Dance Troup for members that wanted to dance.) They did a Great job, and added a lot to many of our rituals.

Element of Air Chant

>Air is the healer, be healed, be healed
>Air is the messenger, listen, listen
>Air is inspiration, be inspired
>And ride on the wings of golden light!
>Air's communication, speak your truth
>Air is new beginnings, begin now, begin now
>Breath of the four winds lift me up
>To ride on the wings of golden light!

Bubbles: *Pass out bubble so all can blow them into the sky*

HPS: Fill the lungs and you are born!
           Breathe through joy and breathe through strife,
           The rhythm persists throughout your life,
           Till your last gasp, when the veil be torn
           First, there's life, then there's death
           The rhythm of being is in the breath

All: Breathe in, breathe out!
           With our breath, we sing and shout!

HP: There's magick in the air!
           Prana, Mana, Chi!
           Giving life to you and me
           And all life everywhere!
           Inhale deeply, suck it in
           And let the healing now begin!

All: Breathe in, breathe out!
           With our breath, we sing and shout!

HPS: Breezes warm and gentle blow.
           Power comes with the storm
           And brings the chance to transform.
           Wind often brings us rain or snow.
           We fly our kites or soar aloft
           On the air, both strong and soft.

All: Breathe in, breathe out!
           With our breath, we sing and shout!

HP: We honor the airy ones
           With gossamer or feathered wings enabling them to fly
           Who ride upon the winds and populate the sky.
           And 'ner forget the fairy kin nor dragons in the sun.

Charlyn Scheffelman (Lady Nytewind)

All: Breathe in, breathe out!
With our breath, we sing and shout!

Chant, leading into a spiral dance.
Spirit of the Air, carry me home
Spirit of the Air, carry me home
Spirit of the Air, carry me home to myself

Closing:

East: Eurana, Lady of the Eastern wind,
Eagle, butterfly, sprites, and sylphs,
We have been honored by your presence,
Your gaiety and laughter,
And your bright promise of Spring.
We shall take with us memories
Of gentle breezes and good, clean air.
Hail and farewell.

North: Boreana, Lady of the north wind,
Gnomes, Dryads and tunneling creatures,
We have been honored by your presence
Your challenges and guidance,
And deeper mysteries.
We shall take with us memories
And deeper understanding
Into the coming chill of winter.
Hail and farewell.

West: Zephrina, Lady of the Western wind,
Undines, Merfolk, and aquatic life,
We have been honored by your presence,
Your love and compassion,
Shared visions and pain healed.
We shall take with us memories
Of wood fire burning and Fall turning.
Hail and farewell.

South: Nona, Lady of the South wind,

Salamanders, dragons, and lions,
We have been honored by your presence,
Your passion and truth,
And the warmth of the summer sun.
We shall take with us memories
Of glowing embers and heart songs.
Hail and farewell.

Dismiss Circle: *(This is the standard for all of our circles)*
May the circle be open but unbroken
May the Lord and the Lady be ever in your heart.
Merry meet and merry part, And merry meet again.

Bardic Circle & Journey, 2ⁿᵈ Night: 2004

People gathered around the fire to share stories, poetry, feelings, drumming, dancing, or whatever they wish until the wee hours of the morning. Guides took people throughout the night (singly or in very small groups) to visit all 1-5 installations.

Journey through the 5 Qualities of Air

1. Air is the healer—be healed

Thoth – (Egypt) and a servant, who holds the caduceus, plays singing bowl and helps with the flash.

Set: A 10x10 gazebo, walls covered with Egyptian-looking drapes, a blow-up life-sized mummy and several statues (Thoth, Anubis, Sekhmet, Bast, scarab, pyramid) and other objects from Egypt placed on covered tables. I made a caduceus and had a suitable Egyptian rug for the floor. Characters should be dressed like an Egyptian king (or queen) and servant.

Needs: Egyptian incense & burner, lighter & charcoal, candles & holders, crystal (or brass) singing bowl, Ignition thing (from a magic store w/ flash cotton), Fire extinguisher.

King/Queen: *Servant is also present playing singing bowl*
"Welcome to the Temple of Thoth, God of all learning and hidden knowledge: God without parents, who precedes all others and the "Source of the Word". Thoth gave man the power of logic and taught him to arrange his speech patterns and write down his thoughts. His creative will power fashions reality, and his word becomes manifest in the world.

He is first known in the line of great magicians and miraculous healers known as Hermes Trismegistus. The oldest book in the world says of him "Man's guide is Thoth, who makes the books and illumines those who are learned therein, and the physicians who follow him, that they may work cures."

Behold the caduceus he carries (show it), ancient symbol of bodily alchemy, and modern symbol of medical and healing arts. It represents the seven ancient forces of alchemy: the staff represents the energy channel of salt (the human spine), and the entwined snakes represent the elements of Sulfur and Mercury (also known as the kundalini). The base of the staff represents the element of Earth. Water is the staff's hidden power as a universal solvent; the two wings represent Air, and Fire is contained in the solar disk at the top. Thus are the seven stages of Alchemical transformation and healing represented and contained in this magickal staff.

In order for you to continue your journey into the meaning of the element of Air, you must experience the healing power of the caduceus. Please close your eyes and concentrate on the condition you would like to be healed in your body **or** your life as you hold and feel the power of this magickal staff.

*(As they hold the staff, one of the characters runs a finger up the spine **quickly** while the other ignites the flash paper in front of the visitor's closed eyes.)*

Go now, and continue your journey through Air."

2. Air is the messenger—listen

Set: This tent was white, draped with white, silver and gold. A silver tarp covered the ground. Mercury wore silver tights and traditional silver costume with a silver half-mask, winged hat, and boots. Grecian columns were made from 8" diameter concrete form tubes covered with corrugated plastic. A two inch (or more) thick square of foam insulation board with a hole cut to fit a paint can (full) provided footing for the columns. Greek statues sat on small tables covered with silver or gold cloths, silver and gold lanterns and little white light strings strung on the ceiling provided lighting and atmosphere. Grecian pedestals held Greek statues.

Needs: Charcoal & lighter, incense, floor covering, fire extinguisher, weights for columns (full gallon pain cans fit inside the columns) CD: *Abaracadabara* by Jeff McBride.

Mercury (Opening of the ears)
"Welcome, welcome. I am Mercury, fleet of foot and swift of thought! Welcome to my temple! I am known the messenger of the Gods, for only I can pass between the worlds at will. I carry messages from the Gods to humans and to each other, as I pass swiftly between heaven and the underworld to do their bidding.

But I am here tonight to connect with you, to remind you that the small voice within that advises and warns you, that guides and speaks to you sometimes in your dreams, should be heeded! Often, I bring messages to you, and you will hear them but not 'Listen' to them. Messages are not a one-way street, you know. I hear you talking to your Gods. Do you not expect an answer? And if the answer comes but you do not act upon it, I am affronted! Mine is not an easy job. Humans all too often forget that I exist!

Perhaps the problem can be addressed by fine-tuning your hearing!

(Look in the person's ears, hem & haw while you examine them).

Perhaps a bit of magick will help. *(play abaracadabra while pantomiming pulling "stuff" out of the ears with a "shoop" sound. You are symbolically pulling 'webs' from the ears, so be very dramatic about it).*

Yes! There were doubts in there; doubts about what you hear being true; doubts about yourself and your ability to communicate with your Gods! There were doubts that you might be thought of as "crazy" – by yourself or by another! There were doubts that you are not GOOD enough to be of concern to your Gods!

I have removed a great many of these doubts, so continue your journey and remember to LISTEN – LISTEN – LISTEN to your intuition and to your Gods, for they are the same!"

3. Air is inspiration—be inspired - Cerridwen (Wales)

Drink from the cauldron of inspiration

*(Open crown chakra using D'Lite – a magician's
trick that lights up - on the forehead)*

Set: 10x10 tent with walls draped in black. The wall on the right was decorated to represent spring, with tapestries of the Celtic tree of life, flowers, an image of the Green Man, a maiden Goddess statue, Moons, etc. The left wall represented fall, with wheat, grapes, suns, stag horns, Mother Earth statue, cornucopias, leafless tree, etc. On the back wall, a black table held a large cauldron with a black bowl inside, dipper & small paper cups, and a statue of Hecate, Cerridwen or another crone.

Needs: Celtic incense & burner, charcoal & lighter, Ivy garland for table, candles & candle holders, Black mask & robe for witch, Fire extinguisher, a magic trick called Delite (to wear on the thumb) and a delicious hot tea for the cauldron.

Crone:

"Welcome to the Temple of the Triple Goddess. I am the Shape-shifter Cerridwen, Crone, and Goddess of death, regeneration, magick, herbs and inspiration.

The altar on your right represents the Maiden, the Earth Goddess of Spring. She, along with the Green man, brings new life and new growth to the world after the long sleep of winter. Their love awakens the world once again to the light in that turning of the wheel, causing the plants to flourish and the fields and flocks to be fertile.

The altar on your left represents the Mother, the Goddess of the Harvest time. It is she who ripens the fruit and the grain and blesses the crops that are gathered in the fall. Her beneficent blessings insure that there will be food to sustain life through the long winter.

Yet when the harvest is done, it is I who cause the world to be dormant and the cold of winter winds to blow. In this time, if you turn to me, I will guide you in your dreams and prepare you for the next turning of the wheel.

We are three, yet we are one, for as the Great Wheel of the Year turns, we transform from one to the other, ever keeping watch over the seasons, the fields and the flocks. In this way is balance obtained. In this way is the wheel kept turning, passing from light to dark and to light again.

Before me is the Great Cauldron of Inspiration and knowledge. All who drink the Grael within, brewed with nine magickal herbs and infused with a spark of enchantment, may thereafter receive the gifts of inspiration, divine knowledge, and foresight. This, I offer to you. *(Serve the tea)*.

Go forth on your journey into the element of Air and remember that Air is Inspiration. Be now inspired."

4. Air is communication—speak your truth

Tirawa *(Pawnee God of Speech)*

Set: A tent, as teepee-like as possible, contains Native American décor. I was lucky to be able to borrow a wolf hide and a buffalo hide, had dream catchers, drums and other objects to use. The character can be either male or female, adjusting the wording to fit, and is dressed as Native American as possible.

Needs: Tobacco, Peace pipe, Rattle, Drum or Shamanic drum CD, and Sage incense

Blessing the Throat Chakra: Speak Your Truth

"Welcome to the lodge of the Great Tirawa, God of the Pawnee and giver of human speech, which he gifted to mankind many long years ago. I now bring his message to you. *(Smudge with sage).*

Words have power, and by giving man the power of speech, Tirawa gave him power—the power to express himself, to create with his voice the prayers and praises offered to the Gods, and to tell others of his thoughts and feelings.

Some time ago, man learned to corrupt that power in an attempt to please others—to keep the peace or to be accepted by his peers, and even to speak falsely and deceitfully to others.

Man must re-learn to use the power granted by Tirawa as it was meant to be: speaking of his true feelings and thoughts, to be empowered by his words. He must be confidant in who he is, giving his word as his honor and allowing himself to let his spirit shine through his spoken and written words. Only then can men learn to trust in each other.

The power to speak resides here, in the throat. The smoke of the sacred pipe has the ability to purify, sanctify and re-initiate you into the power of your words.

(Shake rattle all around the person, chanting some (probably fake) Indian language, then do the pipe ceremony. When done, say something like) Go forth and Speak Your Truth!"

4. Air is new beginnings—start now: *Ganesha, Lord of Obstacles*

Set: 10x10 gazebo, draped with Ganesha and other East Indian tapestry, Ganesha statue and other Indian deities, altar with candles & candle holders, Sitar music plays in the background. There are cushions on the floor.

Needs: Flowers, rice, fruit, 3 brass bowls, tray & spoon, red kum-kum, dish & water, Nag Champa incense & holder, oil lamps, temple bell, flash cotton, sparkle powder, clear marble and a lotus (fake) flower.

Determine if the obstacle is of the head (lavender), heart (green) or will (yellow) by the colored flower they choose. To remove obstacles: Dab flash cotton with sparkle powder and burn in the lamp. Mark visitors forehead w/kum-kum.

Display lotus – (by Karen Eddy written specifically for this event) "Greetings, seeker: I am Shiddhi of achievement, a consort in this house of

Ganesha. It occurs to me as you've entered…that…it seems…as though you are here to…ask for a boon of Ganesha…to ask that obstacles be removed… and to launch a new beginning…?

Well, Ganesha's large ears hear all requests. Ganesha's wisdom speaks and writes your universe into existence because Ganesha IS <u>AUM</u>. Ganesha powers the Kundalini, comes from the root, from Earth. Ganesha's trunk uproots the greatest obstacle: a tree, boulder……or blockage - yet it can discern among the most tender blades of grass, or lift a needle from the ground. So it is that the elephant-headed Ganesha rides on a mouse, to show the power of balance between great things and tiny, hidden things.

Whatever you want to begin in your life, first ask Ganesha to clear obstacles, and to make it happen. Ganesha, we honor You with these offerings. *(Throw: rice, spooned water, white flower - on image)* Seeker, close your eyes. Breathe deeply from your belly. Inhale. Feel your belly to be a void within you. *(ring <u>BELL</u> - wait for sound to finish)*

As you breathe, see this void begin to fill with a yellow mist. *(<u>BELL</u> - wait for sound to finish).* See the mist begin to form a shape: the shape of the elephant-headed one, Ganesha. *(<u>BELL</u> – same)*

Ganesha, within, clears obstacles to grant your new beginnings. Discern now the flower, which most represents your obstacles. *(Seeker chooses a colored flower).*

Ganesha, hear now our plea. Remove this seeker's obstacles. Clear the blockage in this seeker's Mind/heart/will (solar plexus). *(Hold up flash cotton)* Like your tiny omniscient mouse, Ganesha, *(APPLY FLASH-COTTON TO CHAKRA)* let this small cotton absorb all the negative energy. Absorb the blockage in this seeker.

> Oh, Ancient One of strength and might,
> Come and aid us in this plight.
> Push through all that's in our way,
> Let it fall and crumble this day.
> So our path is clear and free.
> As we will, so mote it be!
> *(BURN FLASH COTTON IN FLAME)*
> AUMmmmm

(To image) Ganesha, with your light
    You have consumed this seeker's plight.

Charlyn Scheffelman (Lady Nytewind)

> We've surrendered all problems at your feet,
> Knowing you'll solve each problem we meet,
> As all blockages we've surrendered into your power,
> Now we leave you our chosen flower.

(*Direct seeker's colored flower to image and with 4th finger, apply the red paste to seeker's third-eye*).

Your issues are transformed for you. (*Offer first initiation item*) With this glass emblem of Air, we recognize and honor Ganesha's power, inside you and outside you. Protect it, and use this piece to remember all you have learned. (*Open doorway*) Now, go - follow your liberation."

Closing Ritual – last morning before breaking camp

Due to copyright restrictions, all rituals have been edited to comply with copyright laws. If you have questions, please contact me. Three dots indicate there is more information I cannot reveal.

HPS: Oh, that I could live within the Air,
And dance upon the backs of clouds…

HP: And be of such a mind, so divine
That all regions would spring forth
To my discerning ear…

HPS: That on the wind which blows
From a Portal of Air
There would sing many voices…

HPS: Thus concludes our journey through the element of air, Breath of the Goddess. It is our hope that you have had an enjoyable weekend. Please accept our thanks for your presence at this first Montana festival.

I'd like to offer special thanks to our guest teachers, Ariel, Don, Chet, and Elizabeth for their beautiful contribution to this work, and to Bob and Norma, Priest and Priestess of Desert Moon Circle in Las Vegas, for their love and support.

Thank you too, to all the MMC members who worked so hard to accomplish this weekend.

Spirit of Fire:

Sing or play *I am the Fire* from *Fire of Creation* CD: by Abigail Spinner McBride

> *I am the fire and the Union of Opposites*
> *I am the mystery*

Charlyn Scheffelman (Lady Nytewind)

> *I am calling you, in your dreams*
> *I am bringing you home, to me.*

End with: I invite you to SummerFest, 2005, **Fire, Her Spirit!**

HP: Power of the four winds,
Eurus! Notus! Zephyrus! Boreas!
Winged angels, Raphael!
All sylphs, fairies, and creatures of the air!
Your presence has been evident
Throughout this Portal of Air!
Through the breath of the Gods,
We felt thee!
Through the beat of wings,
We felt thee!
Through the whispering wind,
We felt thee!

Honored ones, we offer our gratitude for your presence and
for the lessons and experiences you've given us. Stay if you
will, but go if you must. We bid you 'hail and farewell!

HPS: We thank you, Cardea, Queen of the Winds,
Opener of every door in the future
Closer of every door in the past
Help us to live truly in the Now, knowing
You are our Guide through the corridor of life.
Heart of the Wind, we thank you
Keeper of the keys to all wisdom
Your zephyr brings love with knowledge.
Stay if you will, but go if you must,
We bid you 'Hail and Farewell'

East: Ancient ones of the East, Portal of Air,
We thank thee for your presence here!
For dancing winds and sylphs of air
Winged ones, and birds of flight,
For power of thought, and spoken word

Healing ways and golden light
With Her breath, out and in,
With new knowledge, we'll begin.
Stay if you will, but go if you must
We bid you hail and Farewell!

North: Ancient ones of the North, Portal of Earth,
We thank thee for your presence here!
For Wee Folk, Elves, and Gnomes
Earth below, and sky above,
Creatures large and creatures small,
Seeds that grow, and flowers that bloom
With Her Body beneath our feet,
We've gathered for this Merry Meet
Stay if you will, but go if you must
We bid you hail and Farewell!

West: Ancient ones of the West,
Portal of Water,
We thank thee for your presence here!
For Merfolk and water sprites,
The Mother's love and Secrets deep,
For lovers, sisters, brothers, friends,
And compassion that never ends.
By her blood, circling round
Love unconditional we've found.
Stay if you will, but go if you must
We bid you hail and Farewell!

South: Ancient ones of the South,
Portal of Fire,
We thank thee for your presence here!
For Salamanders, and spirits of fire
Sparks and flames that transform
For the love and passion of life's flame
And fulfillment of will and desire.
With her Spirit as the spark
From this place we now embark.

Charlyn Scheffelman (Lady Nytewind)

> Stay if you will, but go if you must
> We bid you hail and Farewell!

Dismiss Circle

> May the circle be open, but unbroken
> May the Lord and the Lady be ever in your heart.
> Merry meet and merry part
> And merry meet again.

Mountain Moon Summerfest – Air 2009

Tuesday

2:00 pm on: Check in
5:30-7:00: Dinner
7:00-8:00: Arrows of Intention & Required Sacred Fire Orientation
8:15-9:00: Talent show
11:00 – Dawn: Opening Ritual & Sacred Alchemical Fire Circle

Wednesday

Dawn-9:00 - Breakfast
11:00-12:00 - Beginning Drumming
12:00-1:00 – Lunch
1:15-2:45 – Aromatic Air
3:00-4:30 – Sacred Heart Songs, Part I
4:45-6:00 pm – 2012: Prophecies & Predictions
6:00-7:30 pm – Dinner
11:00 pm – Dawn - Ritual and Sacred Alchemical Fire Circle

Thursday:

Dawn-9:00 am - Breakfast
11:00-12:00 – Vibratory Air: Sounds of Your Heart Tones
12:00-1:00 - Lunch
1:15-2:45– Sacred Heart Songs; Part II
3:00-4:30 - 2012: Can we Prepare?
4:45-6:00 - Whistling Jugs
6:00-7:30 – Dinner
7:30-8:30 – Arrows of intention
11:00 pm - 3:00 am? Ritual & Sacred Alchemical Fire Circle:

Friday:

Pack up camp - 9:00 am-10 am - Brunch:
10:00 am –10:30 am - Closing ritual, Finish camp cleanup & vacate by 11:00am

Rituals from Air 2009 - Four Winds, 1st Night Ritual

By now, many people were working all night at the fire circle. Since each night's fire begins with a ritual, I reused some of the information from the 2004 Air event by bringing it into the circle during the night as you will see. Pick a time when the energy starts to drop, then have Ganesha and/or Mercury enter the circle. Ganesha to remove obstacles brings her kum-kum, incense, flash cotton, and sparkle. She wears a gray robe and elephant mask, and flame color stuff. Mercury, in costume, repeats pulling "stuff" from people's ears, etc.

Needs: Censor, Altar of Magic incense, lighter, charcoal, baskets of bubbles, CD player & CD, athame and sword, feather fan, book, stand, weights, light, witch ball & fairy, silver water bowl & mermaid, crystal, light & gnome, sun & dragon, flute, sparkler, rain stick & drum, bubble machine & bubbles.

(Smudge at the gate, admit all), Cast & seal circle: Dance, using bubble machine, then light the fire; play *Behold there is Magick*, from *Enter the Center* CD: by Jeff & Spinner McBride.

Same quarters as in 2004 but calling cross quarters.
East: (flute
South: (gong & sparkler)
West: (rain stick)
North: (drum heartbeat)

HPS:

Breathe with me! The breath units us! *(breathing together ritual)*. We call to the spirits of this place this land, this sky and all that has it's being here. With honor and respect, we call you. With humble hearts, we call you. With gratitude and love, we call you. We have gathered in this holy place to seek guidance, to give thanks, and to strip away that in ourselves which is not part of our true nature.

We seek our highest good. For three suns we will walk this land in peace and love, with respect for all that is, seeking to transform and improve our lives and our spiritual beings. Spirits, we ask that you aide us in our quest.

HP: Aeolus, Father and King of the four winds, Viceroy of the Gods, we call to thee! Be present tonight with your children as we give honor and praise to your being! Come from the vast caves of Aeolia, Thou King of the winds!

> Hail unto Thee, Who art the Winds,
> Who sweepest across the face of the Earth…

HPS: Cardea, Queen of the Winds, Keeper of the doors, we call to thee! Bring the freshening breeze in to our lives, So that we may breathe deeply of life!
Lady of the wind of Change, Scatter the stale dust from our minds…

Element of Air Chant - (Pass out bubbles)

> Air is the healer, be healed, be healed
> Air is the messenger, listen, listen
> Air is inspiration, be inspired
> And ride on the wings of golden light!
> Air's communication, speak your truth
> Air is new beginnings, begin now, begin now
> Breath of the four winds lift me up
> To ride on the wings of golden light!

Ganesha: *(These actors can enter at any time during the night that's appropriate to do their parts)*

I represent Ganesha, Lord of Beginnings and Lord of Obstacles, Patron of Arts and Sciences, and the Deva of Intellect and Wisdom. I perceive that many of you hope to seek a new beginning here tonight, yet feel hindered by obstacles, real or imagined, that stand in your way.

Know that my mighty trunk can uproot the greatest obstacle; a tree, a boulder; whatever stands in your way…yet it can discern amongst the most tender blades of grass, or lift a needle from the ground. So it is that I often ride on a tiny mouse, to show the power of balance between great things and tiny hidden things.

Whatever you want to begin in your life, first ask me to clear the obstacles, and to make it happen. My large ears hear all requests. My wisdom speaks and as I speak, I write your universe into existence, for I **am** AUM!

Seeker, close your eyes. Breathe deeply, from your belly. Feel your belly to be a void within you. As you breathe, see this void begin to fill with a yellow mist. See that mist begin to form a shape-- the shape of the elephant-headed one, Ganesha. Your inner Ganesha will clear your obstacles to grant you new beginnings. *(pass incense)*

Let this incense of sacred herbs absorb all negative blocks from your conscious and subconscious mind, and all negative blocks that hinder you in the material or spiritual world. Add 'an it harm none' and ask Ganasha to clear the blockages in your way as you offer the incense to the fire. Please repeat after me.

> Salutations to Lord Ganesha,
> Whose curved trunk and massive body
> Shines like a million suns
> And showers his blessings on everyone.
> Lord Ganesha kindly remove all obstacles
> From all my activities and endeavors.
> That my way be clear and free,
> An it harm none, so mote it be!

(Play CD, sitar music: After the offering, anoint the third eye with kum-kum, using 4ᵗʰ finger. Say "Your obstacles are transformed for you" & throw color stuff into the flire and leave circle)

Mercury: *(in costume. Have crystal or brass singing bowl near)*

I am Hermes, also known as Mercury, Messenger of the Gods! I am the son of Zues, Great king of the Gods and Maia, Goddess of the Clouds and the Pleiades. I dwell between the worlds, for I travel swiftly between the world of the Gods, the world of men, and the underworld of the dead.

I perform many deeds at the behest of the Gods. Zeus often sends me to deliver dreams or to travel with a mortal to help keep him or her safe. For Hades, I guide the dead into the Underworld. It was I who interceded between Hades and Zeus for the release of Persephone in order to appease her mother, Hecate who did then released the world from winter.

But I am here tonight for you—each of you! Often I whisper messages in your ears, but you do not hear me. The Gods speak to you often, but tire of your failure to hear them.

Too often your rational, conscious minds tell you that what you hear or think is only your imagination! You are blocked by emotions; by fears and thoughts chasing themselves around and around in your minds: dwelling on the past, which cannot be changed. Worrying about what might, could, or should happen in the future, instead of listening to guidance from without and from within.

Tonight, my helpers and I will remove those blocks, so that you may clearly hear the messages of the Gods. Close your eyes. Listen to the powerful sound of the crystal bowl."

Dance and trance until sunrise!

At Dawn: (Best to have everyone memorize this before the event)
Solar Salutation, by Katlyn Breene

The Sun rises

We lift out hands unto it

To be reborn
Like the day

Golden rays pierce our hearts

Like arrows of light
Dispelling the illusion
Releasing the night
Solar alchemy
Filling each cell of our body
Transforming, transmuting
Lead into purest gold
As above, so below
The Sun sees itself in the fire
In each other, We see God

2nd Night Butterfly Maiden - 2009

Needs: Native American costume, butterfly tokens

Cast & seal circle *(with elements to drum beat)*

East: *(eagle)* Great Spirits of the Air, We call thee to attend us with Feathered Counsel.

By the dreams of the bright-winged spirits, reveal to us an understanding of our path and teach us to live in balance. Help us tend the wisdom in our hearts that we may live and act in harmony with our planet. Hiyaka!

South: *(rabbit)* Great Spirits of Fire, We call thee to gather at our Hearth of Compassion.

Tend the embers of protection and shelter to fashion for us a gleaming shield of strength and vitality. Under your potent magick, may we safe-guard The pulse of life around us. Hiyaka!

West: *(dolphin)* Great Spirits of the Waters, We call thee to attend our Harbor of Devotion. As you nurture the teeming life of your vast oceans, may we restore your wheel of balance, that you might feed both air and fountain for plants and animals wild and tame, giver of life's magic rain. Hiyaka!

North: *(deer)* Great Spirits of the Earth,
We call thee to attend us in your Womb of Creation. As the Silver Horns have cycled once more and the Great Spirit has taken his Bride, may we, too, revivify the gardeners' tutelage and skill. Convey us on our journey to remember and cherish your caved and artesian secrets. Hiyaka!

HPS:
　　Black Elk said "Everything the power of the world does is done in a circle. The sky is round, the earth is round like a ball, and so are all the stars. The wind, in its greatest power, whirls... the sun comes forth and goes down in a circle. The moon does the same... even the seasons form a great circle in their changing and always come back again to where they were before. The life of a man is a circle... and it is in everything where power moves."

We come together in this circle in the same way indigenous people all over the earth have for untold centuries. We come to express our joys and our pain, to honor the ancestors, the spirits of the elements, the earth, and the otherworld, and to pray for our planet and our own spiritual growth.

HP: From above, Great Spirit of the Sky World,
We call thee to attend us from your Starry Realm.
Guide our spirits in our quest for balance in the universe.
Hiyaka!

HPS: From Below, Great Spirit, Earth Mother,
We call thee to attend us from your Ancient and Wise realm.
Give us the wisdom to commune with the elements
in accord with the Ancient ones for balance on this Planet.
Hiyaka!

HPS: *Tells the Papago legend of Butterfly Maiden.*
http://www.ya-native.com/Culture_SouthWest/legends/
ThePapagoButterflyLegend.html

HP: Butterfly Maiden, we call to thee!
Come, bring your powerful medicine!
Help us to know our own minds,
That we may transform our lives through wisdom.
You, with the beauty of Gaia's colors, Dance gaily in our world.
You are truth and beauty, and the promise of beauty at the end the trial.
Come to us, sweet Maiden, Come!

BM: *A Papago American Indian legend:*
I was not always as you see me, for I began life as a small egg. When the life within the egg grew, it became too tight, too crowded. One day, it hatched. What emerged was a caterpillar, which spent her days crawling along the ground and in the trees searching for food.

HPS: But this was only the beginning, for the caterpillar is but the beginning of a miracle. The caterpillar, knowing not why, began one day to spin. She spun and spun until she had created for herself a cocoon which encased her whole body.

BM: I slept within this cocoon for many days, all the while growing and changing—into something else. When the time was right, I opened the cocoon and found, to my surprise that I had beautiful wings! I flew to taste the flowers, and to float above the grass! I flew into the branches of the trees and gazed at my reflection in the pool. I had transformed into a creature of beauty!

You, also are not the person you were years ago as life, for you, too, is a process—a miracle; ever changing, ever evolving, ever seeking to know yourself and to connect with the divine. It is possible that one day you, too, will find yourself transformed into the most beautiful creation you can be, full of joy and compassion, seeking only to express the light within.

I am here tonight to aide you in your quest to identify and transform some things that may be negative in your life into positive expressions of beauty; to assist you in your own transformations into the highest expression of good. Here to help us the great Tirawa

Tiriwa:

I (am, or represent depending on male/female) the Great Tirawa, God of the Pawnee and giver of human speech, which he gifted to mankind many long years ago. I bring his message to you.

Words have power, and by giving man the power of speech, Tirawa gave him the power to express himself, to create with his voice the prayers and praises offered to the Gods, and to tell others of his thoughts and feelings. But some time ago, man learned to corrupt that power in an attempt to please others—to keep the peace or to be accepted by his peers, and even to speak falsely and deceitfully to others.

Man must re-learn to use the power granted by Tirawa as it was meant to be; speaking of his true feelings and thoughts, to be empowered by his own words. He must be confidant in who he is, giving his word as his honor and allowing himself to let his spirit shine through his spoken and written words. Only then can men learn to trust each other.

The power to speak resides here, in the throat. With this sacred rattle and powerful magickal oil, I have the ability to purify, sanctify and re-initiate you into the power of your words. *(Shake rattle for each person, then anoint the throat chakra*

Go forth and speak Your Truth! *(Leave circle)*

Chant:

Oh, Great Spirit, (Oh, sacred mystery)
Earth, wind, sky, and sea
You are inside, And all around me.

Cerridwen enters: *(Needs cauldron & bowl, D'-lite magic trick, dipper & cups, tea)*

I am Cerridwen, Crone and Shape-shifter, Goddess of death, regeneration, magick, herbs, and inspiration.

As the Maiden, I am the Earth Goddess of Spring. She, along with the Green man, brings new life and new growth to the world after the long sleep of winter. Their love awakens the world once again to the light in that turning of the wheel, causing the plants to flourish and the fields and flocks to be fertile.

As the Mother, I am the Goddess of the Harvest time. It is she who ripens the fruit and the grain and blesses the crops that are gathered in the fall. Her beneficent blessings insure that there will be food to sustain life through the long winter.

Yet when the harvest is done, it is I the Crone, who causes the world to be dormant and the cold of winter winds to blow. In this time, if you turn to me, I will guide you in your dreams and prepare you for the next turning of the wheel.

We are three, yet we are one, for as the Great Wheel of the Year turns, we transform from one to the other, ever keeping watch over the seasons, the fields and the flocks. In this way is balance obtained. In this way is the wheel kept turning, passing from light to dark and to light again.

I bring to you the Great Cauldron of Inspiration and knowledge. All who drink the Grael within, brewed with nine magickal herbs and infused with a spark of enchantment, may thereafter receive the gifts of inspiration, divine knowledge, and foresight. This, I offer to you. *(Fill and pass cups of spiced hot tea)*

Go forth on your journey into the element of Air and remember that Air is Inspiration. Be now inspired. *(Leave circle)*

Chant:

Hecate, Cerridwen. Dark Mother, Take Us In
Hecate, Cerridwen. Let Us Be Reborn

BM: Take this token of the work you will do here—the transformation of your physical, emotional, material or spiritual self and your life, into your highest good. *(Pass butterflies and leave the circle.)*

Chant:

> We are a circle moving one with another
> We are moving together, we are one. *(Repeat)*
> I am spirit, and I flow in you
> You are spirit and you flow in me.

All night fire continues; small groups are taken away to the Temple of Thoth, where...

Thoth:

Welcome to the Temple of Thoth, God of all learning and hidden knowledge, God without parents who precedes all others and the "Source of the Word". Thoth gave man the power of logic and taught him to arrange his speech patterns and write down his thoughts. His creative will power fashions reality, and his word becomes manifest in the world. He is first known in the line of great magicians and miraculous healers known as Hermes Trismegistus.

The oldest book in the world says of him "Man's guide is Thoth, who makes the books and illumines those who are learned therein, and the physicians who follow him, that they may work cures."

Behold the caduceus he carries, an ancient symbol of bodily alchemy, and modern symbol of medical and healing arts. It represents the seven ancient forces of alchemy: the staff represents the energy channel of salt (spine), and the entwined snakes represent the elements of Sulfur and Mercury (kundalini). The base of the staff represents the element of Earth, Water is the staff's hidden power as a universal solvent, the two wings represent Air, and Fire is contained in the solar disk at the top. Thus are the seven stages of Alchemical transformation and healing represented and contained in this magickal staff.

In order for you to continue your journey into the meaning of the element of Air, you must experience the healing power of the caduceus. Please close your eyes and concentrate on the condition you would like to be healed in your body or your life as you hold and feel the power of this magickal staff.

(Hand staff to each person in turn. As before, one person runs their finger

up the visitor's spine and the other triggers the flash paper before their closed eyes. Temple set-up, Egyptian theme.)

At Sun Up:

All Recite the *Solar Salutation* by Katlyn Breene

HP: From above, Great Spirit of the Sky World,
You have honored us with your presence,
Your guidance and protection.
Continue to aid us in our quest for balance in the universe.
Return to your Starry Realm with our gratitude. Hiyaka!

HPS: From Below, Great Spirit, Earth Mother,
You have honored us with your presence,
Continue to aid us in our quest for balance on this planet.
Return to your Ancient and Wise Realm with our gratitude. Hiyaka!

East: Great Spirits of the Air, we thank you for attending our Sacred Circle and for your wise council. Stay if you will, go if you must. Nay-ah!

North: Great Spirits of Earth, we thank you for attending our Sacred Circle and for helping us tend the needs of your gardens. Stay if you will, go if you must. Nay-ah!

West: Great Spirits of the Waters, we thank you for attending our Sacred Circle and for helping us restore the balance of water to our planet. Nay-ah!

South: Great Spirits of Fire, we thank you for attending our Sacred Circle and for giving us strength and protection as we seek to balance your blessing of heat with the blessing of rain. Stay if you will, go if you must. Nay-ah!

Dismiss Circle

Third Night: The phoenix Bird 2009

Needs: black cover cloth, red fans, CD – Born live and die, bird girls, bottle of 'tears', temple of sun incense, censor, fan, Phoenix character dressed in a red leotard with red wings and feather headdress.

Cast & Seal Circle: *(cross quarters; meaning stand opposite your quarter, facing into the center of the circle and your true quarter. A large group, or circumstances that might be hard to hear, such as by a rushing stream, will have trouble hearing you otherwise.)*

East

> Eurana, we call thee! Lady of the Eastern Wind
> Be with us this night as we call airy sprites…

South

> Nona, we call thee! Lady of the Southern wind,
> Be with us this night as we call dragons of power…

West

> Zephrina, we call thee! Lady of the Western wind,
> Be with us this night as we call Undines of the deep…

North

> Boreana we call thee, Lady of the northern wind,
> Be with us this night as we call earth-dwelling gnomes…

Statement of Purpose; HPS

Tonight we gather to celebrate our final fire circle together for this event. We come to rejoice in our being, our likes and differences and the process we have set in motion to bring real and positive changes into our lives and our spiritual selves. We rejoice in the power of transformation—the power to become more akin to our ideal selves. *(Light fire)*

HP: Though we celebrate all winged creatures and all spirits of the element of air, tonight we call one winged creature that typifies the alchemical process we have been experiencing. We call to the Phoenix bird, the quintessential being of transformation!

All that is; is born, lives and dies. While here, in this physical existence, we all do the best we can, given the challenges and rewards we have agreed to deal with in this lifetime. We grow and learn, and if wise, we strive to be the best spiritual being living in the flesh that we can be.

HPS: In this time of the world, most of us have come far from living off the land, loving this planet and living in harmony with it, with the animal kingdom, and with each other. We forget the power of the elements—so powerful are they, that we are left helpless in their wake. And so out of touch are we that we are surprised when they give us a glimpse of their might.

The Air has the power to blow away all in its path through terrifying tornadoes and hurricanes. The Fire can consume all, transforming it to ash; even sometimes spewing from the bowels of the earth tons of molten, burning rock. The Water floods the land when the rivers swell or in thousand foot waves; tsunamis. The Earth—the earth has but to shake and cause man's structures to fall, the ground beneath us to split open, land to form or disappear. When this happens, all elements are involved, as the earthquakes cause volcanoes to erupt on land or under the sea, and that causes rampant fire and enormous tidal waves, which cause powerful winds that feed the flames, blow down all in its path and carries ash to distant places. Let us all be humbled by the power of the elements. *(pause)*

So what can we do, we mere mortals, in the time we have here on this earth? We can do exactly what we have been doing these past few days. We can learn, grow, honor nature and transform ourselves into the highest beings we can attain, and, like the phoenix bird, we will live, die, and be reborn.

HPS:

> Bird of life, bird of death
> Come to us at our bequest!
> From your fateful fiery nest
> We dare disturb your final rest
> Come with feathers red and gold
> With your magick powers of old
> From death to life again it's told
> Renewed, revived, your wings unfold.
> *(HP & HPS remove the cover from Phoenix and fire is lit.)*

Phoenix:

It is likely that you have heard of me, for I am a most magickal creature, known by different names in many different lands. I am the miracle of resurrection, rebirth and the immortality of the soul! I am the miraculous resurrection following total destruction. I represent the completion of the alchemical process, for the universe itself, is born in fire, dies in fire, and is reborn in an eternal cycle.

(CD – Phoenix dances with fans; fade & pause at drum section, gets tears from West)

My tears have the magickal power to heal your wounds, whatever they may be. If it be your will, come forth and feel the regenerative power of fire and I will share my healing tears with you. *(Resume music softly, participants come receive a few tears)*

> My yesterdays were burned by Phoenix fire
> Yet in the death's ash, embers of hope remain
> New dreams gave birth from despair
> Covered with ashes, I mourn what was
> To remember what will be no more
> But I am the Phoenix, and I shall rise
> With renewed passion glowing red, yellow, orange
> Ashes will give way to flame
> I am the Phoenix, I will soar again,
> Transformed and renewed to live again!

HP: So when the new-born Phoenix first is seen
Her feathered subjects all adore their queen,
And while she makes her progress through the East,
From every grove her numerous train's increased;
Each poet of the air her glory sings.

--Poem by John Dryden, *The Poems of John Dryden:*
Volume One: Phoenix, 1649-1681 p. 128

Closing Ritual – in the morning before breaking camp

I used the same ritual as 2004, changing the "thank yous" and information concerning next year's camp.

Workshops & Activities Offered during the Air Camp Events: 2004

***Sacred Breath,* 2004:** Chants taught by Karen Eddy.

***Arrows of Intention,* 2004 & 2009:** Debra Harris. Each person will need to set an intention for the week-end's work and make/decorate an arrow signifying this intention. Instructions and materials will be explained at this time, though you will have until Saturday evening to complete your arrow as you are so moved.

***Sacred Smoke,* 2004:** Barbara Merriman on creating incense to honor the element of air. Come hang out, get acquainted and engage in this sacred work. You may take the incense home or throw it in the campfire to honor air/fairy world or aide your intention.

Aromatic Air, 2004: The Art of Aromatherapy: Ariel Fernandez. Study and experience the power of sacred scents carried on currents of air in this workshop. We will experience a variety of ways to use essential oils for connecting with the Divine, and together, we will create a blend to honor a Goddess.

Pranayama: Yoga Breath Work, 2004: Elizabeth Klarich. In many cultures throughout the world, Air is sacred for the energy and life force it contains. Learn to purify and revitalize your physical, mental and spiritual bodies through the ancient practice of pranayama.

Vibratory Air I: Sounds of the Drum, 2004: Chet Leach. Rhythmic sounds vibrate through the air, creating a resonance in our hearts and souls. Learn polyrhythms that lift the spirit and twirl the dancers. No previous experience is necessary. Some drums and percussive instruments will be provided.

***Vibratory Air II: Sounds of Your Heart Tones: An introduction to the power of sound,* 2004.** Ariel Fernandez. Find and express your unique heart tones, creating a deeper connection to all life and to the Divine. No musical ability is required.

Bardic Storytelling: Myth and Oral Traditions, 2004: Don R. Larson. Utilize the same skills taught to musicians and actors to develop your oral communication or storytelling abilities (projection, modulation, rhythm, costuming, instruments and props). Bring a chant, poem or story that is meaningful to you. It's best to have it memorized, but at least be very familiar with your material. If it be your will, you may gift your story/song/poem to the Bardic Fire Circle Saturday evening.

Winds of the Ancients, 2004: *A Peruvian Whistling Vessel Experience*; Ariel Fernandez. This is a unique opportunity to travel on waves of sound to other dimensions! We will be assisted by reproductions of the ancient shamanic whistling vessels sacred to the Pre-Colombian people of Peru. Together, we will create a vortex of sound to connect with our Divine Purpose.

Workshops & Activities Offered during the Air Camp Events: 2009

Fire Circle Orientation: Alchemy, The Emerald Tablet, and the Fire Circle; C. Scheffelman

So glad you all are here! I know many were unable to return, but we also have many new faces. This event is different; the intention, and the orientation. We will experience air, but work with the Alchemy of the fire, transformative element, can transform us.

There is an Ancient artifact that has surfaced several times during recorded history. This artifact is called The Emerald Tablet, for it is reputed to be made of a large, green, glowing stone. The inscription on this tablet is not carved into the stone but raised up from its surface. Several ancient books were found with this unexplainable artifact. No one knows the origin of the tablet or the accompanying books, though some say they were written by Thoth, later passed to Hermes also known as Hermes Trismajestis. Theories of its age range from 10-30,000 years old.

History records the presence of this book three times – first in the hands of the pharaoh Aknaten, who revised Egyptian society using the principles discerned from the tablet; then discovered by a boy genius in Turkey who, after years of studying the tablet, became a renowned healer and holy man, and finally, the tablet was recovered by Alexander the Great, who put it on display in Heliopolis.

What also is known about the tablet is that it consists of seven rubrics, or paragraphs which, when applied to one's life, can elevate one's spiritual vibration enough so that one could perform miracles of healing and transmutation (water into wine, etc). From this tablet thus began the science of Alchemy; a practice of spiritual evolution, proven by the transmutation of metals, i.e. lead into gold.

Each night begins with a ritual that sets the tone for the night's work. Please do NOT miss the rituals, which have been planned with intention, love, gifts and magickal workings for YOU by the hard-working members of MMC. This collaborative effort to ensure the mindful creation of the ritual/ alchemical container for the magical Work of the night.

First; enthusiasm (ego).
We release the ego and our agendas by throwing our crap into the fire. This is Nigredo, the blackening, for, in the lab, the alchemist will heat the prime material until it is ash (calcination), then will dissolve it in a solvent (dissolution). (Separation) as people let go…. During the night, people may make offerings to the fire; chants, poetry, personal declarations, songs, dance…please wait for an appropriate time to do this, but do not be shy—we co-create this event, and your contributions are always welcome.

Albedo (white). Deep trances, releasing pain to states of ecstasy. (This can get noisy.) In the lab, material whitens and softens. Energy is quieter and lighter as we move toward dawn (stages of conjunction, fermentation, and distillation)

The final stage is Rubedo (red). The above and the below are united in the heart; the energy becomes stronger and purer at sunrise, a period of silence; solar adoration let the light enter the cells – grounding.

Points to remember - Trance work can be anything from anger to ecstasy.

- We will keep you safe
- Do not touch, bother or speak to anyone unless eye contact
- No pick-ups
- We will rattle (no more than two people)
- Deep trance- do not touch, cover or speak to during
- Keep all mundane conversation out of the circle
- Food altar in the dining hall, be sure to drink water
- Drums covered or lain down are not to be used
- No rings, etc. while playing drums

- Seating is for drumming only.
- Help maintain the energy – chant, rattle, smudge, feed, tend the fire

You deserve this for yourself – stay up and engaged all night. Magickal things happen!

Aromatic Air; The Art of Aromatherapy, 2009: Ariel Fernandez came to work with us again! Experience the power of sacred scents carried on currents of air in the Art of aromatherapy workshop. We will experience a variety of ways to use essential oils both for connecting with the Divine and how to safely experience their healing powers.

Vibratory Air; Sounds of Your Heart Tones: Ariel Fernandez. An introduction to the power of sound. You will be guided to find and express your unique heart tones, thus creating a deeper connection to all life and to the Divine. No musical ability is required... All are welcome!

Winds of the Ancients; A Peruvian Whistling Vessel Experience: Ariel Fernandez. A unique opportunity to travel on waves of sound to other dimensions. We will be assisted by reproductions of ancient shamanic whistling vessels, sacred to the ancient Peruvian people. Together, we will create a vortex of sound to connect with our Divine Purpose.

Sacred Poetry & the Bard, 2009: Draco Alexander. This is a special 2-part workshop on Sacred Poetry, and how it applies to the Alchemical Ritual Fire Circle. The first part of the workshop will include an introduction and interactive lecture, discussion about sacred spoken-word poetry, and what roles it plays in the fire circle. This first part is intended to educate, enliven, and inspire, as well as initiate the participants into the practice of sacred spoken word poetry. The second part is a hands-on workshop, where Participants will get down and dirty, with paper and pencils to actually create their own sacred poetry. We will discuss ways to open yourself to the power of Air: Her Breath, in order that the inspiration can flow smoothly from energy to written word on paper. During this workshop, we will also discuss confidence, and the role it plays in the delivery of sacred spoken word at the fire circle. This part is intended to inspire confidence and to be a practical hands-on practice in writing sacred spoken word in order to inspire the participants to bring their heart-songs to fire that evening.

Fire Circle Alchemy, 2009: *Lady Nytewind.* Ancient mysteries and modern magic blend together; creating the community fire circle, which is, for us, the elixir of life. In this workshop, you will learn the techniques that go into creating a vessel in which you can transform your personal lead into gold. Our workshop focuses on practical tools for transformation and provides an outline for the magic that happens in our community. Together, we will explore the Mysteries of the Fire Circle, and how to create safe, sacred space in which to become our highest vision. Drink deeply of these sacred secrets and prepare to be trance-formed in this fun exploration of symbol, ritual, and metaphor.

Prophecies and Predictions for 2012, 2009: Shannon Kahler & Lady Nytewind. What do the predictions, both old and new, have to say about the year 2012? We will discuss both the psychic and the scientific possibilities regarding cycles and changes that may affect our planet and people in the near future.

2012; Part 2: Can we Prepare? 2009: Shannon Kahler & Lady Nytewind. What can we do to give ourselves and our families the best possible chance to survive anything from a power outage to global disaster? Preparedness alleviates fear. Preparation is a positive step toward facing the future as calmly and optimistically as possible.

Optional Craft Project, 2004 & 2009 - The Prayer Arrow

The arrow is more than just a weapon for hunting and fighting. It is a tool for stalking food for the soul and fighting tyrants of the spirit. The prayer arrow is often specially made and personalized with emblems and tokens of the owner's power sources. It could then be used in meditation and as a focus for petitions to the Great Spirit. The shaft of the arrow represents the element of Earth and the physical body, it is symbolic of manifestation.

The wet rawhide used for binding the arrowhead and the flight feathers to the shaft represents the element of Water. As the rawhide dried it shrank tight to hold the head and the flight feathers firmly to the shaft. Such binding was likened to the tightening of the spiral force and to one's own emotional energy.

The arrowhead was fashioned from stone or metal both being tempered by fire, so the arrowhead represents the element of Fire. It was a reminder that the Fire energy is good when used wisely but that it can also be dangerous. The flight feathers direct the path of the arrow through the element of Air and represent the Spirit. The feathers control the arrow as Spirit controls all aspects of the being from its sacred place within. It is considered an act of power to use the arrow to send your intention to the Great Spirit.

As with other spiritual items the act of creating the prayer arrow is as important (or even more important) than the physical item created. The thoughts you hold in your head as you create will remain with your arrow. Remember this is a physical form to hold your intentions and send them to the Great Spirit. Actions should follow intention.

A basic guide to creating your Arrow of intention

1. Set your intention
2. Choose your materials; 2 feathers (fletch), 1 dowel (shaft), 1 rubber tip (arrowhead), and one black end with a notch (nock) to create a basic arrow. Then your personal choices for decorative materials.
3. Cut short side off the shaft of the feather and trim both ends of each feather to the length of the example.
4. With glue gun attach the first feather to the dowel about one inch from the tapered end. Then glue the second feather directly opposite of the first feather. Wrap each end of the fletch with sinew.

5. Attach nock (the black thingy) with the glue gun to the tapered end of the arrow *aligning the notch with the fletch (see example).*
6. Attach the arrow head with a bit of hot glue to the opposite end of the nock.
7. Decorate your **Arrow of Intention** to your heart's delight.
8. At the appointed time, we will shoot our arrows into the woods, sending our intentions to the Gods.

Charlyn Scheffelman (Lady Nytewind)

Air – Installations 2004

Installations: These were thematically decorated places (tents or cabins) where people could go to further explore the qualities and meanings of the elemental theme of the camp. Some were quiet places to reflect and meditate. These installations were available throughout the duration of the camp.

There were three "keys" (necklaces with a charm) so that the installation would not become too crowded for an effective spiritual experience. People took one "key" to go in and returned it when they were through. No one could enter without a necklace, so sometimes there would be a wait until one was returned. This worked well to prevent too many people inside at one time.

At other times, costumed actors were there to teach something concerning the theme element. These were visited throughout the night, as small groups were brought by Guides to visit. The guides chose people who were willing to leave the fire circle for a while. (At our first Summerfest these installations compiled the "Journey", as we were not ready to introduce people to the Alchemical Fire Circles at that time.)

In 2004, we set up five environments which I have described in the body of the "Journey" that people were taken on during the Bardic Circle on the second (last) night.

Air – Installations 2009

There were two installations the second year of air: The ***"Temple of Thoth,"*** set up in a tent as in 2004 and performed by actors the same way. People were escorted by guides during the night to experience this "healing". As you can see, the other parts played during Air 2004 were brought into the circle in the middle of the night to perform the same parts, but to the whole group at once in the circle.

The other was the ***"Portal of Air,"*** where people could honor the Fairy world. This tent was decorated with fairies, angels, and things that appeal to those beings. I'm afraid I can't remember specifics about the décor. We had three decks of tarot cards at small stations with these signs:

> "We honor those beings that assist us when we are born into this world and when we leave it, and who watch over us while we are here. Blessed be the Angels. May they assist us in our quest to heal ourselves." *(Please draw an Angel card)*

"We honor the many inhabitants of the Fairy world and thank them for their presence and their assistance. Blessed be the fairies. We ask that they assist us in our efforts to carry their light into our own dimension." *(Offer incense, make a wish, bless & eat a silver-covered almond.)*

(Please draw a Fairy card)

"We honor the many manifestations of winged life, messengers all. Blessed be the winged creatures of the earth. May they carry our messages to the Gods."

(Blow bubbles and send your messages to the fairy world)

Fire Her Spirit; 2005

Schedule of Events

Thursday:
- Check in, 2:00-?pm
- An evening with Isaac Bonewits: 4-6:30 pm (dining hall)
- Dinner: 6:30-7:30 pm
- Required Sacred Fire Orientation: 7:30-8:30 pm. (Classroom building)
- Opening Ritual, drum, and dance till dawn: 11:00 pm

Friday:

- Friday: Breakfast dawn-8am
- Rest, relax, enjoy the scenery
- Lunch: 12:00-1:00
- Bardism 101: 1-2pm (Classroom building)
- Drumming w/ Cindy: 2-3:30 (Fire Pit) or Dance—The Rhythm Inside (TBA)
- Mask Mysteries 3:45-5pm (Classroom building)
- Alchemy of the Fire Circle 5-6:15 pm (Classroom building)
- Dinner: 6:30-7:30
- Required Sacred Fire Orientation for late comers 7:30 (Classroom building)
- Sacred Fire Circle: 11:00-dawn

Charlyn Scheffelman (Lady Nytewind)

Saturday:

- Breakfast dawn-8am
- Rest, relax, enjoy the scenery
- Lunch: 12:00-1:00
- Being a Pagan Man 1-2pm (Classroom building)
- Drumming w/Chet: 2:15-3:45 (Fire Pit)
- Ritual for Empowerment 4:00-6:00pm (TBA)
- Dinner: 6:30-7:30
- Sacred Fire Circle: 11:00-dawn

Sunday:

- Sunday: Breakfast dawn-8am
- Rest, relax, enjoy the scenery
- Lunch: 12:00-1:30 pm
- Closing ritual: 2:00 pm
- Clean up camp, pack up
    1. Please be sure you have all your belongings.
    2. We want to leave things better than we found them, so please help keep the camp free of garbage, litter, cigarette butts, etc. Police the grounds and your cabin before you leave.
    3. No smoking inside cabins or buildings, please.

Opening Ritual 1st Night. 2005: Dragons

("Salt," "Water," "Charcoal," and "Incense" were taken from D.J. Conway's book *Dancing with Dragons)*

Needs: Central fire, 2 tiki torches w/string tied on for each participant, dragon incense & censor at East, salt, water, bowl, knife, athames, two swords, gong player, sparklers, sharp knife and dragon masks for the four quarter people, priest, and priestess.

The dragon was created from hula hoops covered first with red plastic table cloths, then with scales of all colors cut from other plastic cloths and attached. The head was carved from blue insulation board, painted. A stick was inserted so the lead person could hold it up.

Cast circle:

HP: *(Dancing with Dragons,)*

Salt: Blessings upon thee, o creature of earth.
        Let all imbalance and impurity be cast from thee,
        Salt of earth and sea, purified be.

(Hold up and say...Draconis! Draconis! Draconis!)

HPS: *(from Dancing with Dragons)*

Water: Blessings upon thee, o creature of water.
        Let all illusion and impurity be cast from thee.
        Water of land and sea, purified be!

(Hold up and say...Draconis! Draconis! Draconis!)

(Add salt to water, both say) By Dragon Power, I call you purified!

HPS: *Seal circle with holy water saying*: I do purify and consecrate all this circle may hold

HP: *(from Dancing with Dragons) (charcoal)*
Blessings upon thee, o creature of fire.
Let all weakness and impurity be cast from thee
Fire of Dragons, fire of earth,
Be ye purified to bring power forth.

(Hold up and say...Draconis! Draconis! Draconis!)

HPS: (from *Dancing with Dragons*) *Add incense, say:*
Blessings upon thee o creature of air.
Let all confusion and impurity be cast from thee.
I call thee purified.

(Hold up, say...Draconis! Draconis! Draconis!)

Both: *(from Dancing with Dragons)*

Incense magickal, incense bold, Awake the dragons as of old.

HP: *Seal circle with incense saying:* I do purify and consecrate all this circle may hold.

East:
We stand at the gate of mystery and call to the ancient power
of the east:
Dragon of the Eastern sky,
On gossamer wings you swiftly fly
Come bring to us your knowledge of old,
Of magick and secrets yet untold.
Come, Eastern dragon, take to the sky
Quickly now, to our wish comply
Lend to us your second sight
Illuminate us with wisdom and light!
We call your ancient name aloud
Harken to our call Sairys (sair'-iss)! *(Strike gong)*

South:

> We stand at the gate of mystery and call to the ancient power of the south:
>
> Dragon of the Southern sky
> On fiery wings you swiftly fly.
> Come bring to us your protective Fire
> Your strength and passion we desire.
> From caverns deep within the earth
> Your presence here condones our worth.
> Dragon ruler of fire and will,
> Your ancient name echoes still.
> We call your ancient name aloud
> Harken to our call Fafnir! (faf'-near)
> > *(strike gong twice)*

West:

> We stand at the gate of mystery and call to the ancient power of the West:
>
> Dragon of the western sky,
> On opaque wings you swiftly fly.
> Come bring to us your second sight
> And strengthen us in dark of night.
> Mysteries revealed and magick you tell
> Secrets of life and death as well
> From watery depths you bring us peace
> We call your ancient name aloud
> Harken to our call Naelyan!
> > *(strike gong 3 times)*

North:

> We stand at the gate of mystery and call to the ancient power of the North:
>
> Dragon of the northern sky,
> On silver wings you swiftly fly
> Com bring to us your mysteries deep
> Awaken, now from your current sleep.
> From caverns deep within the Earth
> Wise one who grants us our rebirth

Grant us good health and wisdom as well
Guide and protect all with whom we dwell.
We call your ancient name aloud
Harken to our call Grael (grail)
(strike gong 4 times)

HPS: Once mighty dragons roamed the earth,
Soared in the sky, danced on the waves,
And tunneled in caves.
Until the advent of spiritual dearth.

HP: The world was theirs--never doubt
Lashing tails, shining claws
Gave prospective enemies pause.
Until the spiritual light went out.

HPS: The Ancient ones ruled with wisdom and grace,
conjured up storms, caused earth to quake,
molded the land and formed the lake.
Until doubt caused them to leave this place.

HP: Dragons danced and dragons sang,
frolicked with pleasure and
Joy without measure.
Until the tolling death bell rang.

HPS: Hunted by man who sought to kill,
Banished by doubt and disbelief,
Dragons retreated to find relief.
Between the worlds, they abide still.

HP: Their magical presence can still be found
Attending ritual, aiding spell
protecting man and keeping him well
Behold! The dragons are all around.
(light fire)

HP: *(From Dancing w/ Dragons)*
Light of the Spirit, symbol of sun,
Be with us now 'til this ritual is done…etc.
(hold up the sword)

HPS: *(From Dancing w/ Dragons)*
Dragon of Darkness your power will run
Until the time that our magick is done….etc.
(hold up the sword)

HP: By the Power of Ferrum Paenus, this sword of Magick, I call thee!
HPS: By the Power of Halycon, this sword of Magick, I call thee!

(Touch swords together to ignite, stick in the ground to extinquish)

Knot Magick: HPS:

See here, the strings that tie you to failure. See here the strings that bind your creative expression. See here the fears, restrictions, self-doubt, guilt, child memories—the blocks that build the dam that holds back the perfect expression of who you are!

Take, each of you, a string. Contemplate! Look into your inner mind and heart and find those things that are not 'you'—things that have been put upon you by yourself or others that hold you back!

Tie a knot for each thought that comes to your mind—each doubt, each block, tying it tight with intent and passion!

(give time to do so)

HP: *(Cut each string)*
I release you from your obstacles! Place them into the fire where they will be transformed by the power of the flame!

Chant: *(while strings are cut and put in the fire)*
By Dragon Fire, we are purified: by Dragon Magick, we transform

Charlyn Scheffelman (Lady Nytewind)

Quarters Pass out & light sparklers) (MOVE ALTAR) Chinese-style dragon enters to drumbeats and gong held by 5-6 people, circles around several times then leaves the circle.

Chant: *(began to move around the fire)*
    It starts, very quietly,
    It starts, in the heart.

(The Alchemical Fire Circle begins (description elsewhere) until the dawn.)

At Dawn: (Best to have everyone memorize this before the event.) ***All recite the Solar Salutation***, by Katlyn Breene. This is standard for every fire circle to greet the sunrise!

    The Sun rises
    We lift out hands unto it
    To be reborn
    Like the day
    Golden rays pierce our hearts
    Like arrows of light
    Dispelling the illusion
    Releasing the night
    Solar alchemy
    Filling each cell of our body
    Transforming, transmuting
    Lead into purest gold
    As above, so below
    The Sun sees itself in the fire
    In each other, We see God

HP: Dragon of Darkness, O Ancient one,
    This full moon ritual now is done.
    With loving hearts, we bid you farewell
    And gratefully thank you for aiding our spell.
    Your secrets revealed by the light of the moon
    Teach us, and guide us, and keep us in tune.

HPS: Dragon of Light, O Ancient one,
This sacred ritual now is done.
With loving hearts, we bid you farewell
And gratefully thank you for aiding our spell.
Your wisdom and strength, like the light of the sun
Will always stay with us, though ritual is done.

North:

Mountain dragon, O mighty Grael
Whose steadfastness will never fail.
Thanks to you for attending our rite
And keeping us safe this sacred night.
Stay if you will, go if you must
In perfect love and perfect trust.
Hail and farewell!

West:

Naelon, mighty Water Drake
Whose boundless love we gladly take.
Thanks to you for attending our rite
And keeping us safe this sacred night.
Stay if you will, go if you must
In perfect love and perfect trust.
Hail and farewell

South:

Fafnir, mighty dragon of fire
Burning with passion, aflame with desire.
Thanks to you for attending our rite,
And keeping us safe this sacred night.
Stay if you will, go if you must
In perfect love and perfect trust.
Hail and farewell!

East:

Sairys, Dragon of wind and sky,
Whose thoughts and inspirations fly.
Thanks to you for attending this rite,

And keeping us safe this full moon night.
Stay if you will, go if you must
In perfect love and perfect trust.
Hail and farewell!

Dismiss Circle:

May the circle be open but unbroken
May the Lord and the Lady be ever in your heart.
Merry meet and merry part,
And merry meet again.

Review

Isacc Bonewits, one of our guest speakers that year, wrote a lovely review concerning this event, which I am proud to include in this work. He was a great guy and a great druid, and is missed by the entire Pagan community!

By Isaac Bonewits: "Last night (Thursday), the festival held its opening circle, which was not what most festival-goers think of as such. First there was an hour-long ritual briefing earlier in the evening, then everyone was sent to their tents to nap. When the ceremony began at 11:00 pm, it was an intense, all-night ritual, focused around the alchemically transformative power of the sacred fire and the drums. It seems that many of the drum circles now being done in the western part of the USA are more structured than those in the east, and are designed to produce deep trances and psychologically important changes, rather than just the ecstatic joy I'm used to seeing in eastern Pagan festivals."

"While the first hour was a familiar Wiccan style rite, the organizers (Mountain Moon Circle) had obviously spent a great deal of time and effort on costumes, including spectacular masks and ceremonial props and including a five-person Chinese dragon! Then the drumming started out very low and slow while the participants moved slowly around the fire softly chanting "It starts, very quietly, it starts in the heart. It starts in the center, it starts from a spark". This was one of a dozen fire chants I've never heard before that the organizers provided people with lyric sheets of in their registration packet."

"For the Mountain Moon Circle, the fire dancing is specifically an alchemical ritual designed to help people burn away the dross of their spirits. Alas, I still have most of my dross, since my medications don't let me stay up all night, but from the scarcity of people around at 11:00 the next morning, it appears that three-quarters of the attendees were dancing most or all of the night."

Ritual Second night: The Emerald Tablet

Needs: Central fire, 5 hand torches, incense, white shawls, (costumes for Dark Lord, Fear, Ego, King, Distillation)

Cast circle: (quarter calls author unknown, printing 8 lines...)

East:

> Air breathe, air blow
> Make the Wheel of Magick go!

South:

> Fire hiss, fire burn
> Make the Wheel of Magick turn!

West:

> Water flow, water wave
> In Ancient Mother's hidden cave

North:

> Earth spirit, spirit Earth,
> In the Mother find rebirth

Emerald Tablet: (recite the Emerald Tablet)

In truth, without deceit, certain, and most veritable –

That which is Below corresponds to that which is Above, and that which is Above, corresponds to that which is Below, to accomplish the miracles of the One Thing.

And just as all things have come from the One Thing, through the meditation of One Mind, so do all created things originate from this One Thing, through Transformation.

Its father is the Sun: its mother the Moon. The Wind carries it in its belly: its nurse is the Earth. It is the origin of All, the consecration of the Universe; its inherent Strength is perfected if it is turned into Earth.

Separate the Earth from Fire, the Subtle from the Gross, gently and with great Ingenuity. It rises from Earth to heaven and descends again to Earth, thereby combining within Itself the powers of both the Above and the Below.

Thus will you obtain the Glory of the Whole Universe. All Obscurity will be clear to you. This is the greatest Force of all powers because it overcomes every Subtle thing and penetrates every Solid thing.

In this way was the Universe created. From this comes many wondrous Applications, because this is the Pattern.

Therefore am I called Thrice Greatest Hermes, having all three parts of the wisdom of the Whole Universe. Herein have I completely explained the operation of the Sun.

(Speaker and the four quarter people light the fire with torches).

HPS: (Lines from *A hymn to the Sun* from Ancient Egyptian scrolls)

Thou arisest beauteous in the horizon of heaven, O living Aton, Beginner of life, when Thou didst shine in the eastern horizon and didst fill every land with Thy beauty.

Thou art comely, great, sparkling, and high above every land, and Thy rays enfold the lands to the limit of all that Thou hast made, Thou being the Sun.

Being far off, yet Thy rays are upon the earth. Thou art in men's faces, yet Thy movements are unseen. When Thou settest in the western horizon, the earth is in darkness after the manner of death.

HP:

O Gladsome light of the holy glory of the eternal logos, Heavenly, sacred, blessed Helios. Having come to the rising of the Sun and beheld the dawn of morning. We praise the source of wisdom and light. At all times Thou art worthy, thou art worthy of praise in song. As King of Heaven and Giver of Life, Therefore the world glorifies thee! Lord of the Sun, we evoke thee! Join us in our workings to turn our lead into purest gold!

Lady Moon, Thou arisest in all your beauty bright. O Living Luna, shine on us here and fillith the night with your silver beam. Unlock the gate of dream; rise bright and clear on earth and sky and sea, your magic mystery, its spell shall cast.

HPS:

O Secret queen of power, silvery light of the enchanted night, Heavenly, sacred, blessed Luna; having come to the setting of the sun and Beheld the mystery of the darkening vault of heaven and your orb of mystic light.

We praise your ever vigilant, eternal power. At all times Thou art worthy, thou art worthy of praise in song. As Queen of Heaven and Giver of Life Therefore the world glorifies thee!

Lady of the Moon, we evoke thee! Join us in our workings to turn our lead into purest gold!

Calcination: The Dark Lord

I lurk just around the corner from your security. I threaten to make you face the false selves you have become.

Do you rely on your job, your accomplishments to define yourself? It doesn't interest me what you do for a living. I want to know if you dare to dream, to meet your hearts longing.

I want to know if you can sit with pain, yours or another's without moving to hide it, or fade it, or fix it. It doesn't interest me how old you are. I want to know if you will risk looking like a fool for love, for your dreams, for the adventure of being alive.

I want to know if you can disappoint another to be true to yourself if you can bear the accusation of betrayal and not betray your own soul. I want to know if your ego can withstand the fires of change, for change you, I will! I am with you always, and I WILL make changes in your life, whether you want them or not!

Dissolution: Gentle Goddess

I am the wounds that lie in your subconscious. Wounds gained in childhood, or from things too painful to remember. Wounds gained, perhaps, in previous lifetimes; wounds that govern your thoughts, actions, and reactions—without your conscious knowledge.

I am the 'shadows' within you that must be brought into the light, recognized and vulcanized, painful though that process may be.

I am also the waters within you—the waters of life! Only by probing your subconscious, burning the dross of lead you find there and charging it with your emotions can you be healed.

Tears of salt; a physical symbol of your calcified anguish, and of water; the solvent universal, must be allowed to flow until the pain is dissolved.

Cry. Only your ego stands between you and the dissolution of your pain.

Separation – Ego: *(a young man in medieval costume walks calmly in to circle)*
I control my life. I like it the way it is.

FEAR: *(costumed in a black robe with a scary mask, Fear boldly comes into the circle)*

I! I am FEAR--the menace that keeps you from obtaining the reality of your dreams! Never visible to the eye, but sharply felt in the heart!

I was born of ignorance and nursed by misbegotten thoughts! I am the father of despair and the brother of procrastination!

I am the enemy of progress and the tool of tyranny!

Ego: I AM afraid! You are bigger than me!

Fear: I have darkened more hopes and stifled more ambitions, shattered more dreams and prevented more accomplishments than history can ever record!

Ego: No! I'll fight you!

Fear: I look into your heart and see self -doubt! I see the fear of lack! Not enough, not enough, not enough! Not enough love! Not enough money! Not enough strength!

Not enough time! Not enough—courage!

Ego: *(screams and runs from the circle)*

Fear: I am a shape shifter. I wear many disguises.
I can masquerade as caution, sensibility, or doubt.
But whatever I am called, I am still FEAR!

King: *(larger man in medieval costume enters)* Fear! I have come to vanquish you!

Fear: Ha! This you can only do through change, and change is what you fear most!

King: I have been through the fires of calcinations and dissolved my past pains in dissolution. I am ready now to separate that which is my good from that which does me no good!

Fear: Then show me! *(battle with swords begins)*

King: You have no power but that which I give you! And I give you power NO MORE!
(King deals the death blow, then turns to all:

Separate yourself from that which separates you from your own true self, and from others.

Chant: *(begin to circle fire)*
We are opening up in sweet surrender
To the luminous love-light of the one!
We are opening, We are opening
We are opening, We are opening

Fire circle continues: drum, dance & trance work throughout the night to greet the sun.

At Dawn: *Solar Salutation*, by Katlyn Breene (Best to have everyone memorize this before the event.)

HP

Lord of the Sun, we greet thee…
Accept our praise and gratitude
And for joining us in our workings this night.

HPS:

Lady of the Moon…
Accept our praise and gratitude
And for joining us in our workings this night.

East: (Farewell to the elements by Maria Kay Simms, *A Witches Circle: Rituals and Craft of the Cosmic Muse.*
Soft warm winds now fly away
Our blessings go with thee…

North:

Earth of green and flowers of spring
Our blessings go with thee…

West:

>Cool water of lake and spring and sea
>Our blessings go with thee…

South:

>Fire of Sun and hearth and heart,
>Our blessings go with thee…

Dismiss Circle

>May the circle be open but unbroken
>May the Lord and the Lady be ever in your heart.
>Merry meet and merry part
>And merry meet again.

Third night: Honoring the Goddess Pele'2005

Needs: Volcano form in separate fire bowl (I had one on wheels to bring in, and had made a volcano with a cone-shaped fireworks fountain fitted into the top), leis, CD: Drums of Bora Bora, fire staff, white gas, wet towels, basket of fat wood, sword, and Hawaiian headdresses for HP & HPS. *HP/S wear no rings!! – HP/S set drums nearby*

HPS casts Circle: **Quarter people** *– seal all 4 elements (carry around the circle) to drum beat and rattle*

Fire Lighting: *(with flint)*

East:

> We call upon the Great Goddess Hina, she of many forms.
> She who transmits the sacred sound of cosmic vibration. ..

South:

> We call upon the Great Goddess Papa, wise woman.
> Keeper of the Sacred Mysteries of Divine magnetism…

West:

> We call upon the Great Goddess Kapo, wise seer.
> She whose holy breath nourishes the children of the waters…

North:

> We call upon Great Goddess Laka, medicine woman.
> She who causes the land to bloom and grow green…

Statement of intent: HPS:

The Ancient Ones believed Primal Source to be a conscious energy field without Form. The original highly evolved Starseeds freely practiced Nature Spirituality. This system honored one Source of Creation…One Breath…a genderless name that held within it the characteristics later known as Mother… *the Feminine Sacred* … Goddess.

HP:

Soon after the Destruction of the Motherland, the deity was made into a one-minded male God by Earthman. This energy of "Power-Over" first began in Atlantis and spread throughout the World. The Ancient Teachings of the Holy Land of Mu became cloaked in veils of secrecy. Eventually, dogma and physical control took dominion over the Goddess and her children, creating the illusion that possession of Spiritual Truth gives one the right to claim ownership of sovereign sacred laws and myths.

HPS:

Hawaii is a Place that still holds the remembrance of Creation Spirituality. There is a lineage of Polynesian Goddesses who have survived the near extinction of Feminine Divinity. Planet Earth IS a Goddess Creation.

(Quarters pass leis to all)

HPS:

Io, since before time began, You are the unmanifested, infinite source of creation. You breathe forth the Mana which pervades space and gives all living creatures the power to live. By sending Your Mana across the darkness, the Sacred Flame flashes to life.

Io, we search for life and light in this dark night. We have lit the sacred fires and call You into this Sacred One, to bring the potential for creation and truth into our space. *(Place headress on HP.)*

HP:

I am Io, who breathes light into your darkness. I transform your night into creation. I am the flaming gateway you cross to face your fears and there find your power.

To focus your work: I call for Uli! -- the generative force, the Light and Life of the Sun. Uli, from Your Celestial Realm, bring us knowledge of Your Feminine Alchemy.

We call upon Your wisdom, stored in the Central Sun of the Pleiades, to be the lens for these souls' night! Come through this Sacred One, to illuminate this space. *(Place headress on HPS.)*

HPS:

I am Uli, She who guides you toward your highest fulfillment. I help you choose your most difficult challenges. Then I weave them from magnetic strands, to tie your Mana into this place and form.

Through me do you focus stamina and courage to transform your darkest fears. This night will you begin to raise your face, eyes, and hands to claim your truest self, and honor the divine in all!

Enter Tahitian Dancers – HP moves; HPS dance in place

All Sing Hawaiian song
> Eh ma-lama eekay hayeeow
> Eh ma-lama eekay hayeeow

HPS Speaks: Yes! Take care and nurture this sacred land, this temple!
> Eh malama pohnoh, eekay hayeeow

HPS Speaks: Do what is right for this sacred Earth
> Earth *(scoop up earth, rub fingers together)*
> And sky *(lift arms)*
> Sea *(wave motion, left to right)*
> And stone *(hand front, waist level, then clench fists)*
> Hold this land in sacredness *(take hands, circle moving right.)*
> *(Dancers pick up others and eventually get all participants involved)*

HPS:

Pele' is honored as the Spirit of Fire. She is the male principle contained in the Feminine. We summon Her to clear and purify all that is not needed. She challenges and assists with bringing forth that which lies dormant in the very core of your Being. Pele' awakens you to fully experience - and creatively use - your gifts.

HP:

Pele' guides Her devotees to Greater Wisdom. She is the Keeper of Emotions, always willing to share Her "knowing," and lessons of Transmutation. Volcano Goddess Pele' was born as a flame In the mouth of her Earth Mother ~ Haumea ~ and of Wakea, Sky Father. Pele is granddaughter of Great Sky Goddess Papa, and Great Granddaughter of the Great Mother Goddess Creatrix Uli. *(gesture to HPS)*

HPS:

Pele'! Come, be with us tonight and bless our gathering with your presence! Remind us of the passion that lives within each of us and help us transform the divine spark within to a beacon of flame!

(wheel in volcano... Pele enters)

Pele':

I appear to you tonight in my human form, though you may also know me as an old woman, hitchhiking on a deserted road, or I may appear as a dog, most especially as warning of an impending volcanic eruption.

I have the ability to CREATE earth: with every outpouring of lava from my crater-womb, new land is born! I am the Primal Source in action! I am the raw power of the flame!

I have the power to break the dams you have created within yourselves— to transmute the limitations you've held in your psyche into free-flowing vitality, creativity, and psychic awareness! Place those limitations into this fatwood, that they may be reduced to ashes in the volcanic fire!

(Quarters pass 'fatwood', give time to charge and place into volcano)
(Light Fire Staff from fire: CD #3 - Light Volcano and fire-spinners light up)

Pele': I leave you now, but call upon me whenever you have need of my power, for I am within you always. Aloha! *(leave circle)*

HP/S: Chant: *(call and response)*
　　　My soul is awakened (all repeat each line given)
　　　My awesome power is released
　　　I am free
　　　I am revitalized
　　　I am full of fiery passion
　　　　　(Repeat to build power)
Drummers immediately drum like mad! -- FireDance!!!

Sunrise: *Solar Salutation*
　　　HP/S ALWAYS need to be back in garb for closing, if they have changed.

HP:

You have lit the sacred fires and called upon <u>Me</u>, Io, to find your highest truth and create your Self anew. Long have I burned life and light into your Dreams. You have ventured the flames of my gateway and explored the realms of your highest potential. I fly now, on these burning rays of the Sun. Now can you shake out your wings and live your highest life. *(remove headdress)*

HPS:

I, Uli, the Light & Life of the Sun, have wielded the Magick of the

Caduceus this night, to focus your soul toward your highest fulfillment. Many trials and travails have you endured in your quest. Many knots have you faced, broken, and woven into new Dreams. Your courage and stamina is rewarded; you stand before me transformed! You have claimed your Divinity. I return to my Celestial Realm among the Pleiades, ever ready to inspire you - wherever your wings shall take you. *(remove headdress)*

East:

> Hina, Great Goddess and Guardian of the Heavens, thank you for bringing us the power of your love and the light of illumination, perception and creativity.
> Thank you for guarding this portal this night. Go if you must, stay if you will, we bid you 'Hail and Farewell!'

North:

> Laka, Great Goddess and Guardian of Nature and Sunshine, thank you for bringing us rejuvenation, restoration, and healing, and for reawakening us to our true selves.
> Thank you for guarding this portal this night. Go if you must, stay if you will, we bid you 'Hail and Farewell!'

West:

> Kapo, Great Goddess and Guardian of the night, thank you for pointing the way for us to manifest our Divine Essence and for keeping us safe during the hours of darkness.
> Thank you for guarding this portal this night. Go if you must, stay if you will, we bid you 'Hail and Farewell!'

South:

> Papa, Great Goddess and Guardian of the Spirit Realm, thank you for bringing us your power of healing, comfort and care, and for showing us the way with your love light.
> Thank you for guarding this portal this night. Go if you must, stay if you will, we bid you 'Hail and Farewell!'

Dismiss Circle

Closing Ritual – in the morning before breaking camp

HPS: (unknown author so able to print only 8 lines)
Sparkles of the Fairies Flame
Will o' the Wisps on summer nights

HP: Balefire crackling on the hill
The flickering light of candles' flame

HPS: Here befoe the flickering flame
Where ancient powers reign

HP: Ancient ones of red and gold
Of sparkle, crackle, trance…

HP: Father of Sunlight,
We thank thee for attending our festival.
Your passion, energy, and joy have been with us
As we've transformed in the fire of spirit.
Go if you must, stay if you will,
We bid you 'Hail and Farewell'

HPS: Mother of Midnight,
We thank thee for attending our festival.
Your compassion and love have been with us
As we've probed our subconscious
And transformed in the fire of spirit.
Go if you must, stay if you will,
We bid you 'Hail and Farewell'

Dragon Dance (We used our Chinese dragon again because it was so much fun!)

HPS:

Thus concludes our journey through the element of Fire, Spirit of the Goddess.

It is our hope that you have had an enjoyable weekend. Please accept our thanks for your presence at this, our second Montana festival.

I'd like to offer special thanks to our guest teachers, Isaac Bonewits, Cindy Spagna, Karen Eddy and Kim Clausen for their beautiful contributions to this work, and to Bob and Norma, Priest and Priestess of our parent circle, Desert Moon Circle in Las Vegas, for their continuing love and support.

Thank you too, to all the MMC members who worked so hard to accomplish this weekend. You are loved and appreciated by the God and the Goddess—and me!

We also give thanks for the beautiful land on which we've created our sacred play...yada yada

HP: Yada yada
A Witches Circle: Rituals and Craft of the Cosmic Muse, Maria Kay Simms

East: Soft warm winds, now fly away
Our blessings go with thee...

North: Earth of green and flowers of spring
Our blessings go with thee...

West: Cool water of lake and spring and sea
Our blessings go with thee...

South: Fires and flame, embers now
Our blessings go with thee...

Dismiss Circle
May the circle be open but unbroken
May the Lord and the Lady be ever in your heart.
Merry meet and merry part
And merry meet again.

We invite you to SummerFest 2006, **Earth, Her Body** and will inform you of the location as soon as it is secured. Till next your magic forth we call, Fare well and Blessed Be!

Schedule Fire - 2010

Thursday:
2:00pm – 6:00 check in
6:00 – 7:30 Dinner
7:30 – 8:30 Required Sacred Fire circle orientation for newbies
8:30 – Talent show
11:00 – Opening ritual, drum, and dance till dawn

Friday:
Dawn – 9:00 am Breakfast
12:00 – 1:00 Lunch
1:00 – 2:30 Dance to Awareness
2:45 – 4:15 Alchemy
4:30 – 5:45 Drumming
6:00 – 7:30 Dinner
11:00 – Ritual, drum, and dance till dawn

Saturday:
Dawn – 9:00 am Breakfast
12:00 – 100 Lunch
1:00 – 2:30 Intuitive Healing
2:45 – 4:15 Yoga
2:45 – 4:15 Beginning Chain Maille
4:30 – 5:45 Beginning Fire Spinning
6:00 – 7:30 Dinner
11:00 – Ritual, drum, and dance till 3 or 4

Sunday:
10:00 – 11:00 Brunch
11:00 – Closing ritual
11:00 – Clean up camp, pack up and vacate by 1:00 pm.

Mountain Moon Circle's Summerfest: rituals from "Fire– 2010"

Since it had been five years, and attendance had increased, we decided to use the rituals from the first fire event: *Dragon, Emerald Tablet, Pele'* and part of the *Closing Circle.*

However, this was also Lughnassadh, so we modified the Pele' ritual to accommodate the burning of the wickerman as follows.

Ritual 3, 2010 - Pele' and Harvest

Needs: Volcano form, leis, CD: Drums of Bora Bora, fire staff, white gas, wet towels, corn dollies, headdresses, rattler & drummer, quarter décor. Conch shell

Cast Circle: *(seal all 4 elements to drum beat and rattle)*

(The ritual was the same as 2005 until Pele' leaves the circle.)

HP:

On this night, the great Wheel of the year turns to the 7th spoke as the harvest begins. On this night we honor Lona, Polynesian God of agriculture and singing. Also on this night, the Grain Gods of many lands are sacrificed so that their seed may bring life to the fields in the coming season.

HPS: *(Prayer for Lughnassadh)* by Scott Cunningham, *Wicca, a Guide for the Solitary practitioner.*
O God of the ripening fields, Lord of the grain
Grant us the understanding of sacrifice
As you prepare to deliver yourself under the sickle of the Goddess
And journey to the lands of eternal summer.
O Goddess of the Dark moon
Teach us the secrets of rebirth as the Sun loses its strength
And the nights grow cold.

HP: *(hold up corn dolly)*
I am the ancient God,

Lord of the Ripened Harvest,
Sacred King, giver of riches and of protection since before time began,
I give to you, as of old,
My strength and gift of life and power.
(offer corn dolly to the fire, all others do the same)

HP/S: *Chant: (call and response)*
My soul is awakened
My awesome power is released
I am free
I am revitalized
I am full of fiery passion

(Repeat to build power)

FireDance!!!

At Dawn: *Solar Salutation*, by Katlyn Breene

HP: You have lit the sacred fires and called upon <u>Me</u>, Io, to find your highest truth and create your Self anew. Long have I burned life and light into your Dreams. You have ventured the flames of my gateway and explored the realms of your highest potential. I fly now, on these burning rays of the Sun. Now can you shake out your wings and live your highest life. *(Remove headdress)*

HPS: I, Uli, the Light & Life of the Sun, have wielded the Magick of the Caduceus this night, to focus your soul toward your highest fulfillment. Many trials and travails have you endured in your quest. Many knots have you faced, broken, and woven into new Dreams. Your courage and stamina is rewarded: you stand before me transformed! You have claimed your Divinity. I return to my Celestial Realm among the Pleiades, ever ready to inspire you - wherever your wings shall take you. *(Remove headdress)*

East:
Hina, Great Goddess and Guardian of the Heavens, thank you for bringing us the power of your love and the light of illumination, perception and creativity. Thank you for guarding this portal this night. Go if you must, stay if you will, we bid you 'Hail and Farewell!'

North:

Laka, Great Goddess and Guardian of Nature and Sunshine, thank you for bringing us rejuvenation, restoration and healing, and for reawakening us to our true selves. Thank you for guarding this portal this night. Go if you must, stay if you will, we bid you 'Hail and Farewell!'

West:

Kapo, Great Goddess, and Guardian of the night, thank you for pointing the way for us to manifest our Divine Essence and for keeping us safe during the hours of darkness. Thank you for guarding this portal this night. Go if you must, stay if you will, we bid you 'Hail and Farewell!'

South:

Papa, Great Goddess, and Guardian of the Spirit Realm, thank you for bringing us your power of healing, comfort and care, and for showing us the way with your love light. Thank you for guarding this portal this night. Go if you must, stay if you will, we bid you 'Hail and Farewell!'

Dismiss Circle

Closing Circle – Fire 2010
Same as 2005, except--

Dragon Dance – We brought the Chinese Dragon back in to dance around.

HPS:

Thus concludes our journey through the element of Fire, Spirit of the Goddess.

It is our hope that you have had an enjoyable weekend. Please accept our thanks for your presence at this, our Montana festival of Fire.

I'd like to offer special thanks to our teachers, for their beautiful contributions to this work, and their continuing love and support.

Thank you too, to all the MMC members who worked so hard to accomplish this weekend. You are loved and appreciated by the God and the Goddess—and me!

And we give thanks for the beautiful land on which we've created our sacred play...yada yada

HP: Yada yada

Open Circle

Workshops & Activities Offered during the Fire Camp events: 2005

The Fire Circle: We used the camp's volley ball court and a fire bowl, so fire danger was minimal. The colored flags were cut from plastic table cloths purchased at the dollar store and fastened to rope. A portable garden arch provided the entryway. We were very fortunate to have a Native American Fire Tender that volunteered his services at all the camps he attended (which was most of them). Thank you, Reese Johnson!

Fire Circle Orientation: by Jeff & Spinner McBride, Michael Wall, and Dr. Joshua Levin

(With permission)

Since the dawn of time, human beings have gathered around the fire to make music, to dance, and to weave magic in the fire light. In the past thirty years, there has been a resurgence in our Western culture for this type of ritual, a reawakening of the shamanic spirit. What is happening during the course of an all-night fire? After observing the ritual process for a number of years, and comparing stories and experiences with others, we have found that the alchemical model is a useful tool for understanding the all-night sacred fire circle ritual.

While fire circles and drum circles range from very informal social gatherings to all-night intentional magical workings, here we will focus on the style of intentionally created magical drum and dance fire circles that have been evolving for the past thirty years. One of the main differences in our rituals is the "container" which we create. In the alchemical tradition a container or vessel is often hermetically sealed to outside influences. At our fire circles the participants enter the vessel with the intention of doing their magical work.

Every fire circle ritual is different, but there are some elements common to all. In alchemy, the Magnum Opus, or "great work," is the creation of the "philosopher's stone," which has many magical qualities. This philosopher's stone has the amazing power to turn all that it touches into gold, or to spiritualize matter. Basically, as we see it, we're using a pattern that we know works to change and grow more fully into our souls. We are turning lead into gold, on many different levels.

We see the primary goal of staying up all night, drumming, dancing and singing, creating spontaneous group ritual and more, at a fire circle as an alchemical process. Each one of us is involved, on some level, in the great work. We accelerate the processes of personal growth by accelerating the fire of Nature, which transforms the lead of our lives into the gold of Spirit. One of the basic ideas behind many alchemical traditions is that of transmuting or purifying one thing from a "lower" form into a "higher" form. When we consider the history of Alchemy, we find many different traditions.

At a certain point, due to the sulfur, or energetic heat that is released from fire, drums and bodies, these blocks of salt liquify within us. Our vessel overflows, and this liquefied salt pours out of our body through salt sweat and salt tears. This overflowing of emotion and experience of deep feeling is a natural part of the alchemical process. We see it as a release, which leads to real ease. Real ease in life is what connects us to Spirit, Above and Below, mercury, Alchemical mercury is often compared to Akasha, Chi, Prana, Hyle, or Spirit.

By going through these processes, we become illuminated, in the truest sense.... not guru-sitting-on-a-pillow illuminated, but shedding-new-light-on-our-lives, illuminated. When issues come up, friends often say, "what's the matter?" Let's examine the "first matter", or prima materia of alchemy. The prima materia is often referred to in alchemical literature as darkness, chaos, excrement and lead. To transform lead into gold, or to spiritualize matter, early alchemists and we at the Fire, utilized the following formula "Solve and Coagula," or, dissolve and recombine.

The first part of the Work of Alchemy is "solve" or to dissolve, to melt down, to liquify. Could this be some of what is happening at the fire circle?

In his alchemical writings, Carl Jung described the dissolving process of alchemy as "breaking down the boundaries of the ego, and allowing the chaotic material of the unconscious to pour forth where it can be inspected by consciousness." The second part of the Work of Alchemy is "coagula" or to come back together, to rejoin, perhaps ourselves, others, or a new understanding.

In one of Terrence McKenna's last lectures, "Unfolding the Stone," he speaks of the Nigredo stage, that it is "the Saturnine world of what we would call manic-depression, despair and chaotic near-psychotic state of unbounded hopelessness, and that it is a precondition, then, for the alchemical work, through the stages of the alchemical opus." ... hardly a territory to dance through with ease and grace.

In our observation, this release signals the transition from Nigredo to Albedo, from the blackening and burning away of the ego and/or issue, to the dissolving of boundaries and getting more connected to the Self and/or others.

The second part of the Great Work is the Coagula, simply put, coming back together after the purifying process of an alchemical distillation. Often, at the fire circle, we have observed this as how we integrate lessons and experiences we have at the fire circle into the fire that night, into our relationships in community, and how we walk our path during the rest of the year on our much grander circle around the fire of the sun.

A quick review of the seven stages of the alchemical process: (see D.W. Hauck, The Emerald Tablet):

1. **Calcination**– (first chakra, Saturn, survival) The issue or issues within the physical container are brought up and heated by the Fire.
2. **Dissolution**– (second chakra/Jupiter, blending) The element is dissolved in the sea of emotions.
3. **Separation**– (solar plexus chakra/Mars, choosing) A choice is made to separate or release from the "issue," (of energy, tears, or intense physical movement), and in so doing separate from the things which separate our individual egos from others and Self.

4. **Conjunction**– (heart chakra/Venus, joining together through love) The shift to Albedo, the white, soft stage of the Work. The coming together of Self and ego, or the individual and the community. An important step; often it gives us deeper understanding of our Self in relation to our ego. At the fire circle, deeper connections are forged between the person releasing and the other dancers that receive or catch the energy and assist gently through the process.

5. **Fermentation**– (throat chakra/Mercury, speaking) Refining, skimming the crud that rises to the surface off the top, to find a purer solution. This is the stage this issue of releasing or "popping" is in right now. We have had the experience of burning, dissolving, separating, and joining together. Now, we are speaking our truth and separating the subtle from the gross as we continue to refine.

6. **Distillation**– (third eye, Moon, introspective visioning) At this stage of the Work, we have a pure, refined solution. We gain insight and understanding through "processing" our issues through the alchemical laboratory that is our body. By contemplating the past, while being engaged in the present, we can now make informed choices about how to move and interact at the Fire, or out in the world in the future.

7. **Coagulation**– (crown chakra, Sun, illuminating) The beginning of the Rubido phase of the process, in which our spiritual gold is realized. Consciously connecting to Spirit, releasing the light within matter, dissolving the boundaries between inner and outer experience. We bring our experiences and knowledge into the world, moment by moment, remaining in the flow. We connect with our highest selves, connect with Spirit, and with the earth. Also at this stage, we experience an accelerated rate of synchronicities.

At this point in the alchemical work, we re-enter the Fire, with our hearts connected to community and to Spirit. As we dance the Fire, the circle of life, new issues will arise in us, and the refining process begins again.

The alchemical furnace and container that is the Alchemical Fire Circle is very much like the laboratory of our body. Both are continually evolving: processing blocks, and issues, pushing boundaries, and separating the "subtle from the gross, gently with great ingenuity.

Remembrance: *Over the years, we have had wonderful guest teachers. We were fortunate enough to have Isacc Bonewits (Arch Druid Emeritus) teach* *several workshops at our 2005 event. Isaac Bonewits was one of North America's leading experts on ancient and modern Druidism, Witchcraft and the rapidly growing Earth Religions movement. He is the author of Real Magic, Authentic Thaumaturgy, Witchcraft, Rites of Worship, and The Pagan Man: Priests, Warriors, Hunters and Drummers. He is no longer with us, as we lost him to cancer in 2010, and is sorely missed, but widely remembered and honored for his contributions and achievements.*

An Evening with Isaac Bonewits: Songs, stories, rants, and wisdom presented in a coffeehouse Q&A style on whatever topics the participants have in mind or Isaac is currently obsessing about.

Ritual for Empowerment; Guided meditations, invocations and evocations designed to put each participant in touch with her or his own 'Source of Inner Strength."

Being a Pagan Man. Based on his book, *The Pagan Man: Priests, Warriors, Hunters and Drummers*. This workshop will cover some of the issues and concerns raised by Pagen men and boys and discussion will focus on the men and boys in the audience.

Bardism 101: Effective use of Performance Arts in Ritual, Poetry, music, chants, and drama can make a break a ritual in terms of generating and focusing the psychological, and therefor psychic, energies of the participants. This introduction by Isaac will prepare participants for the Sacred Fire Circles.

Alchemy of the Fire Circle for Personal Transformation; Lady Nytewind. Just as the alchemists worked to transform physical lead into gold, they worked to transform their souls to a higher spiritual level. This workshop focuses on the structure and use of the Sacred Fire Circle to transform the lead (shadows) within ourselves into gold and, as a result, make needed transforms in our lives and spirits.

Mask Mysteries, Bindura. Masks give us an outlet to understand, celebrate, and "play out" our inner work. You will learn about the meanings and uses of masks and how masks relate to your personal and spiritual life. You will also learn about movement, acting, and personification. Masks let "Fire - Her Spirit" breathe through you! This class will assist all attendees with their Summerfest project.

2010

Dance to Awareness: Madeline Martin has been teaching American Tribal Belly dance for 7 years. She has studied mediation for 25 years and is an EFT practitioner. She developed a movement mediation called "Dance to Awareness" which is a movement meditation through the Chakras. It is designed as a tool to experience Awareness. When we are Aware, we are in our Power and who we truly ARE. We will be exploring each of the seven energy centers of the body in great detail through Dance, meditation, and, sound. No prior dance experience required, only willingness and a desire to move. There is no right way or wrong way to dance, surrender yourself to the beat, lend your ear to the music and your body will follow, have fun and feel great!

Alchemy; What is it and Why Should I Care? Charlyn Scheffelman gives A brief introduction to the seven stages of Alchemy that influence our lives whether we know about them or not. Learn to work with this process and go with the flow rather than fight against it.

Intuitive Healing: Learn how to use your connection with Spirit and use your intuition to heal yourself and others. We will discuss different healing modalities, different tools, releasing blockages that inhibit energy flow, Use creative visualization and meditation. Class will include using intuitive healing on pets.

MMC Drummers: Drumming for the circle: No experience is needed in order to contribute to the energy of the drum circle. Get involved with drums and other percussion instruments that a necessary ingredient of the trance. The drums drive the energy of the circle and the dancers drive the drummers. Come, have fun and participate. Please bring pliers for this class.

MMC Fire Spinners: Bring any fire toys you may have. Safety and technique will be discussed and we will work with a variety of fire play equipment.

Beginning Chain Maille, Todd Kintz. Please bring pliers for this workshop.

Optional Craft Project; 2010

Corn Dollies:

1. Choose four husks about the same size. Lay them on top of one another. Tie the pointy ends together close to the top for the body of the doll.

2. Take two husks in each hand and fold them over the string so the string is inside. The fold will form the top of the doll's head.

3. Pull a string around the husks and tie to make the head.

4. To make arms, take another husk, trim the pointed end straight across with scissors, then roll the husk into a tight tube. Tie each end of the arm tube or braid with a piece of string.

5. Put the tube between the body husks below the head so that an arm sticks out on each side. Make a waist for the doll by tying a piece of string around the body husks below the arms. This helps hold the arms in place.

6. Wrap a husk around the back of the neck and criss-cross it across the chest to make shoulders. Tie it to the doll around the waist.

7. To make legs for a boy, separate the body husks below the waist into 2 parts, tearing from the bottom if necessary. Tie each section at the ankle.

Fire – Installations, 2005

Portal of Fire: In a 10' x 10' gazebo, I draped the walls with red and yellow fabric.

I had looked up the Mayan birth sign for each attendee and put them in an envelope in the tent. There were *Mayan Oracle Cards* to draw and information about the Mayans, their calendar, their gods, and their predictions.

Fire – Installations, 2010

Mayans: I used the Mayan theme again, as everyone was anticipating 2012. The décor was somewhat different. There were pictures and information about the Crystal Sculls, and Crystal Scull message cards to draw. There were pictures of the *Miracle of Teotihuacan* and information concerning that event. Again, I had the astrological information for each attendee ready for them in the installation.

Temple of Bridgit: Using a 10'x20' tent, we divided the space into three sections by hanging walls of fabric.

As described previously, people were brought from the fire circle in small groups to explore the installations. Three people, one in each section, were costumed as one form of Bridget.

The first section was for her properties as a healer, herbalist, and Goddess of the hearth. It was decorated with a paper fireplace with chimney (a Christmas decoration thing) and hung with strings of herbs and dried flowers. Homey atmosphere; rag rug, wooden chair – as if a little cottage.

Guide:

You are entering the dwelling of the ancient Goddess who has been known by many names: By Brigit, Bride, Brigantia, Bridey, Briggidda, Breede and others she is known. Tonight She has chosen to reveal the wisdom of her four fires to you.

Brigit #1 as Herbalist *(Irish dress, corset, etc.)*

"I was born near the waters of the magick well at the instant the sun rose into the sky. Out of my head came a column of fire. I broke some away to become my Hearth Fire. All the medicinal plants of the earth gathered in my house, and with their leaves, flowers, barks, and roots, I create healing teas.

From my heart streams forth the Fire of Compassion. Know that healing will take place only if you have a compassionate heart. Think of that which you would like to heal in your life and drink this tea of wellbeing that I offer you."

(Each visitor received a small cup of tea, then is passed to the next section.)

The walls of the second section were black and silver, with red sparkly fabrics, candles crystals, and other beautiful things. Brigit is seated.

Brigit #2 as Inspiration   *("fantasy dress, otherworldly)*

"Out my head came the Fires of Inspiration. I taught mankind to make the talking marks so they could remember what they did not want to forget.

When they could write these things down, they were inspired to write poetry and to put down their thoughts and ideas as well. They found the beauty in words.

Let this flame represent the fiery passion of your soul. (I had a magic trick that changes a lit match into a red rose, which she executed at this point.) Be inspired to use this fire to create beauty."

The third stall was open to the outdoors. It was decorated with armor, swords, shields, knives, etc. and highlighted with florescent paint and black lights. A fire in a small burner sat just outside the tent.

Brigit #3 as Smithy *(plain brown dress, leather apron and boots)*

"Out of my hands came the Fire of the Forge. People flocked to learn from me the secret of using fire to soften iron and bend it to the shapes of their desires. They called this smith craft and made wheels, pots, and tools that did not break. They forged swords and weapons of martial arts with which to defeat their enemies. Follow me to the Fire of my Forge.

Here are pots of molten lead, which may be used to divine your future or bring you a message from the Gods. Dip and pour a little into the water with your question or desire in mind. Go now and see what you have wrought."

(When finished the lead piece was given to them to keep. I used wheel weights for the lead, and the shapes could be read like wax readings, etc)

Earth Her Body, 2006

Portal of Earth will be open until Tuesday morning.
Temple of Gaia, Sunday & Monday.

Schedule for 2006 - Saturday:
Check in, 3:00-5:30pm
Dinner: 5:30-7:00 pm
Required Sacred Fire Orientation: 7:00-8:30 pm & Purification Sweat Lodge:
9 pm
Opening Ritual, drum, and dance till dawn: 11:00 pm

Sunday: Breakfast dawn - 8 am & 11-12:00—Qi Gung
Lunch: 12:00-1:00
  1:15-2:45 – Drumming (Billy & Cindy) &
  3:00-4:30 — Crystal Healing Basics
4:30-6:00—Required Sacred Fire Orientation for late-comers
  Dinner: 5:30-7:30
Ritual & Sacred Fire Circle: 11:00pm -dawn

Monday: Breakfast: dawn - 8am
  11-12:00 – Herb walk
Lunch: 12:00-1:00
  1:15-2:45 - Bach Flower Remedies & 3:00 - 4:30 - Exploring
  Crystal Healing
  4:45-5:45 - Qi Gung
Dinner: 6:00-7:15

Charlyn Scheffelman (Lady Nytewind)

7:30-8:30 – drumming (Billy & Cindy)
Ritual & Sacred Fire Circle: 11:00pm - 3:00am

Tuesday: Breakfast 7-9am
Pack up and clean up camp
Lunch: 11:00am-12pm
Closing ritual: 12:00 pm
Vacate camp by 1:00pm

Mountain Moon Circle's Summerfest: rituals from "Earth – 2006"
Opening Ritual 1st Night, the Ancient Ones (or not)

This year we had a surprise opening ritual, even for us! A group of Native Americans came, some of which were regulars attendees for other SummerFests. They offered, and we accepted to have them do a pipe ceremony and opening ritual. Which they did perform.

2nd Night 2006: Egyptian Alchemy

On altar: Small tall altar, Purple & gold cloths, Eye of Horus & stand, lighters, a dish of incense w/sparkle & Vesta. Torches each side of altar, 2 propane burners in tubs, 2 pots of lead & tin foil, book, stand & light, 2 dippers, 2 bowls of water *(N & S)*, Pieces of lead for each participant *(E & W)*, Kephi incense, burner & lighter West, Holy Water East, Canopic jars & statues at quarters

Cast & Seal Circle:

East: Qebhsennuf (Kebsnoof),
We respectfully ask your presence at the Eastern gate.
We ask that you bear witness to our rites,
And guard this sacred space from the East.
Your light comes to us, may our light come to you
So mote it be!

South: Duamutef
We respectfully ask your presence at the Southern gate.
We ask that you bear witness to our rites,
And guard this sacred space from the South.
Your light comes to us, may our light come to you
So mote it be!

West: Insety
We respectfully ask your presence at the Western gate.
We ask that you bear witness to our rites,

And guard this sacred space from the West.
Your light comes to us, may our light come to you
So mote it be!

North: Hapi (haahpi)
We respectfully ask your presence at the Northern gate.
We ask that you bear witness to our rites,
And guard this sacred space from the North.
Your light comes to us, may our light come to you
So mote it be!

Statement of Purpose: HPS:

As did the Ancient Alchemists, we seek this night to transform ourselves—to rid ourselves of that which is not part of our greater good—the lead that holds us back from our true spiritual progress, turning it into gold, as pure as the light of the sun that brings the dawn. This is deep work—work that changes us and changes our lives. Through the transformative power of fire, we can effect these desired changes in ourselves and in our lives.

Light Torches:

HP *(from Egyptian Book of the Dead)*
The shining eye of Horus comes.
The brilliant eye of Horus comes.
It comes in peace,
it sends forth rays of light unto Ra, the Sun, in the horizon,
And it destroys the powers of Set, the powers of darkness,
According to the decree.
It leads them on and it takes possession of Set,
And its flame is kindled against him.
Its flame comes and goes about and brings adoration;
It comes and goes about heaven in the train of Ra
upon the two hands of thy two sisters, O Ra.
The Eye of Horus liveth, yea liveth.

HPS: *(Light fire)*
The fire is laid, the fire shines; *(throw in incense and sparkle stuff)*
The incense is laid on the fire, the incense shines.
Your perfume comes to us, O Incense;

May our perfume come to you, O Incense;
Your perfume comes to us, O Gods;
May our perfume come to you, O Gods
May we be with you, O Gods, may you be with us, O Gods,
May we live with you, O Gods, may you live with us, O Gods.
We love you, O Gods, may you love us, O Gods.

Emerald Tablet: *(Author unknown, attributed to Thoth)*
In truth, without deceit, certain, and most veritable –
That which is Below, corresponds to that which is Above, and that which is Above, corresponds to that which is Below, to accomplish the miracles of the One Thing. And just as all things have come from the One Thing, through the meditation of One Mind, so do all created things originate from this One Thing, through Transformation.

Its father is the Sun: its mother the Moon. The Wind carries it in its belly: its nurse is the Earth. It is the origin of All, the consecration of the Universe; its inherent Strength is perfected if it is turned into Earth.

Separate the Earth from Fire, the Subtle from the Gross, gently and with great Ingenuity. It rises from Earth to heaven and descends again to Earth, thereby combining within Itself the powers of both the Above and the Below.

Thus will you obtain the Glory of the Whole Universe. All Obscurity will be clear to you. This is the greatest Force of all powers because it overcomes every Subtle thing and penetrates every Solid thing.

In this way was the Universe created. From this comes many wondrous Applications, because this is the Pattern.

Therefore am I called Thrice Greatest Hermes, having all three parts of the wisdom of the Whole Universe. Herein have I completely explained the operation of the Sun
(Speaker and the four quarter people light the fire with torches).

HPS: *(The Golden Ass by Lucius Apuleius, Late 2nd century Adapted)*
O Great Goddess, Soul of Isis
Heart of the Sun, hear our call!
You are Nature,
The Universal Mother,
Mistress of all the elements,
Primordial child of time,
Sovereign of all things spiritual,

Queen of the dead,
Queen also of the Immortals,
The single manifestation of all Gods and Goddesses.
Enter now this consecrated shrine.
Make Thy presence known to all who are present
Aide these, Thy people, in reaching the source of all things.

HP:

Oh Great God, Soul of Osiris
Lord of Eternity, hear our call!
Your forms are manifold
Your attributes are majestic
Universal Father,
Guide of the underworld
Whom the Gods glorify,
Lord of the celestial world,
All hearts are at peace as they behold thee.
Enter now this consecrated shrine.
Make Thy presence known to all who are present
Aide these, Thy people, in reaching the source of all things.
(Pieces of lead are passed to all)

HPS:

This piece of lead, mined from deep within the Earth, symbolizes the lead that lies deep within you—that which 'weighs you down' in your life, keeping you from reaching your highest good. Hold it…charge it with the thing that needs to be transformed in yourself, or in your life.

HP: *(2 hold water pots, quarters go FIRST)*

When you are ready, come place your 'lead' into the melting pot. From that pot, take a small dipper of lead and pour it into the water. This produces for you a talisman—one that represents your transformation. See in it what you will. Use it to help you in your process this night.

(Participants bring their lead to one of the two melting pots, throw it in, then ladle some into the water to cool it. They take the cool lead with them. Meanwhile, belly dancers are getting ready)

MMC Belly Dancers Perform! And the fire circle begins! Dance and trance until dawn.

Chant

> Burn Fire, Burn Bright
> Pure Vision Come To Me
> Guide My Path Tonight
> With Your Strength and Light

Dawn – All recite the *Solar Salutation* by Katlyn Breene

HPS:

> Beloved Isis, we bid you farewell.
> Guide our steps on the true Path.
> May we never falter in Thy presence
> Nor do harm or disfavor to Thee.
> Answer our soul's desire for Maat.
> May Thoth aid us in perfect judgment
> May we always go in graciousness with the Gods.
> So mote it be! *(Extinguish torch)*

HP:

> Beloved Osiris, we bid you farewell!
> Watch over us as a good shepherd watches over his flocks.
> May we never falter in Thy presence
> Nor do harm or disfavor to Thee.
> Answer our soul's desire for Maat.
> May Thoth aid us in perfect judgment
> May we always go in graciousness with the Gods.
> So mote it be! *(Extinguish torch)*

East:

> Wise Qebhsennuf *(Kebsnoof)*,
> We thank you for bearing witness to our rites,
> And for Guarding the Eastern Gate.
> We bid you Hail and farewell!

South:

> Mighty Duamutef
> We thank you for bearing witness to our rites,
> And for Guarding the Southern Gate.
> We bid you Hail and farewell!

West:

> Compassionate Insety
> We thank you for bearing witness to our rites,
> and for Guarding the Western Gate.
> We bid you hail and farewell.

North:

> Great Hapi (haahpi)
> We thank you for bearing witness to our rites,
> And for Guarding the Northern Gate.
> We bid you Hail and farewell!

Dismiss Circle

3rd Night – Celtic Tree Ritual by Isaac Bonewits

Ritual 3 - Celtic tree ritual

Needs:

Pine tree, apple bell w/mallet, corn meal & bowl, cauldron w/water & small bowl, 3 coins, **branch for asperging**, holy water, Celtic circle incense, censor, charcoal, fire chemicals, bread, 2 chalices of wine, staff

HPS:

To the Druids, Celts, and many others, wood from sacred trees have magickal properties. This was reflected in the Celtic <u>Ogham</u> runic alphabet, wherein each letter represents a particular sacred tree. Celtic divination is also based on the uses and importance of these sacred trees.

Some trees provide food, some wood for making hunting weapons; others are sacred to the fairy-folk or to the Gods. In Celtic creation stories, trees were the ancestors of mankind, the elder beings of wisdom who provided the alphabet, the calendar, and entrance to the realms of the Gods—a connection to the world of the spirits and the ancestors, living entities, and doorways into other worlds.

Long after the Druids of old had vanished into the mists of time, the lore of trees continues as a vital part of Celtic myth and folklore. Countless Irish legends revolve around trees. For instance, one could fall asleep next to a particular tree and awake in the fairy realm!

In Celtic legends of the Gods, trees guard the sacred wells and provide healing, shelter, and wisdom. Trees carry messages to the other realm, and confer blessings. Trees can be seen in the Irish countryside festooned with ribbons and pleas for favors, love, healing, and prosperity.

The interlaced figures known as Celtic knots represent sacred trees and plants, and the sacred animals of the forest. The Green Man or foliate god, is the animus of nature; the spirit of the forest and of the hunt, and is pictured as a spirit face in the form of gathered leaves and sprouting tendrils.

Without trees and the gifts they give us, life would be impossible.

East:

Hail to the Eastern groves of dawn, of Alder trees breathing in soft spring breezes. Tree of the Spring Equinox, symbol of resurrection and renewed life. Doorway to the fairy realm, which is concealed within thy trunk!

Bran' the Blessed's sacred tree. Tree of the Raven, Bran's totem animal. He carried a branch of Alder during the 'Battle of the Trees' in times of old.

Tree of legend, from which the first man was formed, while the first women came from the Rowan.

Tree which bleeds, when cut, your red blood dyed the faces of Sacred Kings in ritual, and the green dye made from you clothes the Faeries and the Green Man. Tree of which ritual pipes and whistles are made.

We give thanks to the Eastern groves of dawn, of Alder trees breathing in new life.

South:

Hail to the Southern groves of midday, of Oak trees standing strong and proud. Beneath thy branches and in thy groves, the Druids meet—for all of their meetings and teachings are closely connected to the tree dryads, the Spirits of the Trees.

The Oak tree, mighty, strong, enduring and steadfast; the symbol of the High King and his ancient and spiritual link to the land.

Sacred fuel for Midsummer fires; you stand at the doorway of the great turning point of the year; the Summer Solstice when the sun reaches the height of its power and strength, and turns to begin a new cycle of decline.

Mistletoe, the sacred herb which grows on you, is harvested by Druids Summer Solstice.

We give thanks to the Southern groves of midday, of Oak trees standing strong and proud.

West:

Hail to the Western groves of twilight; of apples dancing, their starlight within. You stand at the heart of Avalon, the Otherworld, known also as the Isle of Apples. Old sagas tell of heroes crossing the western sea to find you in this magickal land, which is ruled by Fairy Queen, Morgan le Fay and is the land of fairy and of the dead. It is where King Arthur was taken to be healed by his sister, Morgan.

You are the bearer of magickal fruit, food of the people of Faerie, fruit which has the power of healing, youth and rebirth. The sacred pentagram is at the core of your fruit. Your apples are a source of basic sustenance and your branches a provide shelter and fuel for cooking and warmth.

The Druids cut your branches for divining rods, the sacred plant, Mistletoe, is often found growing upon you. You are the source of life and knowledge. It is from the apple that we receive healing, renewal, regeneration and wholeness, especially after being wounded, exhausted, ill, or lost on our ways.

We give thanks to the Western groves of twilight, of apples dancing, their starlight within.

North:

Hail to the Northern groves of midnight, of yew trees arching to the otherworld.

These ancient trees, some thousands of years old, link us to our ancient past. You are trees of death—and immortality, and symbols of the rebirth of the sun at Winter Solstice.

You are one of the nine sacred trees for kindling Sabbat fires—one of the five sacred trees brought from the Otherworld at the division of the land into five parts. Known as the Tree of Ross, the World Tree, one of the Seven Chieftain Trees, the Offspring of the tree that is in Paradise, and The Witches Tree, you brought lasting plenty to Ireland where you are used in sorcery and magick!

We know thee as the tree of resilience—as darkness is the matrix from which light springs forth, and it is out of death that life arises.

Here Druid Priests their altars place and sun and moon adore. We give thanks to the Northern groves of midnight, of Yew trees arching to the otherworld.

We give thanks to the Northern groves of Midnight, of yew trees arching to the otherworld.

HPS:

Hail to the Inner groves of notime, of ancestral root and branch and tree. I give thanks to the Inner groves of notime, of ancestral root and branch and tree.

Druid 1 (*rings bell 9 times*)

We have come here to stand as one to honor the Shining Ones!

Charlyn Scheffelman (Lady Nytewind)

Druid 2:

> We come together on this sacred night
> To celebrate the Earth,
> To win from chaos a peaceful time
> In which to gain our harvest.

Druid 1:

> Let us proclaim peace for without peace, no work can be done.

East: Let there be peace in the East

South: Let there be peace in the South

West: Let there be peace in the West

North: Let there be peace in the North

ALL:

> Let there be peace throughout the world. Biodh se! (bee shay) So be it!

Druid 1:

> We revere the nature spirits, our ancestors, and the Gods and Goddesses of our tribe and of this place. Through the magic of the sacred fire, the holy well, and the great tree, we offer our rites.

Druid 2:

> Let us now reverence the earth who is our mother, our home, and indeed the substance of our very bodies.

ALL: *(kneel and touch the earth)*

Druid 1:

> Beloved mother of all, from whose starry womb the green earth springs; you are the bearer of all life. Accept our offering, and bless and uphold this rite.

Druid 2 *(offers corn meal to the World Tree Offering bowl)*

Tree Meditation - Seer:

When e'er we stand in a sacred place
Beneath the Sun's or Moon's bright face,
In a circle's rim or shady grove,
Our spirits go to the Gods we love.
Let all our minds go clear and free,
and form the image of a tree,
A youthful sapling of the glade,
Whose budding branches cast no shade.

Around this tender, supple youth,
Are seen its sturdy forbearers growth,
Those forest Elders strong and wise,
Who nurture those of lesser size.

So close your eyes, and in your mind
Become one of the spirit kind.
Cast off your cares and disbelief,
and enter tree from root to leaf.

Relax and breathe and center well,
Then let the peace within you swell
Until it is a thing profound.
Now send it deep into the ground.

In every little tender root
Feel water flow, and then transmute;
The sap will flow through every vein,
Our links to our ancestors regain.

Now let the sap rise in a flood,
And race to every branch and bud;
Each branch extend into the air,
Each leaf unfold in green so fair.

The gentle zephers toss each bough,
And to you calming breaths endow,

While rays of golden summer light
Give warmth and lend their power's might.

Let water rise and fire descend,
And lively air the branches bend;
Thus firmly planted in the Earth,
The elements give us rebirth.

Now let the green entwine,
And form our sacred grove divine.
With branch and root our circle form,
And magic from mundane transform.
We all are rooted just the same,
We feel the same supernal flame,
We drink the water free to all,
We hear the gentle airy call.
Now let us feel our spirits surge,
And into one great spirit merge.
To let the Lord and Lady know
That we are ready here below.

N: Stand tall and Proud. Sink your roots deeply into the Earth.
S: Reflect the light of a greater source.

W: Think long term
E: Go out on a limb

N: Remember your place among all living beings, for each yields its own abundance.

E: The energy and birth of Spring
S: The growth and contentment of Summer

W: The wisdom to let go of leaves in the Fall
N: The Rest and quiet renewal of Winter

E: Feel the wind and the sun and delight in their presence

W: Look up at the moon that shines down upon you and the mystery of the stars at night

N: Seek nourishment from the good things in life
S: Simple pleasures; Earth, fresh air, light. Be content with your natural beauty

W: Drink plenty of water
E: Let your limbs sway and dance in the breezes. Be flexible.

N: Remember your roots

ALL: Enjoy the view!

Druid 1: *(invokes the Awen)*
Power of inspiration, attend to us.
Voice of the fire of wisdom,
Voice of the well of inspiration,
Voice of the sky above,
Come into our hearts' shrine.
Make us aware of every good or ill.
O Brigit, guide our rite in the way of truth.
I call you to make our hearts clear within us,
Power of inspiration in this holy place,
Power of inspiration at this holy time.
Power of inspiration, be with us!

ALL:
Biodh se! (bee shay) So be it!

Druid 1 *(fills a small bowl with water from well, offers Silver)*
Sacred waters that flow and swirl beneath all being, accept our offering. Let us know the elder depths within ourselves the source of all, the well of elder wisdom. *(Dump water back into well)*

ALL:
Sacred well, flow within us!

Seer: *(offers oil to the Fire)*

Sacred fire that consumes and transforms, true and holy light of the Shining Ones, accept our offering. Sacrificed and sacrificer, let holy flame warm our spirits and our lives.

ALL: Sacred fire, burn within us!

*(**Druid 2** draws water from the Well while **Seer** lights a smudge stick from the Fire. **Seer** censes and **Druid 2** sprinkles the Tree)*

Seer:

Sacred pillar, boundary of all worlds, stand at the center of the sky, stand at the center of the sea, stand at the center of the land on which we dwell. Let us be deepened in your depths, Raised to your heights, Strengthened in your strength.

ALL: Sacred tree, grow within us!

*(Seer gives smudge stick to **Druid 1** and takes ale to south entrance to make an offering of ale to the Outdwellers)*

Druid 1:

This place I name, this land I do claim, while I and my own are upon it.

Outsiders! You who choose not to assist in our stated purpose, whose voice will not harmonize with the tune we play this day; Your function we honor. Your purpose we respect - for you are among the many faces of the great mystery. But as a gift calls for a gift, we offer and pray, asking only this: Till the bell is rung, and the rite is done, let there be peace between us!

*(**Seer** makes an offering of ale to the Outdwellers. As he returns to the circle, **Druid 2** meets him at the entrance and asperses them)*

We purify you from the Outsiders' influence.
We cut you off from them,
That you might return to the people.

*(**Druid 1** smudges, **Druid 2** asperses the Pagans).*

Druid 1:

Sacred is this land to us, sacred is all land to us, and it is the world in which we walk. We are supported and sustained by the land, valleys, fields, hills, spires of peaks, depths of forest and desert down to the shores holding before the waves.

Seer:

Waves of the Sea, touches of the Otherworld endlessly dancing to rise and recede at our shores. Across the waves the ancestors rest and the sea gives and claims as it will, all the while pushed by the breath of the skies.

Druid 1:

Skies above, the very world of the Gods of our people, with shining eye, sweeping winds and blessings raining down. The secret of lives written in mysteries of star and cloud.

Druid 2: *(Thump staff 3x for land, swing staff around body for sea, make spiral in air for air)*

We are here in the Sacred Center of the worlds of land, sea and sky. Here the Gates Between the Worlds may be opened. Through the gates of Fire, Well and Sacred Tree we send love, worship and offerings to the Powers and They send us blessings in return.

*(**Seer** makes an offering to Manannan, saying)*

Manannan, Lord of the Gates, Lord of Wisdom, open the ways for us. We walk in your holy ways; we walk the Sacred Road. Share your magic with us; ward us as we walk in safety. Manannan mac Lir, accept our sacrifice.

(Seer makes an offering of chemicals to the Fire)

*(**Druid 1** then opens the Gates, saying):*

Now, Shining Ones, join your magic with ours and let the fire open as a gate. *(Makes an opening awen over the Fire)*

Let the well open as a gate.
(makes an opening awen over the Well)

Let the tree be the crossroads of all worlds. Open as a road to our voices and to the spirits.

Charlyn Scheffelman (Lady Nytewind)

(makes an opening awen before the Tree.)

Let the gates be open!

ALL: Let the gates be open!

Seer:
We children of the earth call out to the Ancient Ones. Hear us, our ancestors, our kindred, our mighty dead.

To all those whose bones lie in this land, we offer you welcome.

To all our grandmothers and grandfathers, our own beloved dead, blood-kin and heart-kin; ancient tribes of our blood, we offer you welcome.

Come to our fire, spirits; meet us at the boundary. Guide and ward us as we walk the elder ways. Ancestors, accept our sacrifice.

Seer *makes an offering of bread and ale to the World Tree Offering Bowl.*

CD: Gwydion Fairy Shaman: #7, The **trees of Annwfn**, *Trees circle and swirl, enter fairy, Satyr, Mermaid, Unicorn, Gnome, Dragon, troll*
ROUND THE TREE
Round the tree of life we go
Twisting turning quick and slow
Wending, winding to and fro
Beginnings into endings flow

Dawn: Solar Salutation

Closing: Seer
A tree stands faithfully and won't turn away
Like a sign that says 'welcome', it asks you to stay.
The branches reach out and sing to the birds
And down on the sidewalk the twigs spell words.

Deep in the earth the silent roots sleep
One day they awaken and slowly they creep.
Close to the ground there and touching the sky
A tree stands always as the clouds sail by.

A tree weaves a story, a history of time
Look up and listen, and together, we'll climb.

Druid 1:

Having offered to the kindred and received their blessings, we now thank all those who have aided us in our rite. Nature spirits, we thank you!

All: **We thank you!**

Druid 2: Ancestors, we thank you!
All: **We thank you!**

Druid 1: Shining Ones, we thank you!
All: **We thank you!**

Seer: Earth Mother, we thank you!
All: **We thank you!**

Druid 1:

We now return the unused portions of our offerings to the Earth Mother *(do so)*. We call upon the Gatekeeper to close the gates.

Druid 2:

Manannan Mac Lir, join your magick with ours and…
Let the Well be but water
Let the Fire be but flame
And may the Sacred Tree be but a symbol of the world of tree within us all.
Let the Gates be close!

All: Let the Gates be closed!

Seer: Brother and sisters, go in peace and blessings, the rite is ended.
(ring bell 9 times)

Closing Ritual – in the morning before breaking camp

HP: To be of the Earth is to know of restlessness,
HPS: Of being a seed.

HP: The darkness of being planted,
HPS: The struggle toward the light.

HP: The pain of growth into the light,
HPS: The joy of bursting and bearing fruit.

HP: The love of being food for someone,
HPS: The scattering of your seeds.

HP: The decay of the seasons,
HPS: The mystery of death and the miracle of birth.

−Quote from John Soos on Goodreads

HPS:

We came to this place to honor the land upon which we dwell, and to honor the life within us and the life within all things created. We came to change ourselves and our lives for our better good, and now we prepare to take what we have been given here back into our mundane lives.

We came in perfect love and perfect trust, to build bridges between each other, to honor our similarities and our differences and our various paths as Pagan People. We came to honor the Earth, the good, green Earth.

HPS:

Thus concludes our journey through the element of Earth, Body of the Goddess. A Very Special Thanks to you--all the MMC members who worked so hard to accomplish this weekend, and to all of you; first-timers (now members of the Tribe), and especially to those who have returned to share their magick with us all.

Accept our heartfelt thanks for your presence at this event. We hope to see you all again next year for Water, Her Blood.

(Water Woman walks through in a water costume to watery music)
I cannot find the poem, but can include a few lines.

HP: A mountain is she, standing as the highest peak...

HPS: Canyons fill with her; the rising gorge walls her vast domain...

HP: Mother mountain, river mother rooted in glacier's path, embracing our bones cupped in the hands of time...

HPS:
Mother Mountain, river mother, arc of her breast caressed by sky whose winds are lover's hands, a mountain is she.

Honored ones, of Earth and Sky, we offer our gratitude for your presence and for the lessons and experiences you've given us. Stay if you will, but go if you must, we bid you 'hail and farewell!

East:
Ancient ones of the East, Portal of Air,
We thank thee for your presence here!
For dancing winds and sylphs of air
Winged ones, and birds of flight,
For power of thought, and spoken word
Healing ways and golden light
With Her breath, out and in,
With new knowledge, we'll begin.
Stay if you will, but go if you must
We bid you hail and Farewell!

North:
Ancient ones of the North,
Portal of Earth,
We thank thee for your presence here!
For Wee Folk, Elves, and Gnomes
Earth below, and sky above,
Creatures large and creatures small,
Seeds that grow, and flowers that bloom

Charlyn Scheffelman (Lady Nytewind)

With Her Body beneath our feet,
We've gathered for this Merry Meet
Stay if you will, but go if you must
We bid you hail and Farewell!

West:

Ancient ones of the West, Portal of Water,
We thank thee for your presence here!
For Merfolk and water sprites,
The Mother's love and Secrets deep,
For lovers, sisters, brothers, friends,
And compassion that never ends.
By her blood, circling round
Love unconditional we've found.
Stay if you will, but go if you must
We bid you hail and Farewell!

South:

Ancient ones of the South, Portal of Fire,
We thank thee for your presence here!
For Salamanders, and spirits of fire
Sparks and flames that transform
For the love and passion of life's flame
And fulfillment of will and desire.
With her Spirit as the spark
From this place, we now embark.
Stay if you will, but go if you must
We bid you hail and Farewell!

Dismiss Circle

Mountain Moon Circle's Summerfest Schedule: Earth 2012

Thursday: Check in after 2:00 pm
6:00-7:00pm Dinner
7:00-8:00 pm Required Sacred Fire Orientation
8:30 pm Talent Show
11:00 pm Opening Ritual, drum, and dance till dawn

Friday:
First Breakfast at dawn; 9:00-10:00 second breakfast
12:00-1:00 Lunch
1:00-2:30 The Magick of Crystals
2:45-4:00 Flower Power; Healing with Flowers
4:15-5:30 Drumming in the Circle
6:00-7:30 Dinner
11:00-dawn Ritual and Sacred Fire Circle

Saturday
First Breakfast at dawn 9:00-10:00 second breakfast
11:00-12:00 Earth Energy Yoga
12:00-1:00 Lunch
1:00-2:30 Crystal Healing for Animals
2:45-4:00 Lesser Banishing Ritual of the Pentagram
4:15-5:15 Metal Magick
6:00-7:30 Dinner
11:00-3:00 Sacred Fire Circle

Sunday
10:00-11:00am Brunch
11:30 am closing ritual - Clean up camp, pack up and vacate by 1:00 pm

Opening Ritual 1ˢᵗ Night, the Ancient Ones

Needs: arrow, Incense pot w/charcoal & cedar, feather fan, Cloth for ties, bowl & tobacco, twine for ties, quarter tables w/leather & plastic covers, 4 dream catchers, drum, 5 black cloths to hide women, 6 black lights, Tribal Neon Paint & brushes, table w/masks, book, stand and lights, Hoop

Cast Circle: *(Use arrow. Participants are smudged and seated. Torches are extinguished and 5 women crouch in the circle covered by black cloths)*

Creation: *(A voice speaks, using a black light to illuminate the air designs on her face)*

I am the Ancient One. I have had being since time began. My home is here in the void of space. I see the stars and the moon, the sun and the comets that streak by. I sit upon my cloud and observe all that is beautiful and interesting, but yet, I feel that something is missing.

Below the cloud upon which I sit is nothing but a watery wasteland. I shall, by my powers, see what I can create from the hairs of my head. *(plucks a hair and drops it. First woman emerges from under her cloth))*

A: Woman, have you given any thought to what you will do? *(To Earth woman w/light)*

E: Yes, I have. I will become the Earth. I will become mountains and caves, trees and stones, rivers and plains. In that way, I will become a mother to all living things. They will all grow from my soil and swim in my oceans, run through my forests and burrow deep into the ground. They will fly, crawl, walk and swim, and I will create deserts and rainforests and all manner of environments in which they will dwell. Everything will come from me, and after these things have lived upon me for a long time, they will die and return to me.

A: This is a very good thing. I am pleased with your decision. *(Drops another hair)* Woman, what will you be in the scheme of things?

W: I will be Water, Old One. All will depend upon me to have its being. I will quench the thirst of every living thing great and small. Both fauna and flora, and all that walks, swims, flies or crawls will have need of me. I will provide a place for the fish and all the creatures of the oceans, the seas, the rivers and the streams to live. I will cleanse all things with falling rain, and Earth's creatures shall bathe in me for their pleasure and survival.

A: I am very pleased! *(Drops another hair)* Woman, what would you be?

D: I would be a woman who would bear many, many children. But my children will be strong! They will be aggressive and intolerant. They will rely upon violence and destruction. They will fight with each other and cause wars, turning against each other at the slightest provocation. They will commit murder and do many terrible things, causing much pain and grief, and they will often do so in the guise of righteousness. *(cackle)*

A: What you have created will upset my new world with trouble, strife and violence! *(Drops another hair)* Woman, what would you be?

L: I will also bear many, many children. My sons and daughters will be big and strong, too, but they will also be kind, intelligent, wise and good. They will invent many useful things and honor the earth. They will respect the creatures of Earth's creation, taking only what they need to survive. They will plant and grow and harvest Earth's bounty, never forgetting to thank her for her abundance. They will spread peace and goodwill amongst men wherever they walk and promote harmony with the earth and with each other.

A: I am grateful to you, for you shall begin a peaceful and respectful race of people to live in my new world. *(Drops another hair)*

F: *(without being asked—has light)* Old one, I will become the element of Fire. I will be hidden in the center of the Earth, and shall aide Mother Earth in the creation of mountains and valleys as She sees fit. I will also exist in all things as the powerful spark of life, causing all to have its being until it is called by the Mother to return to her.

I will exist for the good of the people so that they may warm the food that they eat and protect themselves from cold weather. I will light the people's way in darkness so that they might make use of the dark hours as well as the sunny ones.

A: This is an important thing to be; Fire! Be the things you are—the mothers of good and bad, the mothers of Earth, Fire, and Water! *(Other elements go to their quarters.)*

At first, there will be much trouble and unhappiness in this world because of the third woman's choice. Eventually, however, the world will return to balance between humans and nature, and all of you will live in harmony in the universe. *(Goes to Air's quarter).*

(Light quarter torches, then center fire. The peace pipe is lit, offered to the six directions then passed to the East)

East: *(stands to receive pipe, offers prayer to the East, then puffs and passes it to each person clockwise)*

South: *(stands to receive pipe, offers prayer then puffs and passes it to each person clockwise)*

West: *(stands to receive pipe, offers prayer then puffs and passes it to each person clockwise)*

North: *(stands to receive pipe, offers prayer then puffs and passes it to each person clockwise)*

HPS: Breathe with me! The breath unites us! *(breathing together ritual)*

We call to the spirits of this place—this land, this sky and all that has it's being here. With honor and respect, we call you. With humble hearts, we call you. With gratitude and love, we call you.

We have gathered in this holy place to seek guidance, to give thanks, and to strip away that in ourselves which is not part of our true nature. We seek our highest good.

For three suns we will walk this land in peace and love, with respect for all that is, seeking to transform and improve our lives and our spiritual beings. Spirits, we ask that you aide us in our quest.

Prayer Ties:

You will receive a piece of cloth, some tobacco, and a strip to tie it with. Place your prayer into this tobacco offering and tie it shut, then tie it to the rope that unites us. *(hold up the rope)*

It will be present at the Sacred Fire until the last night when all will be burned and your prayers sent to the Gods. If it be your will, materials will be available during our time together to make more prayer offerings in colors that signify each element.

(Long string, squares of cloth, tobacco and short ties are passed by the quarter people. Drum heart beat accompanies the making of the prayer ties, and when all are done, they are tied to the long string which is then removed to the boundary of the circle.)

Evocation of First Original Clan Woman:
Talks with Relations is the Mother of Nature who welcomes all life forms into her Clan. She is the keeper of rhythm, teaching us to find our own rhythm and to respect the rhythms of all living things. In this way, we may be accepted, as wild creatures are willing to accept some humans without fear.

Each life form has a Sacred Space and a rhythm. Talks with Relations teaches us to respect the rhythm of all living things. If we learn the rhythm and ask permission, with respect, we can enter the world of those Sisters and Brothers without disturbing the natural order.

Evocation: *Clan Mothers,* by Jamie Sams
This is copyrighted material, so I cannot include it here. She has several books available, but I found this part floating around the internet, so maybe you can find it too.

Shape Shifting: *(Drum is played as all are led into a spiral dance and through the hoop, signifying that their transformation has commenced. Masks are available through the night for those who wish to more fully express their animals.)*

Chants; MEDICINE PEOPLE
We are medicine people
We come from stars
We are holders of the sacred hoop
We carry the fire

FUR AND FEATHERS
Fur and feathers and scales and skin
Different without but the same within
Many a body but one the soul

Charlyn Scheffelman (Lady Nytewind)

By all the creatures are the gods made whole

At Dawn: (Best to have everyone memorize this before the event.)
Solar Salutation, by Katlyn Breene

Clan Mother:
>Clan Mother, Mother of Nature talks with her kin,
>Accept our gratitude!
>We know that you have opened your heart to us,
>And have shared your ancient wisdom this night
>We hold your truth in our hearts
>As we sing our heart songs.
>Your divine rhythm has brought us to the sacred space within.
>By the divine force that connects all life as one, Aho!

East:
>I am that which creates—I am new beginnings.
>I am the messenger that comes from the Gods,
>Bringing you inspiration and healing
>I leave you now with this message....
>Each day begins anew with the sunrise
>Each day is your new beginning.
>Aho!

North:
>I am the ground beneath your feet
>I am that which supports life on Earth
>I am the Mother of the plants and animals in this dimension,
>And I leave you now with this message...
>Take care of the Earth and its creatures
>And you will be taken care of as well.
>Aho!

West:
>I am the waters that support all life
>I am the home of many creatures
>I am the life blood that flows through your veins
>I leave you now with this message...

Your emotions flow within you
Listen to them--acknowledge them
Aho!

South:

I am the fire that burns within you
I am desire, and love, and joy
I am the spark of life in all that is
And I leave you now with this message…
Life is a gift!
You are here to experience it!
Aho!

Dismiss Circle

2nd Night, 2012: Druid Tree Ritual

The tree ritual was also repeated – it had been six years, and we wanted to do it again.

3rd Night, 2012: Khnum

Needs: Natron, water bowl, Egypt incense, burner & charcoal, Khnum & veil, clay figures, fat wood/black candles, singing bowl, CD: Egypt meditation, gold altar cloth, hula hoop, tall round altar.

(Cast circle to singing bowl and admit Quarters to seal the circle)

Holy Water HPS: *(from Ancient Egyptian text)*

O Water may you remove all evil,
As Ra who bathes in the Lake of Rushes,
May Heru wash my flesh,
May Djehuty cleanse my feet,
May Shu lift me up and Nut (Noo-it) take my hand

HP:

It is pure, it is pure. My natron is the natron of Heru and the natron of Heru is my natron.

My natron is the natron of Sutekh and the natron of Sutekh is my natron.
My natron is the natron of Djehuty (Je-**hoo**-ty), and the natron of
Djehuty is my natron.
My natron is the natron of Geb (Geeb) and the natron of Geb is my natron.
My mouth is the mouth of a milking calf on the day that I was born
(Join & stir, hand to Water)

HPS: The fire is laid, the fire shines
The incense is laid on the fire, the incense shines
Your perfume comes to us, O Incense;
May our perfume come to you, O Incense
Your perfume comes to us, you Gods:
May our perfume come to you, you Gods.
(Hand to Air)

HP:

May we live with you, you Gods;
May you live with us, you Gods
We love you, you gods,
May you love us, you Gods.

Both: "May he who enters the temple be pure"
(participants are sprinkled and Smudged)

HP:

Sons of Horus, God of One Face, we call to you to stand at
the portals of the elements—you who are the Guardians of
that which is within and that which is without:

East *(bird)*

Qebhssennuf (Kebsnoof),
Ibis-headed God of the Element of Air
Who brings breath to the lungs to feed the Sa,
The divine strength within us;
Your light comes to us, May our light come to you.
Kebsnoof, son of Horus, by the dawn's first light,
Protect us and guard our Eastern Gate this night.
So be it!

South: *(Jackel)*
Duamutef (Dwa-**moo**-tef)
Jackal-headed God of the Element of Fire
Who brings fire to the belly, giving us the strength
Of our souls and the courageousness of spirit.
Your light comes to us, may our light come to you
O Duamutef, Son of Horus,
Guide us with your brightest light
And protect us with your holy might
So be it!

West: *(man)*
Imsety (Im-**set**-y) human-headed God
Of the Element of Water
The liver within, the purifier of intentions
And emotions to live and love freely with compassion.
Your light comes to us, May our light come to you
O Imsety, Son of Horus,
At the western gate be our guide,
On waters deep and waters wide.
So be it!

North: *(Baboon)*
Hapi (Haahpy) baboon-headed God
Of the Element of Earth
The river, the giver of life who nourishes the aufu
The physical flesh, and the ka, the mind-double.
Your light comes to us, May our light come to you
O Hapy, Son of Horus,
At our Northern Gate, you stand,

All who would enter are at your command
So be it!

Statement: HPS
Tonight we stand in the presence of the Gods to leave behind all that is not true to our soul's purpose. Just as the Gods of the Harvest sacrifice themselves at this time of year and return to the underworld to await rebirth,

we also must sacrifice our weaknesses and faults in order to birth a better life ahead for ourselves and for all who love us.

To assist us in completing this separation and in successfully conjoining our better attributes, we shall call upon the Great God Khnum.

Khnum was the Ancient God of all rivers and lakes, even those in the underworld. As such he was God of the Nile, bringing forth the yearly floods that deposited rich, fertile soil on the fields along its banks. This silt also became a pure, smooth clay which could be formed, and Khnum molded all that exists on his potter's wheel, including other Gods, the world, and people—into whom he then placed the vital essence of life, the soul or Ka. *(Bow before the altar, gently touch your palms to your knees. Unveil the statue of Khnum)*

HP: *(Bow before the altar, gently touch your palms to your knees.)*

Hear me, Khnum, for I am True of Voice! Come forth to dwell in thine image so that I may adore and converse with thee!

O Khnum the Creator, in whom the Elements are united and manifest! Thee, thee I invoke!

Ram-headed Lord with Horns of spiral force! Thee, thee I invoke!

O Thou who wearest the White Crown flanked with the Double Plumes of Truth, Thee, thee I invoke!

O Thou who art glorified in Elephantine! Thee, thee I invoke!

O Father of fathers and Mother of mothers of the pharaohs, the Self-created! Thee, thee I invoke!

O Guardian of the Nile, who brings forth the Inundation! Thee, thee I invoke!

O Modeler of men, whose breath is the breath of life! Thee, thee I invoke into thine image! *(return to the altar)*

HPS:

You have molded and brought with you to this holy place an image of yourself made out of clay. You have worked through the pain, the sorrow, the anguish and the anger of calcination these past two nights as you've given these ills to the fire. Now is the time to let go – to let IT go!

This last time, this last night, the fire shall take it from you. Breathe all that keeps you from being a better you into your wood as you slowly move widdershins around the fire. When you are ready, and ONLY when you feel ready, you will throw the wood into the fire and pass your effigy through the smoke as a sign of your sacrifice and commitment.

HP:

You have also experienced the alchemical process of dissolution as your body has sweat and your tears have fallen. Dissolved, now are those things that no longer keep you from your spiritual path and progress.

When you are ready, and ONLY when you are ready, you will sprinkle your clay body with holy natron, symbolizing the completion of that process.

HPS:

Calcination and Dissolution are the processes of letting go of any negative traits or conditions that stand in your way of spiritual growth. But there are good things in your life and yourself as well, and it is time to separate these positive traits and conditions that are worthy of keeping. Think on these things, and then, when you are ready, and ONLY when you are ready, receive Khnum's blessing and pass through the birthing hoop, symbolizing the start of a new beginning and a new life.

(Play CD of Egyptian music as they do the above, then two people will hold the hoop, while they pass through. HPS holds Khnum before & HP blesses clay figures after they are through the hoop)

Chant:

Hungry flames, lapping, lusting;
Burned away our deepest fears
Separating good from bad,
Ash dissolved in cleansing tears
Conjoined to make a whole new me;
To be the best that I can be.

(Belly Dancers perform then celebratory final fire; add the prayer ties to the fire.)

HP: Great Potter and Modeler of all,
Guide our steps on the true Path.
May we never falter in Thy presence
Nor do harm or disfavor to Thee.
Answer our soul's desire for Maat.
May Thoth aid us in perfect judgment
May we always go in graciousness with the Gods.
So mote it be!

HPS: Great Creator, Ram-headed Lord.
Watch over us, thy created
May we always go in graciousness with the Gods.
So mote it be! *(re-cover statue)*

East:

I Qebhssennuf (Kebsnoof) have attended and witnessed your rites and have given you my protection. May you take the light of knowledge with you as you leave this sacred space tonight.

North:

I Hapi (Haahpy) have attended and witnessed your rites and have given you my protection. May you take the light of wisdom with you as you leave this sacred space tonight.

West:

I Imsety (Im-**set**-y) have attended and witnessed your rites and have given you my protection. May you take the light of love and compassion with you as you leave this sacred space tonight.

South:

I Duamutef (Dwa-**moo**-tef) have attended and witnessed your rites and have given you my protection. May you take the light of strength and passion with you as you leave this sacred space tonight.

Dismiss Circle

May the circle be open but unbroken
May the Lord and the Lady be ever in your heart.
Merry meet and merry part
And merry meet again.

Closing Ritual – in the morning before breaking camp, 2012

East: *(Cast circle hand to hand) I cannot find this poem again, so here are a few lines.*

> I live on a planet, The blue planet
> My feet patter it every day…

South:

> Fire in the sky warms the earth;
> The mighty earth, churning along…

West:

> I gulp its cycled rain
> And so do others.
> We make fountains, lakes, and drains…

North:

> We stir the dust and clay
> And make our marks upon it.
> Life is a Mystery…

> *-Poem by John Soos*

HP: To be of the Earth is to know of restlessness,
HPS: Of being a seed

HP: The darkness of being planted
HPS: The struggle toward the light

HP: The pain of growth into the light
HPS: The joy of bursting and bearing fruit
HP: The love of being food for someone
HPS: The scattering of your seeds

HP: The decay of the seasons
HPS: The mystery of death and the miracle of birth.

HPS:

We came to this place to honor the land upon which we dwell, and to honor the life within us and the life within all things created. We came to change ourselves and our lives for our better good, and now we prepare to take what we have been given here back into our mundane lives.

We came in perfect love and perfect trust, to build bridges between each other, to honor our similarities and our differences, and our various paths as Pagan People. We came to honor the Earth, the good, green Earth.

HP:

I'd like to offer special thanks to our guest teachers for their wonderful contribution to our work, and to all of you, who came and worked and played and made this event possible; who drummed and danced and opened your hearts; who explored the deep, sometimes dark, places within; who dared to come and grow and transform in the presence of the Gods.

HPS:

Thanks to you--all the MMC members who pitched in and helped me so much this year, enabling the preparation for this event to proceed quite smoothly.

And thanks to all of you first-timers, who are now also members of the Fire Tribe, as similar alchemical fire circles occur in Nevada, California, Georgia, West Virginia, Massachusetts, New York, Oregon, Belize, Holland, Hawaii and perhaps other places by now.

HP:

Thanks also to those who have returned to share their magick with us all; accept our heartfelt thanks for your presence at this event. We hope to see you all again next year.

HPS:

Last and not at all least, let's thank Art, (camp caretaker) who willingly puts up with us each year and works hard to make this camp the wonderful place that it is. *(Yell "We love you, Art")*

Chant: *(3x)* **CIRCLE OF LIGHT**
> There's a circle of light around you
> There's a circle of love in your heart

There's a circle of family around you,
There's a circle of you inside me.

Oh, sisters, we love you
Oh, sisters, you help us to grow
Oh, sisters, we love you
My sisters, we want you to know, that....
There's a circle of light around you
There's a circle of love in your heart
There's a circle of family around you,
There's a circle of you inside me

Oh, brothers, we love you
Oh, brothers, you help us to grow
Oh, brothers, we love you
My brothers, we want you to know, that....

East:

Ancient ones of the East, Portal of Air,
We thank thee for your presence here!
For dancing winds and sylphs of air
Winged ones, and birds of flight,

For power of thought, and spoken word
Healing ways and golden light
With Her breath, out and in,
With new knowledge, we'll begin.
Stay if you will, but go if you must
We bid you hail and Farewell!

North:

Ancient ones of the North, Portal of Earth,
We thank thee for your presence here!
For Wee Folk, Elves and Gnomes
Earth below, and sky above,

Creatures large and creatures small,
Seeds that grow, and flowers that bloom

With Her Body beneath our feet,
We've gathered for this Merry Meet
Stay if you will, but go if you must
We bid you hail and Farewell!

West:

Ancient ones of the West, Portal of Water,
We thank thee for your presence here!
For Merfolk and water sprites,
The Mother's love and Secrets deep,

For lovers, sisters, brothers, friends,
And compassion that never ends.
By her blood, circling round
Love unconditional we've found.
Stay if you will, but go if you must
We bid you hail and Farewell!

South:

Ancient ones of the South, Portal of Fire,
We thank thee for your presence here!
For Salamanders, and spirits of fire
Sparks and flames that transform
For the love and passion of life's flame
And fulfillment of will and desire.

With her Spirit as the spark
From this place we now embark.
Stay if you will, but go if you must
We bid you hail and Farewell!

Dismiss Circle

May the circle be open but unbroken
May the Lord and the Lady be ever in your heart.
Merry meet and merry part
And merry meet again.

Workshops & Activities Offered during the Earth Camp Events: 2006

Fire Circle Orientation: Attendance was required on the first night of camp to explain the process and the rules concerning the Alchemical Fire Circles we intended for each night. I varied the presentation so it was different each year. This was vitally necessary, especially for new-comers, to understand the trance work, etc. that they would experience and witness.

The Alchemical Process, by Jeff & Spinner McBride

During the course of an all-night fire, as well as a fire circle succession each night, three distinct time periods, energetic signatures, along with their constituent components, are clearly discernable referenced as follows:

NIGREDO:

The Latin term for the first phase of the alchemical process is Nigredo, meaning "the blackening." In the laboratory, this is the phase where the "Prima Materia," or first matter, is placed into a container and burned to ash, then dissolved to produce a suspension. Within the fire circle, Nigredo is evidenced as a vast expanse of chaotic, often frenetic activity, from the arrival and acclimation of celebrants to the excitement of the fire-lighting ceremony, to highly energized drumming and dancing.

On a personal or transformational level, this is a time when we "burn away and dissolve" whatever stands between us and the Divine. The three stages of alchemy encompassed by the Nigredo phase are:

1. Calcination (root chakra, Saturn, survival): Issues within the physical container (self) are brought up and heated by the Fire, by chanting, drumming, dancing, and other creative expressions.
2. Dissolution (sacral chakra, Jupiter, blending): The issues are dissolved in the sea of personal and collective emotion. Through sweat and tears, salt is released from the physical body, as blocks begin to dissolve.
3. Separation (solar plexus chakra, Mars, choosing): In the alchemist's laboratory, this is the stage when the solution is broken up into its separate components. At the Fire Circle, people begin to sacrifice whatever Lead they've been carrying into the fire to be transformed.

A choice is made to separate or release from the "issue," (energetic discharge, more tears, or intense physical movement), and in so doing separate from the things which isolate our individual egos from others and Self.

ALBEDO:

The Albedo phase, which in orthodox alchemy relates to the whitening process, is a time when the matter in the flask is softening and beginning to purify. Translated to the vernacular of the fire circle, this phase corresponds to a palpable lightening of the energy; perhaps the drumming grows quieter, or the songs and chants move to a place of more richness and depth, or the dancing becomes increasingly lyrical. Coincidentally, this is often the time when the sky begins to grow light. The above and the below are united in the heart, resulting in a vibration of increased purity and strength. The three stages of the alchemical process that comprise the Albedo phase are:

1. **Conjunction** (heart chakra/Venus, joining together through love): The shift to Albedo, the white, soft stage of the Work. This step represents the coming together of Self and ego, soul and spirit, or the individual and the community. An important step; often it gives us a deeper understanding of our Higher Self in contrast to our ego. At the Fire Circle, deeper connections are forged between the person releasing and the other celebrants who witness, receive or catch the energy and assist gently through the process.

2. **Fermentation** (throat chakra/Mercury, speaking): In Alchemy, fermentation is the process of refining, skimming the crud that rises to the surface, to find a purer solution. We have had the experience of burning, dissolving, separating, and joining together. Now, we are speaking our truth and separating the subtle from the gross as we continue to refine.

3. **Distillation** (third eye chakra, Moon, introspective visioning): At this stage of the Work, we have a pure, refined "solution." We gain insight and understanding by "processing" our issues through the alchemical laboratory that is our body. By contemplating the past, while being engaged in the present, we can now make informed choices about how to move and interact at the Fire, and out in the world in the future.

RUBEDO:

The culminating phase of the alchemical process is called "Rubedo," meaning "the reddening," an expression which, within the confines of a conventional laboratory, indicates the material's conversion to a red tint, and presages it's transformation to gold. In the tradition of Fire Circle Alchemy, this can be equated with the sunrise itself. Of this mystery, few words can be said. The stage that corresponds with the rubedo is:

1. **Coagulation** (crown chakra, Sun, illuminating): This begins the phase of Rubedo, the period in which our spiritual gold is realized. This is the stage of consciously connecting with Spirit, releasing the light within matter, and releasing the boundaries between inner and outer experience. We bring our fresh insights and knowledge into the world, moment by moment, remaining in the flow. We connect with our highest selves, connect with Divinity, and with the Earth. Also at this stage, we experience an accelerated rate of synchronicities.

At this point in the alchemical work, we re-enter the fire of our daily lives, with our hearts connected, and our minds set free. As we continue the practice in the circle of life, new issues will inevitably arise within us, and the refining process will begin again.

Both the physical laboratory of the alchemist and the virtual laboratory of the fire circle are very much like the laboratory of the body. Each is in a perpetual state of evolution: processing blocks, pushing boundaries, and, as the Hermetica states, "separating the subtle from the gross, gently and with great ingenuity."

Talent Show:

Since the night rituals didn't begin until 11:00 PM lasting through the night until sunrise, we added a talent show. This was completely voluntary, and a REALLY good ice breaker! It also filled the hours from dinner and orientation until the Opening Ritual and became a tradition.

Bach Flower Remedies, Patrizia Johnson.

Massage therapy has been Pat's chosen profession since 1994. Her training in the healing arts includes: deep tissue, hot stone therapy, Thai Yoga Massage, cranial-sacral, and basic reflexology. She began training in Reiki in 1995, received her Usui Master in March 2002, Karuna Master in June 2002, Sekhem-Seichem Reiki Master in October 2004 and Lightarian Master in June 2005. In 2003, she received certification in the use of Bach Flower Remedies and recently added working with the Perelandra Flower Essences and Microbial Balancing Program as well.

Crystal Healing Basics, Linda Thomas: Learn to choose, cleanse and charge your stones and explore different stones and their uses.

Exploring Crystal Healing, Linda Thomas. Since receiving her certification in crystal healing in January of 1988, Linda has traveled throughout the country doing lectures, classes on crystal healing and helping people in their healing processes. Linda works closely with the Ascended Masters who guide her in her healing work. Through the process of laying stones on the body, an integration of the mental, emotional, spiritual and physical bodies is achieved.

Drumming in the Circle, Cindy Spagna. Cindy has been an active and influential participant in the Spiritual Community of Las Vegas. She has spent the last few years developing her skills as a drummer, working with the Rhythm Tree Revolutionaries, a local drumming circle in Las Vegas, is Musical Director of Desert Moon Circle and she works with Serpentine Splendour Lodge, Ordo Templi Orientis, for whom she has contributed her special understanding of ritual.

Drumming, Billy Woods. Billy has been a professional drummer since 1958, preforming and teaching across the United States. In 1987 he traveled to Egypt, studied with teachers in Cairo and played with a baladi band. He has also studied with Ibrahim Turnem and Souhail Kaspar. He has received several awards and national recognition for his contributions to the quality of drumming within the Society for Creative Anachronism, Inc.

Chi Lil and Drumming, Billy Woods. Chi Lil uses the energy of the earth through Qi Gung exercises for healing, balancing, energy, and well-being. This practice was developed in China over a period of centuries to increase the level of internal vitality through the use of breath, slow movement forms and visualization patterns related to the oriental system of energy meridians in the body.

Optional Craft Project, Medicine Bags 2006 & 2012

We encouraged people to decorate a medicine bag as these would be used for their "gifts". We made the bags from a suede-look fabric and put them and some materials for decorating them whenever and however they wanted to do so.

- Cotton ties, red, white, black and yellow
- A sign explaining colors/directions/attributes for Native Americans
- Paint, etc. for decorating medicine bags
- Loose tobacco

Workshops 2012

Required (at least for newcomers) Orientation

First, Welcome HOME! What happens at this event is different from other gatherings, festivals or events you may have attended elsewhere. Therefore, some explanation is necessary.

Since the dawn of time, human beings have gathered around the fire to make music, to dance, and to weave magic in the firelight. Fire Circle Alchemy is a ritual of transformation derived from a mystical tradition. This process has been evolving for the past sixteen years. We use the "fire of nature" to accelerate growth and change on interior levels. It is a very powerful tool.

The fundamental components of Fire Circle Alchemy correspond to the four elements: voice, which corresponds to Air as breath is essential to the production of human sound; music corresponds with Fire as it supplies the circle with its energy; movement corresponds with Water as it is an external reflection of the constant motion of the fluids within us; and service, or Earth, the foundation upon which all of the other work rests.

Each night begins with a ritual that sets the tone for the night's work. Please do NOT miss the rituals, which have been planned with intention, love, gifts and magickal workings for YOU by the hard-working members of MMC. This collaborative effort to ensures the mindful creation of the ritual/ alchemical container in which the ensuing magical Work will soon transpire.

With the opening Fire ceremony, the alchemical work begins. Please read the hand-out I'll give you for further understanding of this process. To assist you in the work, you will be taken to special places to receive special gifts. We encourage you to make a sacrifice—to try to stay up all night. Sleep deprivation aides this process. Also, if you go to bed too soon, you will miss out on the magickal workings into which MMC has put a lot of loving work. We also realize some of you have physical needs that preclude a night-long vigil. We encourage you to stay until you have received your gifts, nap, then return to the dawn ceremony.

During the night, people may make offerings to the fire; chants, poetry, personal declarations, songs, dance...please wait for an appropriate time to do this, but do not be shy—we co-create this event, and your contributions are always welcome.

As the solar disk begins to rise, there is a raising of the energetic vibration of the group, followed by an interlude of stillness, an intimate pause for reflection, internal and external, juxtaposed with reverence. It is in this space of conscious group connection that the ascendance of the sun is celebrated, a cosmological mirroring of the Gold that has been created during the ritual process, and a symbolic ending of the ceremony.

The Alchemical Fire Circle has a particular structure. The fire in the center of the vessel we create is representative of the Sun, the source of energy, heat, light, and transformation. The metal that corresponds with Sol is Gold -- Attainment. Wisdom. Self-realization. The Sun corresponds with our seventh chakra, the crown, and the foremost connection to Source.

In our Fire Circle tradition, the Moon is associated with the Priest/ess current-nurturing, serving, assisting, and maintaining gravitational balance in any of the planetary orbits. The metal of the Moon is silver, and it corresponds with the sixth chakra, inner vision, intuition, and dreaming.

The closest dance path circling the fire is the Mercury track. It is the fleet footed inner ring of movement. Dancers in this orbit are generally quite energized and active, like Quicksilver, the planet Mercury's metallic match. Mercury is the mediator and messenger, clear communication, the fifth chakra, and the throat.

The Venus track is an intermediate path. This is an orbit of relationship in motion, with self and others. It is not uncommon for people engaging in this ring of planetary dance to be in a light trance, attuned to the sensuality of movement, song, and rhythm. The metal of Venus is Copper. In our paradigm, Venus relates to the fourth chakra and the energies of the heart.

The Earth track, demarcated by corn-meal or flour, is a slow and deliberate moving orbit, for those in a deep trance, doing rattle work, or personal grounding.

Defined by the interior ring of torches, the Mars track is a place to witness and consciously contribute to the creation of the transformational container. People regularly stand in this area with small rattles, providing sonic guardianship and energetic support for others who are active within the inner orbits. The metal of Mars is iron, and the energetic correspondence is one of warrior energy, martial and protective. Disciplined will and third chakra are connected to Mars.

Between the two torch rings is the Jupiter track, an area for interactions with others that are not suited to take place within the ever-moving circles of dance. Not for idle chatter, people partake of food and water; connect with each other through breathing together, hugging or rubbing shoulders. This is not a "social" zone, but a place for conscious encounters or movement of a stationary nature. The metal of Jupiter is Tin, which is a malleable metal, related to blending and balancing of energies as well as to the second chakra.

The ring of Saturn is delineated by the internal perimeter of the circle. The metal of Saturn is Lead, representing "heavy," intense energy; power that needs to be purified, first chakra, survival instinct, and fight-or-flight response all connect here.

On the exterior side of the fire circle perimeter is the "comet's trail," a path for walking meditation which allows those individuals seeking solitude to stay engaged and involved in the energy of the fire circle if it is their will.

It is allowable to create 'nests' (sleeping bags, chairs) outside of the circle where you can rest, yet still be in contact with the work.

Often this process invokes a trance state, whether light or deep. Those of us experienced in the sacred fire circles will be watching you and assisting if necessary, perhaps with rattles intended to deepen the trance, perhaps guiding you out of the path of other traffic or keeping you a safe distance from the fire.

Under NO circumstances should your personal work be interfered with. It is human to ask "what's wrong" or try to comfort someone who is experiencing deep emotion. We come here to 'burn out lead'—and to let out emotions that have been bottled up inside us. If you want or need help, make eye contact. Otherwise, you will be left alone to do your work. Be prepared—people may cry, scream, or enter a state of ecstasy. It's all GOOD!

Earth Energy Yoga, Eryn Braida. Eryn has been interested in nature and all things magical since she was a child. She became interested in divination at the age of twelve and found Wicca at thirteen. She has been doing yoga for eight years and became certified through YogaFit to teach in the summer of 2010.

The Magick of Crystals, Linda Thomas. Linda will demonstrate how to use crystals for healing, chakra balancing, and energy dowsing. You will learn how to choose, cleanse, recharge and activate your stones and crystals and will practice energy dowsing, chakra balancing and basic layouts using only clear quartz points. We will also explore how the emotions contribute to what we experience physically.

Crystal Healing for Animals, Linda Thomas. Linda will talk about the most beneficial stones to use on our pets, then demonstrate how to use them. As many of us are becoming aware of the challenges our animals and pets face, we are looking for healing modalities that will work for them. Knowing that our pets mirror the challenges of their owners, we will discuss different stones and crystals that will help both, Where to place them and how to use them to aid you in making your life, as well as your pet's life, more wonderful.

Nature Magic in the 21ˢᵗ Century, *Richard Fox AKA Renard:* We will explore the difference between science and magick and delve into the mechanics of the universe and four primary influences that determine what a human will experience at any point in time. Each of us has access to the great Gaia Network that connects every living entity that exists on this planet. This presentation will speak to our power and not our weaknesses, looking at ways to reconnect with old paths and forge new paths as metaphysical people. This presentation is based on an article originally appearing in Aontacht magazine.

Lesser Banishing Ritual of the Pentagram, Gwen Gardner. Gwen is the High Priestess of the Garden of the Crescent Moon Coven in Kalispell, Montana. She discovered Witchcraft 1988 and studied with the Sylvan Grove in Seattle in 1993-94. When she moved to Montana took lessons here in and became a 3ʳᵈ Degree High Priestess in the Fellowship of the Elder Path Tradition in 2006. She teaches Wicca 1ˢᵗ, 2ⁿᵈ and 3ʳᵈ degree classes in the Correllian Tradition, which is the path her coven follows.

Qui Gung – Richard (Renard) Fox is the Editor of Aontacht, the global magazine of the Druidic Dawn. Earlier in life, he lived and worked outside in the great American forests for most of 18 years developing his earth magick skills. Today he is a fire druid, who brings his fire dancing and the living flame to audiences around the world.

Herb Walk – Practice identifying herbs in the surrounding area.

Lakota Purification Sweat Lodge Ceremony: Jim Del Duca became a Traditional Sundancer in 1992. He is a member of the Elk Society of the Apsaalooke Sundance, a Pipe Carrier and is privileged to serve as Pipe Keeper of the Medicinehorse-Two Dogs Lakota Sundance. Jim was given the right to build Sweat-lodges and conduct the ceremony by his adopted father Bacheewassee in 1996.

Flower Power; Healing with Flowers, Vicka Lanier. Vicka is a Montana native who loves Mother Earth and enjoys working with people and animals to help them heal. She has been practicing Reiki since 2000 and teaching it since 2002 when she earned herMastership. She also does Karuna Reiki, Theta energy healing, and Flower Essence therapy. Vicka uses all these modalities to help animals heal as well.

Metal Magick, Lord Quiet Bear. AKA Todd Kintz, Priest of Mountain Moon Circle. In this class, we will cover some of the magickal and mundance properties of various metals as well as the use of them in spells combined with gem stones.

Drumming in the Circle, Lady Nytewind, Priestess of Mountain Moon Circle. Drums are the main support for the Alchemical Fire Circles, and all are encouraged to help keep the energy going! In this workshop, you will learn how to participate in the percussion group even if you are a beginner, how to follow the lead drummers, to watch the dancers and trancers closely to see how they are responding to the rhythm and know when to slow, speed up, or maintain the beat.

Optional Craft Project, 2012- The Clay Mini-You

The craft table is always available throughout the event. (Use Sculpy or other brand oven-bake clay and a toaster oven.)

Directions:
- Out of a ball of clay, make an effigy of yourself! Shape it freehand or use the cookie cutter provided, (a gingerbread man metal cutter)
- Be sure to personalize it, whichever you do.
- Make a hole large enough for a ribbon and cut one long enough to wear around your neck.
- Bake your mini-you 15 minutes for each ¼ inch thickness at 275 degrees, but no more than 20 minutes.
- Bring or wear this effigy to the ritual Saturday night to honor yourself and the alchemical process you have experienced during this event.

Installations, Earth 2006

Labyrinth

I was able to rent a 24' plastic labyrinth to spread on the ground. At the center, I placed a white pillar and put a beautiful globe on top. I strung a rope around in the trees and hung painted banners of the other planets, children of Earth, vines and Christmas lights. Music played continuously *(Echoes of Eternity,* by Astarius) and green light sticks were available to help light the way after dark.

Jaguar Woman; (Guide leads participants to the installation one at a time)

This was the first installation that people were taken to, as they would need the Medicine bag to store their gifts.

Intention: Give thanks for the animals

Magickal working: Determine animal totem for this time

Receive animal totem and Medicine bag

Jaguar Woman was robed in jaguar print. She helps interpret the token. Jungle sounds were being played, many stuffed jungle animals were added in this 10 x 10 tent.

Jaguar Woman:

Welcome human! What seek you in my jungle? *(Wait for an answer.)*

This is the wild place, where all animals exist in their true state—as they were in the beginning. It is time for you to take your place amongst your brothers and sisters and to recognize your true nature.

Allow yourself a few moments to reflect on your own truth. Look around at the animal images here and be at one.

Feel the energy emanating from your center. Remember who you truly are and give thanks to the light of that truth.

Now, please reach into this bag and bring forth the symbol of your totem animal. *(Participant chooses)*

This totem animal is your mirror—the reflection of your higher self. You can learn from this animal. It will help you understand and guide you in your life.

Accept this gift of the Medicine Bag from Jaguar Woman. Place this sacred object within it and carry it with you for the next three suns while you walk in this sacred place.

Be humble and give thanks to the spirit guides that give you connection to this earth. Go forth on your journey in peace and love.

(Participants were then escorted either to another installation or back to the fire circle.)

Cave of the Gnome:

A 10 X 10 tent was completely draped in black to resemble a cave. Out of chicken wire, etc, I created stalactites and stalagmites, and out of crumpled tinfoil, painted with florescent paint; giant precious gems. These were lit with black lights. I found a little child's wheelbarrow to pile some of the gems in, had a small hammer, glow sticks for more light, a water well, made out of Styrofoam stones, blue fabric for water, giant mushrooms out of Styrofoam, a foot stool, and more.

The guide would bring in a few people to be greeted by someone in a gnome costume. The gnome has pieces of iron pyrite in it to give to the visitors.

He/She *tells this story:*

Oh! I see you have found your way here, to the womb of the mother! She welcomes all seekers who have true hearts. Here, deep inside the earth, is where treasures lie. We gather them and care for them, and sometimes place them where they can be found and used by humankind. Come, sit—I have a story to tell you.

There once was a young lad that lived in a quiet little village. His parents were simple people who earned just enough to meet their needs. But the lad was not content. Each day, he watched the road that passed by his house. He saw fine carriages in which rode important people. He saw splendid soldiers mounted on beautiful horses and beautifully dressed women.

"Someday," he said to himself, "I shall be one of those important, finely dressed people and I shall own great carriages and beautiful horses!" And so, one day, he bid his parents goodbye and set out to seek his fortune.

Soon he apprenticed himself to an important sword smith. He was quick to learn and skilled with his hands, so in time, his excellence at his craft exceeded even that of his master. So skilled was he that his swords became well-known throughout the land, and soon drew the attention of the King.

The King offered him a fine position as master sword maker for the royal army. He was housed in the palace, wore the finest clothes, rode in the best carriages and owned several beautiful horses. He had achieved all he had set out to accomplish—fame, fortune and high position. But somehow, the young sword maker felt there was something missing. He was not content.

Word came that a great Wizard was coming to visit the palace.

"I shall seek the Wizard's advice", he thought. And so he did.

The Wizard looked into his magic crystal and said "Your father is dying, lad. You must go to him at once".

The lad set out early the next morning for his parent's home. "Father," the lad said, "I have much gold. I can get you the best doctor in the land".

"No," his father said, "I have had a good life and I am old and ready to go on. I have had much love in my life, my wife, my children and my friends. Love is the important thing in this world, not gold or material possessions."

At his father's words, the lad looked into his own heart and saw that what he lacked was love—love of self, and love of others.

Earth Mother and Sky Father gift us with unconditional love. Feel it in your minds and in your hearts. Know that pure gold lies within you, just waiting for you to discover it. It is your true self—your divine soul—that which came to Earth pure and whole. But what you have experienced here—pain, disappointment, lack of love, illness, and abuse, makes you forget who you truly are.

Take this gold stone with you. (*Give each a piece of iron pyrite*). It will remind you that many things that seem valuable to the world may lead you from your true path. The <u>true</u> gold, your highest good and the knowledge of spirit, lies within you always.

(Participants were then escorted either to another
installation or back to the fire circle.)

The Crone Installation *(Ancient wisdom and divination)*

This gazebo was decorated to simulate a comfortable cottage, where an old woman practiced her magick and divination using Celtic Tree Runes. The walls were tan, and there was a cauldron that emitted fog, a round braided rug, and shelves full of magickal items: mortar and pestle, crystal ball, old books and a statue of a cat. Bouquets of dried herbs and flowers hung from the ceiling. There was a large spider web and spider in the corner of the ceiling. Also, I used my paper fireplace again.

The visitor (one at a time) drew a rune for a "reading" from the Crone.

Gaia *(Earth is our nurturing Mother, give thanks for earth's bounty)*

A waterfall fountain sits on a table covered with a blue cloth. The wall opposite the one pictured displayed fruits and vegetables, grain, and other examples of Gia's bounty. A pine tree sits in the other corner. White icicle lights and solar lights were placed for illumination, and a vase of live flowers sat outside the entrance. The statue is by Oberon Zell-Ravenheart, "Gaia'"

(Before entering, each is asked to choose a fresh flower from a vase outside)

Priestess:

Welcome to the Temple of Gaia, Supreme Earth Goddess and Mother of all. I see you have brought an offering. The flower that you hold represents your gratitude for all that the Earth Mother gives you. When you are ready, place it, along with your prayers, in the vase on her altar.

Gaia has given us a beautiful planet on which to live. She has given us many plants which provide food, shelter, and medicines for our well-being. She has given us a myriad variety of animals which have served humans in many ways. She asks only that we respect her and her creations and, when we use them, to do so with honor.

(This involves a magic trick I purchased, changing a seed into a flower)

Our fertile Mother plants a seed in the ground *(show small seed)*. Deep within the womb of the Mother, the seed begins to grow larger and larger. *(show larger seed)*. With the aid of sunlight and water, the seed breaks through the earth. A plant develops, which in turn brings forth its beauty. *(show flowers.)*

Within you, there is also a seed. This seed is the seed of your divine self, the self that is spirit—all that is good in you, and all that you dream to be. Gaia reminds us that this seed also can grow and develop its beauty if given proper attention.

On the bulletin board outside the dining hall, you will find "keys" to the Labyrinth and the Portal of Earth. To enter either of these, you need to take and wear a key. The spiral charms are the keys to the labyrinth and the leaves to the Portal of Earth. Please remember to return them to their place so that others may take their turns.

A labyrinth is a tool for meditation and differs from a maze in that there are no deceptions on the path; no tricks and no dead ends.

This year, the labyrinth was enclosed with leaf-patterned green fabric. At the entrance, a pillar held a bowl of small pieces of lead. The sign read:

> *Enter now this sacred space*
> *That the Goddess doth embrace.*
> *A piece of lead you'll carry in*
> *And bid the alchemy to begin.*
> *It represents what you leave behind*
> *That's not a part of your life's design.*

Another pillar sat in the center. The bowl there contained pieced of Iron Pyrite, or "Fools Gold." A sign there read:

> *Rid yourself of fear and pain*
> *Your spirit then will quickly gain*

Peace and love and harmony.
On your true path, you then will be.
Leave the lead and take the gold
Begin the new; forsake the old.

Crone Installation was repeated, except that we used a cabin which was occupied by two old Crones that argued with each other constantly. They did some scrying or tarot readings for each visitor.

We also repeated the **Jaguar Woman**, with the same kind of setting.

Gnome Woman was essentially the same, except we eliminated the stalactites and stalagmites. Instead, I got some plastic bowls from the dollar store, heated them so I could shape them, painted them inside then inserted glow sticks and attached them to the black walls to make glowing gems. This worked great. The Gnome had big false ears and green makeup and hair.

Portal of Earth: (needed a key to enter, unmanned).
I used a blue 10 X10 gazeebo. Wall hangings included dolphins on one wall, trees on another and artificial grass on the ground. Several beautiful stations were set up on TV tables, etc. to represent needs of our planet.

For Earth, a globe sat on a 4' Grecian pillar and the sign read:
Place your hands upon this globe,
Which represents our beautiful blue and green planet.
Send your prayers, wishes, and energy
To our home, Planet Earth.

A small table to represent Love was draped in pink chiffon with vases of flowers, a mirror, and a large, stuffed red heart. Sign:
No one can truly love unless they first love themselves.
The Gods love us unconditionally,
for they look upon us as young children who will make mistakes.
But through those mistakes, we will grow.

Press this heart to your own as you
Gaze at your reflection in the mirror.
Send all the love you can to yourself;
without condition, judgement or prejudice.

One table had a little stool to sit on. It held a book and pen, an electric incense burner and incense, and a statue of Gia. The instructions were:

You have come before Gaia, Great Earth Mother of many names
To whom many have given their solemn devotion.
What would you ask of her concerning our planet?
If it be your will, please write in the book provided,
Your requests; for the earth, its' people, plants, animals or other.
Then turn on the burner, place a pinch of incense upon a piece of foil,
and send your prayer to Gaia.

Another table was draped in blue and included a statue of Neptune and a jug of blessed water with a water ladle.

Water is the life blood of this planet,
but much has been polluted and destroyed
The water in this vessel has been sanctified and purified.
If it be your will, carry this vessel to the creek nearby;
remove a dipper full of water
into which you will place your own blessings,
as you pour it into the stream.

Another table held lots of crystals and five bowls of sand, a tiny spoon, and little plastic bags, also a deck of Crystal Skull message cards.

The instructions read:
The Earth has blessed us with beautiful stones, including crystals, which hold memory and emit vibrations that improve our health and wellbeing. Be present in their vibrations. Take a card from the deck of mysterious crystal skulls to see what advice they give you.
Next, help yourself to a tiny crystal for your medicine bag.

Sand is the product of wind, heat, pressure, and water upon the rock body of the earth. Find here five different kinds of sand. Take what you will.

Red sand *from the Valley of Fire holds*
the memory of ancient people who drew
sacred symbols upon the canyon walls in the desert.
Gain from it the energy of fire, will and the courage of the warrior.

Golden sand *from Egypt holds the memory*
of a mighty and most accomplished ancient civilization,
whose golden age was one of freedom and prosperity.
Gain from it a connection with the Sun Gods,
knowledge with wisdom, and healing energy.

Black sand *from the shore of the Pacific Ocean*
holds the energy of the Goddess,
the mysteries and the cycle of life.
Gain from it compassion,
and heal your inner being.

Magnetic sand *is the sand of attraction.*
It will bring to you what you ask,
yet always be mindful of the phrase
"be careful what you wish for."
This sand carries the ancient wisdom
of the Earth's deepest core. Feel that connection.

The fifth sand *comes from the shores of the*
Atlantic Ocean – the direction of the sunrise.
It carries with it old memories and new beginnings;
communication and connection with the old Gods.
Let it bring you closer to them and to the guidance they offer.

"Water - Her Blood" 2007

Schedule

Thurs. Aug 2 - Check in after 3 pm - Portal will be open until Sunday morning.
6:30– 7:30 dinner
7:30 – 8:30 Fire circle orientation
8:30 – 9:30 Fire Circle Participation for "Non-Musicians"
10:30 – opening ritual & fire circle 'till dawn

Fri. Aug 3
Dawn – 8 breakfast
11:00 - 12:00 Quantum Physics and the Hidden Power of Water
12:00 – 1:00 lunch
1:15 – 2:30 Meet OZ
2:45 – 4:15 Tarot Star
4:30 – 6:00 Drumming – Making a Joyful Noise
6:30 – 7:30 dinner
11:00 – Water ritual (dancers) & fire circle 'till dawn

Sat. Aug 4
Dawn – 8 breakfast
12:00 – 1:00 lunch
1:15 – 2:30 Tarot star
2:45 – 4:15 Real Wizardry at camp & Women's mirror therapy at studio Sat.
2:30-3:30
4:30 – 6:00 Men's meditation

Charlyn Scheffelman (Lady Nytewind)

6:30 – 7:30 dinner
11:00 – 3:00 Avalon ritual & fire circle

Sun. Aug 5
9:30 – 10:30 brunch
10:30 – 11:00 closing
Vacate camp by 1 pm

Mountain Moon Circle's Summerfest: rituals from "Water– 2007"

Needs: *Egypt incense, oil lamp, a bowl of water, earth, quarter candle jars, tables and covers, music stand, CD & player, white canopic jars, flute, tin, rain stick, drum*

Cast circle: silently, then seal with elements silently while sounds are made. *(East - flute/voice, South – rattle, West – rain stick, North – thunder)*

East: *(Call cross quarters)*
Qebhsennuf (Kebsnoof),
We respectfully ask your presence at the Eastern gate.
We ask that you bear witness to our rites,
And guard this sacred space from the East.
Your light comes to us, may our light come to you.
(light candle) So mote it be!

South: Duamutef
We respectfully ask your presence at the Southern gate.
We ask that you bear witness to our rites,
And guard this sacred space from the South.
Your light comes to us, may our light come to you
(light candle) So mote it be!

West: Insety
We respectfully ask your presence at the Western gate.
We ask that you bear witness to our rites,
And guard this sacred space from the West.

Your light comes to us, may our light come to you
(light candle)   So mote it be!

North: Hapi (haahpi)
We respectfully ask your presence at the Northern gate.
We ask that you bear witness to our rites,
And guard this sacred space from the North.
Your light comes to us, may our light come to you
(light candle)   So mote it be!

HP Light Fire: *(Ancient Egyptian Text)*
The shining eye of Horus comes. *(light fire)*
It comes in peace,
it sends forth rays of light unto Ra, the Sun, on the horizon,
And it destroys the powers of Set, the powers of darkness,
According to the decree.

It leads them on and it takes possession of Set,
And its flame is kindled against him.
Its flame comes and goes about and brings adoration;
It comes and goes about heaven in the train of Ra
upon the two hands of thy two sisters, O Ra.
The Eye of Horus liveth, yea liveth.

HPS Light incense:
The fire is laid, the fire shines;
The incense is laid on the fire, the incense shines.
Your perfume comes to us, O Incense;
May our perfume come to you, O Incense;
Your perfume comes to us, O Gods;
May our perfume come to you, O Gods
May we be with you, O Gods,
May you be with us, O Gods,
May we live with you, O Gods
May you live with us, O Gods.
We love you, O Gods.
May you love us, O Gods.

Charlyn Scheffelman (Lady Nytewind)

HP:

Oh Great God, Soul of Osiris
Lord of Eternity, hear our call!
Your forms are manifold
Your attributes are majestic
Universal Father,

Guide of the underworld
Whom the Gods glorify,
Lord of the celestial world,
All hearts are at peace as they behold thee.
Enter now this consecrated shrine.
Make Thy presence known to all who are present
Aide these, Thy people, in reaching the source of all things.

HPS:

O Great Goddess, Soul of Isis
Heart of the Sun, hear our call!
Great Mother, Great Goddess
Giver of Life and Queen of the dead,
Priestess and magician,
Enter now this consecrated shrine.
Make Thy presence known to all who are present
Aid these, Thy people, in reaching the source of all things.

I am Nature,
The Universal Mother,
Mistress of all the elements,
Primordial child of time,
Sovereign of all things spiritual,
Queen of the dead,
Queen also of the Immortals,
The single manifestation of all Gods and Goddesses.

Though I am worshiped in many aspects,
Known by countless names
And propitiated with all manner of different rites
Yet the whole round earth venerates me.

Both races of Aethiopians,
Whose lands the morning sun first shines upon,
And the Egyptians who excel in ancient learning
And worship me with ceremonies proper of my godhead,
Call me by my true name, namely, Queen Isis.
(Play Music of Ancient Egypt Sacred Movements for Belly Dance troupe.)

HPS:

Nephthys! Anubis! Through you, we shall seek out our shadows and transform them! Come, way-showers, we summon, stir and call thee!
(Enter Nephthys and Anubis in silence, circle the fire in a dance of infinity, drums and others start in)

At Dawn: (Best to have everyone memorize this before the event.) *Solar Salutation,*
HP: Queen Isis, Great Mother, Mysteries revealed,
We bid you farewell.
May we be guided by your love,
Transformed by it
As the phoenix flies forth toward the rising sun.
May we never be beyond your song,
Which is the song of Nature.
So mote it be!

HPS: Nephthys, Veiled Goddess of Hidden Mysteries,
We bid you farewell.
Guide our steps on the true Path.
May we never falter in Thy presence
Nor do harm or disfavor to Thee.
Answer our soul's desire for Maat.
May Thoth aid us in perfect judgment
May we always go in graciousness with the Gods.
So mote it be!

HP: Anubis, Guardian, Opener of the Way,
We bid you farewell!
Watch over us as a good shepherd watches over his flocks.
May we never falter in Thy presence
Nor do harm or disfavor to Thee.

Answer our soul's desire for Maat.
May Thoth aid us in perfect judgment
May we always go in graciousness with the Gods.
So mote it be!

East:

Wise Qebhsennuf *(Kebsnoof)*,
We thank you for bearing witness to our rites,
And for Guarding the Eastern Gate.
We bid you Hail and farewell!

South:

Mighty Duamutef
We thank you for bearing witness to our rites, and for
Guarding the Southern Gate.
We bid you Hail and farewell!

West:

Compassionate Insety
We thank you for bearing witness to our rites, and for
Guarding the Western Gate.
We bid Hail and farewell!

North:

Great Hapi *(haahpi)*
We thank you for bearing witness to our rites, and for
Guarding the Northern Gate.
We bid you Hail and farewell!

Dismiss Circle:

Second Night Ritual - Mari

Needs: Conch horn, central cauldron, pitcher, 4 quarter cauldrons, paper cups, tall altar, blue cloth, Dolphin Dream incense, water/salt/bowl, cauldron stuff.

HPS: Water of Life, be cleansed, be pure, be Blessed by the Mother
HP: Salt of the Earth, be cleansed, be pure, be Blessed by the Father

Jointly:
> Life force combined, water and earth
> Repel the dark, to the light, give birth
> This fluid most holy does now ignite
> Calling but good to our sacred rite.

Cast & seal circle: (I don' think I wrote these quarter calls, so are edited.. .)

East: *(cauldron, cloth, glass bowl, dry ice)*
> Portal of the Eastern dawn, morning bright and clear,
> Bring to us your precious light, your happiness, and cheer...

South: *(cauldron, sand, charcoal, flash paper bomb)*
> Portal of the Midday Sun, shining bright and clear,
> Bring to us your warmth and love, your spirit present here...

West: *(cauldron, glass bowl, everclear)*
> Portal of the Setting sun, eventide; light dimming
> Bring to us compassion, hope within us brimming...

North: *(cauldron, salt, wax shavings, lighter fluid, herbs, leaves)*
> Portal of midnight, sun now dark and cold,
> Bring to us your wisdom, mysteries of old...

HPS:
> Rising river running wild, grotto's pool of deepest green
> Ocean crashing on the shore Its hidden depths unseen
> Power of water, her blood in me!

ALL: *(Respond after each stanza with:)*
Power of water, her blood in me!

HP: Azure lake with flashing fish, the trail of a single tear
Raindrops splashing to the earth, and the perfect scrying mirror
Power of water, her blood in me!

HPS: Within the deep and foaming sea, ancient powers dwell,
King Niksa, Mari, Neptune, Aphrodite on her shell.
Power of water, her blood in me!

HP: Ancient ones of blue and green, of rain and sleet and snow
Grant to us the power of love and the mysteries for to know.
Power of water, her blood in me!

HPS: The blessings of Water, we beseech the Goddess give.
Guide us to her mysteries, and let our magick live.
Power of water, her blood in me!

HP: Mari, Goddess of the Sea, we call to you!
She who is older than time itself,
She who holds men's destinies in her hands,
Mistress of the Mermaids, we call to you!
Come join our sacred circle as we honor the
Sacred waters of the Earth, and of life.
(blow conch shell 3x)

Mari: *From The Egyptian Book of the Dead*

I am Mari, Queen of the Sea and Mistress of the Mermaids. I come to you tonight as the great mystery within your hearts and your dreams. I am your imagination, your intuition, and your inner wisdom—that small voice within you that cries out to be heard.

As if I'd slept a thousand years underwater I wake into a new season. I am the blue lotus rising. I am the cup of dreams and memory opening—I, the thousand-petaled flower. At dawn the sun rises naked and new as a babe, I open myself and am entered by light. This is the joy, the slow awakening into fire as one by one the petals open, as the fingers that held tight the secret unfurl. I let go of the past and release the fragrance of flowers.

I open and light descends, fills me and passes through, each thin blue petal reflected perfectly in clear water. I am that lotus filled with light reflected in the world. I float content within myself, one flower with a thousand petals, one life lived a thousand years without haste, one universe sparking a thousand stars, one God alive in a thousand people.

If you stood on a summer's morning on the bank under a brilliant sky, you would see the thousand petals and say that together they make the lotus. But if you lived in its heart, invisible from without, you might see how the ecstasy at its fragrant core gives rise to its thousand petals. What is beautiful is always that which is itself; in essence, a certainty of being. I marvel at myself and the things of earth.

I float among the days in peace, content. Not part of the world, the world is all the parts of me. I open toward light and lift myself to the Gods on the perfume of prayer. I ask for nothing beyond myself. I own everything I need. I am content in the company of the Gods, a prayer that contains its own answer. I am the Lotus. As if from a dream, I wake up laughing.

Through the sea-water within you, you are all connected to the primordial sea, the collective unconscious, and to me.

I offer you compassion; for I know the pain you've suffered in this world of mortal flesh. I beseech you—do not hide your pain, for to do so would prevent the healing necessary for your growth.

Honor your tears, for they will mend your broken soul. Honor the love I give you and give it to others without condition. Honor the tie that binds you to me through the sharing of this water.

Cauldron for water sharing ceremony *(to be dipped into individual cups, after which Mari leaves the circle)*

MMC Belly dancers – perform Nida

Fire circle begins w/chant "Back to the River." Dance, sing, drum, trance, and express your joys and frustrations until sunrise!

At Dawn: *Solar Salutation,* by Katlyn Breene

HP:

Mari, Great Goddess of the Sea, we've felt your joy and your compassion this night, and honor you with love. We have experienced a connection with

Sea, Earth, Fire, and sky above. We thank you for your ancient gifts and mysteries profound, and for the sea within us, the blood of Goddess found.

East:

> Portal of the Eastern Light begin the day anew
> Messages received this night the dark have brought us through…

North:

> Wisdom gained through ancient rite and rhythm of the drum.
> We leave thee now in gratitude

West:

> Portal of the Eventide, Presence of the One,
> Our soul's we've reexamined, our work this night is done.

South:

> Portal of the Midday sun, bring your strengthening rays
> That all we've done throughout the night sustain us through the days.

Dismiss Circle:

> May the circle be open but unbroken
> May the Lord and the Lady be ever in your heart.
> Merry meet and merry part
> And merry meet again.

Underworld Ritual & Installation – 2007

During the second night's fire, small groups were taken to the Underworld Installation (See description under "Installations") and were challenged along the path by death.

Needs: 3 skull masks for Death, salt crystals, sulfur, incense burner and charcoal, gong, anointing oil, salt candle holders, water bowl, Anubis statue, mummy, black drapes, Khnum statue, Isis statue, Thoth statue, brass bowl, etc.

(Ptah leads the group and encounters the Sobek, the dark shadow side. L = mask on left hand, R = mask on right hand, D = Death's face mask)

D: Do you lie?

L: Liar!

R: Cheater! Sweet-talker! Illusionist, charlatan, deceiver!

D: When you say "there's nothing up my sleeve…"

L: You lie!

D: When you speak of love…

R: Do you flatter? Do you lie?

L: What is your cheapest lie?

D: What do you love to lie about?

R: Perversions? Forgerer! Fibber!

L: Humbug suppressor of truth, sham-bum bull-shitter!

R: Lip service! Hypocrite, white-washing purists!

L: Evasive, truthless fraud!

D: Do you mislead? Misquote? Misconstrue? Gloss over the facts? Know truthfully who you are?

(Death steps aside after pretending to judge them worthy, he lets the group pass and enter Purification temple)

PS1:   Who seeks admittance here?

Ptah:

I, Ptah-kepher-hotep, Son and High Priest of Osiris, ask for entry into the Temple of the Soul on behalf of ones who come to be renewed. Their hearts lie in the Temple of Anubis so that they might heal.

These dead ones have no names, for names have been left behind with all that once was of Earth as they have journeyed now far into the underworld.

PS2: *(to group)*

Are you without fear? Are you clean in your thoughts and deeds? Are you prepared to take the next step on this journey in perfect love and perfect trust? *(All answer Yes)*

Then enter, for your heart has been weighed and you have been found to be honest and worthy of entry. *(Strike brass bowl)*

P: (Oberon – Yeah, Oberon Zell was one of my guests that year)

Behold the waters of Nu, who was the beginning before all—the cosmic ocean—the primal sea from which all came forth. Hold forth thy hands that Nu may Cleanse and renew your emotional body that it may be prepared. *(Anoint/asperge with water)*

PS:

Behold Thoth, he who had no parents but was created out of the void. Through his spoken word, all matter came into being. The Breath is sacred. Inhale the fumes of sulfur, for it shall purify, heal, and renew thy mental and spiritual bodies. *(Inhalation of sulfur smoke)*

P1:

Behold Isis, Great Mother of all, mistress of elements, and daughter of time. She reigns over the realms of spirit and earth. She is Sovereign of Death and Queen of the Immortals. By a gesture, she commands the shining vault of the sky, the gentle breezes of the sea, even the dark silence of the underworld. She is the Lady of life.

Cease your tears now; look within for she abides in you and will come to your aid. She sees the sorrows of your life with compassion. All things will soon change for you, as under her watchful light your life is renewed. *(Anoint with oil)*

PS:

Behold Khnum, the great potter, the creator of the body of flesh. Once formed, the body becomes the receptacle of the Ka or spirit. Through Khnums powerful magick the Ka finds its home in this world.

Great Khnum, cleanse and renew these bodies that they may be prepared to be reborn and renewed. *(Sprinkle with salt)*

Both: *(chant) – use vowel sounds (Gesture for all to leave and return to fire circle.)*

Third Night Ritual - Avalon

Needs: a tree with apples that rolls in (built on a wagon), tall altar, green cloth, 2 Silver branches, Druid Circle incense, 3 silver coins, water bowl, CD & player, chemicals/incense for fire, Bubbles?

Casting & sealing; *(Cross quarters)*

East: (Author Unknown, cannot print the whole thing.)
Air breathe, air blow
Make the Wheel of Magick go!

South:

Fire hiss, fire burn
Make the Wheel of Magick turn!

West:

Water feel, water churn
Make the Wheel of Magick turn!

North:

Earth spirit, spirit Earth,
In the Mother find rebirth

HPS: *(shake silver branch)*

Oh Manannan Mac Lir, Powerful Son of the Sea, Mist-shrouded rider of the maned waves, I ask that you hear my call. Lord of the Otherworld, Bearer of the Silvered Apple Branch, join with us this night, so that you may guide us in our workings. Holder of the magics of the crane bag, accept our offering and open the gates between our realm and yours. *(Throw incense & chemicals on the fire)*

HP: *(shake silver branch)*

I call to the Great Morgan Le Fay, Ruler of the Mysterious Fortunate island-valley of Avalon, where dead heroes reside,

Where falls not hail, or rain, or any snow,
Nor ever wind blows loudly; but it lies deep-meadowed
Happy, fair, with orchard lawns and bowery hollows
Crowned with Summer Sea

Mother Death, Giver of immortality, I ask that you hear me. Join us this night so that you may guide us in our workings. Sea-woman of the Merfolk, accept our offering and open the gates between our realm and yours. *(drop silver coins in water bowl)*

(Play CD The Faerie Shaman by Gwydion, #7, The Trees of Annwfn) as you bring in apple tree and Morgan, Lady of the Lake, Apple girl & and mermaids.) Apple tree was built on a wagon.

Morgan:

Behold, I am the Triple Mother Goddess and Fairy Queen, Priestess of the Old Ways over the sisterhood of nine that inhabit this mystical Isle known as Avalon

As Morgana, I am Goddess of War, Fate, and Death. As Margawse, I am Mother and healer; I am also Sea Woman, Water Fairy, or Mermaid....

I have been much aligned and my reputation corrupted by the monks who came to judge me by their own religious standards--ignorant of my shape-shifting powers and the power of the crone.

This is a refuge for the spirits of the dead, but also a place of magick and healing, for here stands the fabled apple tree whose magickal fruit promises immortality.

I aided the great King Arthur throughout his life by fairy magick, and when mortally wounded, I received him here, where, by staying for a long time, he shall be healed. It was also here, in Avalon, that his sword, the great sword Excalibur was forged.

Vivian

I am Vivian, also known as the Lady of the Lake, or sometimes as Nimue. I come to you from the West, the land of the setting sun, place of the Mysteries of life and death, the Isle of Avalon.

It was I who raised the sword, Excalibur, from my depths and presented it to Arthur. It was I who reclaimed that powerful blade upon his death and accompanied the three faerie queens to Avalon with the body of that slain king.

Apple Meditation: (Author Unknown, a few lines..)

I am the Guardian of the sacred and magickal apples that grow on the mystical Isle known as Avalon, or as Annwn to some, Asgard to others. I ask you now to close your eyes and

Visualize yourself as a small apple seed. Feel roots growing downwards in the earth. Feel them broadening and thickening as you pull in energy to nourish yourself....

Post Meditation:

By your union with the tree, the apples on this tree have become enchanted. By merely touching one and making a wish (of course adding 'an it harm none) your wish may be granted. Come forth with your hopes and dreams.

(Start slow drum beat, encouraging people to come forth, touch an apple with their wish and continue to walk around slowly. When all have done so, drums speed up for all-night fire dance) Bubbles?

At Dawn: *Solar Salutation,*

HP: Guardian of the Sacred Apple Grove, Keeper of the fruit of immortality, we thank you for your presence this night and the gifts of hope you have given us! We bid you stay if you will, go if you must, Hail and farewell!

HPS: Mysterious Lady of the Lake, accept our gratitude for your presence this night. Sorceress, healer, keeper of the revered sword, Excalibur, we bid you stay if you will, go if you must, Hail and farewell!

HP: Morgan Le Fay, Great Queen, Queen of Specters, Queen of the Fairies, Patroness of Priestesses and of Witches, you have honored us with your presence and your magick this night, and for this, we are grateful. we bid you stay if you will, go if you must, Hail and farewell!

HPS: Manannan Mac Lir, Guardian of the Blessed Isles, Son of the Sea, Guardian of the Gates between the worlds, you have honored us with your presence and your magick this night, and for this, we are grateful. we bid you stay if you will, go if you must, Hail and farewell!

East:

Wings of air, wings of light
Thank you for attending this night!
Guided by the Spirits fair.
We have felt the presence of Air
'Ere ye depart for your pleasant and lovely realms,
We bid you stay if you will, go if you must, Hail and Farewell.

North:

Earth Mother, Spirit of Earth
We are anew, through rebirth
Our heart beats within,
To you we are kin,
'Ere ye depart for your pleasant and lovely realms,
We bid you stay if you will, go if you must, Hail and Farewell.

West:

Ocean song, silver moon
With you now we are in tune
To Sprits of Water, we give our due
For giving us life, our thanks to you.
'Ere ye depart for your pleasant and lovely realms,
We bid you stay if you will, go if you must, Hail and Farewell.

South:

Portal of fire, Portal of flame
Our spirits purged of sorrow and shame
For your transformational power
Our gratitude upon you we shower.
'Ere ye depart for your pleasant and lovely realms,
We bid you stay if you will, go if you must, Hail and Farewell.

Dismiss Circle:

Closing Ritual – in the morning
before breaking camp; 2007

Cast the circle Hand to Hand (start in the East/North, going clockwise, say to the person next to you "I cast this circle hand to hand" repeat.

Give thanks to the spirits of the elements and of this beautiful place.

HPS:

Thus concludes our journey through the element of Water, Blood of the Goddess. We hope that you have had an enjoyable and meaningful weekend. Please accept our thanks for your presence at this festival. (Do "Thank yous".

HP: (*Thirst* - Poem by Claude McKay, 1921)

My spirit wails for water, water now!
My tongue is aching dry, my throat is hot
For water, fresh rain shaken from a bough,
Or dawn dews heavy in some leafy spot.
My hungry body's burning for a swim
In sunlit water where the air is cool,
As in Trout Valley where upon a limb
The golden finch sings sweetly to the pool.

HPS:

Oh water, water, when the night is done,
When day steals gray-white through the windowpane,
Clear silver water when I wake, alone,
All impotent of parts, of fevered brain;
Pure water from a forest fountain first,
To wash me, cleanse me, and to quench my thirst!

HP:

We are composed predominately of water, as is this Planet Earth. Let us ever be mindful of how important to us, to all living things and to our home the element of water is. Conserve it, work to stop the pollution of it, and honor it every day.

Great Lord and Lady, we give our gratitude for the mysteries of this element, and for your assistance in helping us gain understanding.

HPS:

As we depart for our homes, we ask that you continue to watch over us and guide us in our daily lives.

And as you depart for your lovely realms, we bid you hail and farewell.

Dismiss elements

Dismiss Circle:

May the circle be open but unbroken
May the Lord and the Lady be ever in your heart.
Merry meet and merry part
And merry meet again.

Mountain Moon Circle's Summerfest: from "Water– 2011"

Thursday: Check in after 2:00pm
    6:00-7:00pm - Dinner
    7:30-8:30 pm - Required Sacred Fire Orientation:
    8:30pm - Talent Show
    11:00pm - Opening Ritual, drum and dance till dawn

Friday:
    First Breakfast at dawn; 9:00-10:00 - Second breakfast
    11:00-12:00 - Yoga
    12:00-1:00 - Lunch
    1:00-2:15 - Reincarnation & Regression
    2:30-3:30 - Drumming Workshop
    3:45-5:15 - Dance to Awareness, Part I
    6:00-7:30 - Dinner
    11:00-dawn - Ritual and Sacred Fire Circle

Saturday:
    First Breakfast dawn 9:00-10:00 - Second breakfast
    12:00-1:00 - Lunch
    1:00-2:30 - Shannon on Quantum Physics
    2:45-4:00 - Dance to Awareness, Part II
    4:15-5:30 - Reading Runes
    6:00-7:30 - Dinner
    8:00 – Séance
    11:00-3:00 - Sacred Fire Circle

Sunday:
    10:00-11:00am Brunch
    11:30am - Closing ritual
    Clean up camp, pack up and vacate by 1:00pm

Pre-Ritual Ritual - 2011

I had an idea I wanted to try, but it had to include a pre-ritual ritual in order to complete the whole process before time to break camp. Since the main rituals for the night usually started at 11:00 PM, We performer this ritual with some people before the fire circle began. The rest were taken from the fire and brought to this installation. It had to be done in small groups, I think of 5. I used a 10'X20' tent w/painted Egyptian theme walls and décor.

Removal of the Heart

Needs: Systrum, Montana gold tea, cups, lidded pot, Kephi incense, burner and charcoal, disk, ahnk, Anubis mask, Statues of Anubis, CD of Egyptian music plays softly; high altar and black cloth, Oils, Feather fan

N: *(Circle widdershins shaking systrum as people arrive. When all are in,)* I am Nephthys, dark sister of Isis, The Shadow self.

A: And I am Anubis, son of Nephthys and Opener of the way.

N: You are here to begin a journey of renewal.

A: You shall participate in the Ancient mystical rites of Sed, as written in ancient times in the pyramid of Unas at Sakkara Egypt.

N: To proceed, you must be willing to experience a shamanic ritual of death, putting your heart into Anubis's hands. By so doing you will be cleansed of the pain and suffering lodged in your body, your emotions, your soul. If you wish to take this journey, please be seated. If not…*(indicate the door)* the way is open.

Accept this elixir. *(pass out)* Imbue it with your intention, inhale the fragrance—feel the vapors enter your body, then drink. As it enters your body, feel the effects of the elixir—the soothing comfort it brings you. As you relax, any remnants of fear or doubt will vanish. *(Collect cups)*

Now lie down and breathe deeply. Let the breath activate your heart center, feeling the love and compassion around you. A golden light of protection surrounds and encircles you now.

A: *(To each individual, whispering in their ear)*

It is right to give yourself to death. I shall gently remove your heart that it may be renewed and healed. *(Anubis gently makes an incision with his athame, removes the heart and holds it up to his ahnk for purification).*

Now you are blessed, O heart, with eternal life. *(He hands the heart to Nephthys, who places it in a fragrant container).*

N:

I place this heart in nectar created by the Gods to take away its burdens. All of the pain and sorrow of your past stories will be removed; all of the grief and death, and all the parts of your heart that hurt shall be relieved. *(sings Geeb, Noot, neteru zep tipi maat heka ab! waving feathers over jar)*

A: *(Anoint by drawing ahnk on forehead; go to next person until all hearts have been removed)*

N: Your hearts will remain here and will continue to undergo an alchemical transformation. Meanwhile, your body must be cleared of all old hurts and pain, disappointment and suffering that has been embedded in its cells, tissues, blood, and bones.

A: Your hearts will be safe while you complete the preparations and go through the process necessary to receive your renewed heart. *(Both help people up and usher them to the door.)*

Avalon: Opening Ritual, Water 2011

I used the same Avalon Ritual from 2007 for the opening ritual in 2011, with some minor changes, as follows.

Needs: a tree with apples that rolls in, tall altar, blue cloth, 2 Silver branches, Druid Circle incense, 3 silver coins, water bowl, CD & player, chemicals/incense for fire, water and salt, 4 cauldrons

HPS: Water of Life, be cleansed, be pure, be Blessed by the Mother
HP: Salt of the Earth, be cleansed, be pure, be Blessed by the Father

Both:

> Life force combined, water and earth
> Repel the dark, to the light, give birth
> This fluid most holy does now ignite
> Calling but good to our sacred rite.

Cast & seal circle:

East:

> Portal of the Eastern dawn, morning bright and clear,
> Bring to us your precious light, your happiness, and cheer.

South:

> Portal of the Midday Sun, shining bright and clear,
> Bring to us your warmth and love, your spirit present here…
>
> Transform all that needs be changed with the power of fire,
> To change our lead to purest gold is what we now desire.
> So mote it be!

West:

> Portal of the Setting sun, eventide; light dimming
> Bring to us compassion, hope within us brimming…
> So mote it be!

North:

>Portal of midnight, sun now dark and cold,
>Bring to us your wisdom, mysteries of old…
>So mote it be!

Statement of Purpose:

Guarded by the Gods of the Underworld, the portal of the West, Water, is the place of death and transformation. It is called by many different names, but always remains the Gate between the worlds of life and death, and often reached by crossing water. Tonight we honor the Celtic tradition and the isle of death called Annwn or Avalon.

HPS: *(shake silver branch)*

Oh Manannan Mac Lir, Powerful Son of the Sea, Mist-shrouded rider of the maned waves, I ask that you hear my call. Lord of the Otherworld, Bearer of the Silvered Apple Branch, join with us this night, so that you may guide us in our workings. Holder of the magics of the crane bag, accept our offering and open the gates between our realm and yours. *(Throw incense & chemicals on the fire)*

HP: *(shake silver branch)(The Passing of Arthur, Idylls of the King by Alfred, Lord Tennyson)*

>I call to the Great Morgan Le Fay,
>Ruler of the Mysterious Fortunate island-valley of Avalon,
>Where dead heroes reside,
>Where falls not hail, nor rain, nor snow,
>Nor ever wind blows loudly; but it lies deep-meadowed
>Happy, fair, with orchard lawns
>And bowery hollows, crowned with the Summer Sea

Mother Death, Giver of immortality, I ask that you hear me. Join us this night so that you may guide us in our workings. Sea-woman of the Merfolk, accept our offering and open the gates between our realm and yours. *(silver coins in water bowl)*

(Play CD – Song of the Mermaid Queen from Journey to the Goddess by Lisa Thiel) Morgan Le Fey & enter apple tree and Morgan, Lady of the Lake, Apple girl & and mermaids.)

Morgan:

Behold, I am the Triple Mother Goddess and Fairy Queen, Priestess of the Old Ways over the sisterhood of nine that inhabit this mystical Isle known as Avalon.

As Morgana, I am Goddess of War, Fate, and Death. As Margawse, I am Mother and healer; I am also Sea Woman, Water Fairy, or Mermaid.

I have been much aligned and my reputation corrupted by the monks who came to judge me by their own religious standards--ignorant of my shape-shifting powers and the power of the crone.

This is a refuge for the spirits of the dead, but also a place of magick and healing, for here stands the fabled apple tree whose magickal fruit promises immortality.

I aided the great King Arthur throughout his life by fairy magick, and when mortally wounded, I received him here, where, by staying for a long time, he shall be healed. It was also here, in Avalon, that his sword, the great sword Excalibur was forged.

Vivian

I am Vivian, also known as the Lady of the Lake, or sometimes as Nimue. I come to you from the West, the land of the setting sun, place of the Mysteries of life and death, the Isle of Avalon.

It was I who raised the sword, Excalibur, from my depths and presented it to Arthur. It was I who reclaimed that powerful blade upon his death and accompanied the three faerie queens to Avalon with the body of that slain king.

Apple Meditation: (same as before)

Sunrise: *Solar Salutation*

HP:

Guardian of the Sacred Apple Grove, Keeper of the fruit of immortality, we thank you for your presence this night and the gifts of hope you have given us! We bid you stay if you will, go if you must, Hail and farewell!

HPS: Mysterious Lady of the Lake, accept our gratitude for your presence this night. Sorceress, healer, keeper of the revered sword, Excalibur, we bid you stay if you will, go if you must, Hail and farewell!

HP: Morgan Le Fay, Great Queen, Queen of Specters, Queen of the Fairies, Patroness of Priestesses and of Witches, you have honored us with your presence and your magick this night, and for this, we are grateful. We bid you stay if you will, go if you must, Hail and farewell!

HPS: Manannan Mac Lir, Guardian of the Blessed Isles, Son of the Sea, Guardian of the Gates between the worlds, you have honored us with your presence and your magick this night, and for this, we are grateful. We bid you stay if you will, go if you must, Hail and farewell!

East:

> Portal of the Eastern Light,
> Begin the day anew
> Messages received this night
> The dark has brought us through
> We leave thee now in gratitude
> For all we have received
> Stay if you will, go if you must
> Your duties now relieved.
> Hail and Farewell!

North:

> Portal of Midnight
> Through the dark, we've come
> Wisdom gained through ancient rite
> And rhythm of the drum.
> We leave thee now in gratitude
> For all we have received
> Stay if you will, go if you must
> Your duties now relieved.
> Hail and Farewell!

West:

> Portal of the Eventide,
> Presence of the One,
> Our soul's we've reexamined,
> Our work this night is done
> We leave thee now in gratitude

For all we have received
Stay if you will, go if you must
Your duties now relieved.
Hail and Farewell!

South:

Portal of the Midday sun,
Bring your strengthening rays
That all we've done throughout the night
Sustain us through the days.
We leave thee now in gratitude
For all we have received
Stay if you will, go if you must
Your duties now relieved.
Hail and Farewell!

Dismiss Circle:

Cauldron of the Sea – 2nd Night Ritual, 2011

Needs: Cauldron of sea water, shells for all, blue altar, quarter shells, ocarina, bullroarer, rain stick, drum, fan, cakes & tea

Cast & Seal Circle

East: *(ocarina)*
> O Air, I call to the Eastern tower,
> Now quickly, lightly, send your power
> 'Till break of dawn and golden light
> Inspire our thoughts throughout the night.
> Let knowledge from the Gods come through
> Messenger thou, on swift wings true.
> O Guardian of the Eastern sphere,
> Come, East. Come be here!
> So mote it be

South: *(bull roarer)*
> O Fire, I call to the Southern tower
> With bright vitality send your power.
> Dance gaily with your flame-red light
> And keep us safe throughout the night.
> Let the transformation begin
> As our lead departs let your light come in.
> O Guardian of the Southern sphere,
> Come, Fire. Come be here!
> So mote it be

West: *(rain stick)*
> O Water, I call to the Western tower,
> With waves of feeling, send your power.
> Flow through us with deep blue light,
> Bringing mystical and magickal sight.
> Our heavy hearts shall find release
> And we shall find our inner peace.
> O Guardian of the Western sphere,
> Come, West. Come be here!
> So mote it be

North: *(Drum)*

> O Earth, I call to the Western tower
> With strength of stone, send your power.
> Help us work through fright and pain
> So growth and wisdom we attain.
> Ancient mysteries, old ones wise,
> Keep near us through the darkened skies.
> O Guardian of the Northern sphere,
> Come, North. Come be here!
> So mote it be

HPS:

Listen to the sounds of the rushing water. Imagine the ocean waves that break into foam and wash up on the sand—soothing, gentle, or crashing against the rocks—powerful, persuasive.

All life on Earth once came forth from the sea, the womb of the mother. High above, the moon this night *is in the watery sign of Cancer, symbol of the mother and her timeless, never-ceasing love. Would that we could drift and dream with her.* (Change or delete as is appropriate for the current moon position.)

HP:

Here, in this time and place may we create a timeless and sacred space between the visible and invisible worlds, where we may call upon the unseen energies to flow ever more strongly within us. I charge that this shall be a circle of unity, of love and of trust, where we may seek and share and grow from the insights that our Gracious Lady may reveal to us. By the love of the Threefold Goddess and her mighty consort, I do bless and consecrate this circle of power. As it is willed, so mote it be.

HPS:

> Rising river running wild, grotto's pool of deepest green
> Ocean crashing on the shore its hidden depths unseen.
> Power of water, her blood in me!

ALL: *(after each stanza, all repeat)* Power of water, her blood in me!

HP:

> Azure lake with flashing fish, the trail of a single tear
> Raindrops splashing to the earth, and the perfect scrying mirror.
> Power of water, her blood in me!

HPS:

Within the deep and foaming sea, ancient powers dwell,
King Niksa, Mari, Neptune, Aphrodite on her shell.
Power of water, her blood in me!

HP:

Ancient ones of blue and green, of rain and sleet and snow
Grant to us the power of love and the mysteries for to know.
Power of water, her blood in me!

HPS:

The blessings of Water, we beseech the Goddess give.
Guide us to her mysteries, and let our magick live.
Power of water, her blood in me!

HP:

I call upon Mazu (mat su), Radiant Goddess of the Sea, Mother Matriarch and Daughter of the Dragon, she who is rooted in the hearts of her people, worshiped in 1,500 temples. Dance with us and be with us tonight. Awaken the spark of the Goddess within us all. *(Blow conch)*

Mazu: (with an oriental accent)

I have been one of you, born in the country you know as Taiwan and my given name was Lin Mo Niang. I taught people how to prevent illness and injury, and I also healed those who were sick

Earth mother say she pray to Kuan Yin for daughter. Kuan Yin came in dream, cause her to eat flower. Next day, she conceives me. When I born, mother say room fill with bright light and smell of flower. She name me Lin Niang, but I never cry, so call me Lin Mo Niang for Mo mean quiet.

When I four year old, I see statue of Kuan Yin in temple. She give me gift of sight, also photo-membering. I learn Chinese medicine, so heal the sick, also teach people to prevent illness and injury.

When I thirteen, entered training of old priest in secret mysteries of Taoism. When I fifteen, looking in pool with friends to see our new dresses, a creature of the sea jumped up from water holding bronze disc in mouth. Friends ran, but I take gift. Gift give mysterious powers.

One time, I weaving, then sleep. See father and brother washed off ship from typhoon wind. I go to them, push brother to safety, then get father, but mother see me and think I sick, so wake me then. Father drown. I go to sea, walk in. Three days, find body of father to bring home.

My earth life was short, only 28 years. I tell mother, time for me to go. I walk to top of mountain where came thick fog, beautiful music, and golden light. Took me up in sky, then came rainbow. In China, rainbow mean dragon here, mean blessing and good fortune.

But as you see, I live on to aide those who call upon me. I keep watch on sailor at sea. I come to warn of storms. I come to rescue them or calm the waters and the winds.

(Shells being passed) Now, tonight, I bring to you the sea. You can always be wherever you wish, in your imagination. Sea have magickal power to clean even most impure and polluted things. Give to the sea your feelings that worry you, emotions that pollute your spirit and keep you from feeling secure. Close eyes and feel floating and drifting on the waves, rocked and safe as you bathe in my waters. Touch yourself, then return touch to water in shell, see all unwanted feelings being washed away, cleansed and changed.

Now pour water back into the eternal sea, container of power to cleanse or consecrate, destroy or create and it shall be returned to the sea to be recycled and reborn, perhaps in your dreams—but soon, as new feelings that support you and give you comfort. Keep little shell nearby as you sleep, as a reminder.

I tell you now, always need balance of kindness and ferocity, masculine and feminine, nature and civilization. But most of all, unity of mind, body, and spirit. Be safe, my children, be at peace—you are loved. *(Depart)*

HP:

In the making and baking of these cakes, we find the hand of the benevolent Sun, which transforms green shoots into golden grain. We consume these cakes that they may give us spiritual and physical sustenance, strength and love.

HPS:

In the picking and brewing of this tea, we find the hand of the nurturing Sea, which transforms her water into rainfall that nourished all. We drink this tea that it may give us spiritual and physical sustenance, strength and love.

Chant: *(begin fire circle)*

Back to the river, back to the sea
Back to the ocean Home to Thee

> Back through my blood, back through my veins,
> Back to the heartbeat, one and the same

At Dawn, recite the *Solar Salutation*

HPS: Our thanks be to Mazu, for her healing, her protection, and her love. We shall be ever mindful to seek balance in our lives and within ourselves. Hail, Mazu, and farewell.

East:

> O Guardians of the East, Spirits of Air,
> Dance on your way with grace and flair!
> Take our grateful love and be now free,
> Hail, farewell, and blessed be!

North:

> O Guardians of the North, Spirits of Earth,
> Dance on to the world with strength and mirth!
> Take our grateful love and be now free,
> Hail, farewell, and blessed be!

West:

> O Guardians of the West, O Water sprite,
> Dance on to the sea with magickal sight!
> Take our grateful love and be now free,
> Hail, farewell, and blessed be!

South:

> O Guardians of the South, Spirits of Fire,
> Dance to the world, your gifts inspire!
> Take our grateful love and be now free,
> Hail, farewell, and blessed be!

Dismiss Circle:

> May the circle be open but unbroken
> May the Lord and the Lady be ever in your heart.
> Merry meet and merry part
> And merry meet again.

3rd Night ritual was conducted by a Guest Circle, "Garden of the Crescent Moon" a Coven from Kalispell, MT

Unfortunately, I do not have that ritual - **BUT – it's time to give back people's hearts!** (They did feel strange walking around without their hearts...) We took them in small groups from the fire circle to the...

Temple of Atlantis – Receiving the Heart

This took place in a 10 X 20 ten, divided into two sections. The first section was sunken Atlantis, watery walls, sunken broken statues and pots, sandy floor, fish, etc. and two chairs occupied by the King and Queen of Atlantis.

The second section was also undersea, containing the pool and 4 mermaids, seaweed, fish, shells, etc. Wish I had pictures.

King:

Long ago, even before the existence of the land you know as Ancient Egypt, we, the people of Atlantis, ruled the world. Our powers of Magick and science were great—so great that we destroyed even ourselves.

Through this destruction, we learned much. We exist now in the otherworld, far wiser than before, and in your world through far memory and tales passed down through many generations, which were finally preserved in writing.

You are here, displaced in time by acts of great magick. You are here to find your true self.

Queen:

It is your nature to strive for the fulfillment of your soul's purpose and passion, but books, workshops, and therapy are not the way. What you seek is already within you. You need only to remember—to come back to the love, wisdom, and freedom you experienced before you entered matter, and while in the womb before you were born.

King:

Your journey has been long and hard. You have visited the underworld after giving up your hearts to the Gods. You have met challenges, and were found worthy.

Queen:

You have been prepared and purified. Khnumn's magick has created a new body and placed within it the Ka, your astral body, fresh and new.

You have been blessed by the Gods and Goddesses of Ancient times. You must now prepare to enter the womb of the Mother, the waters of life, as one by one you will be reborn.

(Play a CD of singing bowls and/or chimes; HP stands at the door to admit one at a time to the birthing chamber. The mermaids simulated water by rippling yards of blue watery fabric and rippling it back and forth to each other. The Guest stood between and was asked to kneel.)

Mermaid Queen: *(She held a hot packs people buy for camping disguised as a heart.)*

Your heart has slept safely in the House of Hearts where it has been renewed. I shall give you back your heart. No more dreams of death, for I bestow the gift of life.

(Apply Heart to chest) May your heart pump again life's power into you, infusing even your hands and feet with spirit. Death is but a dream, from which you now awaken.

Closing Ritual was the same as 2007
Workshops & Activities Offered during
the Water Camp Events: 2007

The two thousand years allotted by their own mythos for the reign of Christianity has now ended. After an Age-long exile, Paganism is returning to the world. Joseph Campbell said it is time for a new myth that includes the whole Earth and everyone on it. Paganism and the Gaia Thesis offer such an all-embracing mythos. This Millennium can be ours if we can seize the day. Come prepared with questions to raise, issues to discuss, ideas to present, and visions to offer.

Paganism in the Third Millennium: Oberon Zell. Drawing upon 45 years' experience as a group founder, magazine publisher, presenter, author, and teacher, he will present a forum-style discussion concerning our identity as modern Pagans, our history, and our future.

Mirror Therapy: Marcela Insignares. Re-evaluate your life, discover your true identity and increase your sense of personal control and autonomy. It is time to discover the real "self", this unique, lasting identity; the source of your thoughts, actions, and emotions; an identity that should remain the same throughout life...

Fire Circle Alchemy: Ritual Technologies for Fire Circle Magic, Nytewind. Ancient mysteries and modern magic blend together to create the community fire circle, which is, for us, the elixir of life.

In this orientation, you will learn the techniques that go into creating a vessel in which you can transform your personal lead into gold. We focus on practical tools for transformation and provide an outline for the magic that happens in our community. Become your highest vision. Drink deeply of these sacred secrets and prepare to be trance-formed.

Charlyn Scheffelman (Lady Nytewind)

An Encounter with the Goddess; a Meditation for Men: Oberon Zell. This is a special workshop for men only. The core of this session is a guided meditation through the realm of personal archetype. Discover the Goddess in Her relationship aspects, as Mother, Sister, Daughter, Lover, and Grandmother. Learn the lessons they each offer to men who can meet them as sons, brothers, fathers, lovers, and grandsons. (Gay men are welcome, but are reminded that one of the aspects encountered will be Goddess as Lover.)

Real Wizardry for the Harry Potter Generation: Oberon Zell. *A Discussion of Modern Wizardry and the Magickal Arts.* After writing the *Grimoire for the Apprentice Wizard,* Oberon created an online School to further such studies. The Grey School offers a 7-year-level Apprenticeship program, culminating in a certificate of "Journeyman Wizard." Oberon will present the Grey School Vision, and show how you can become part of it.

Tarot Basics: Stella Bennett. This workshop will cover some of the history of Tarot, the basics of the individual suits, and major arcana. You will also learn how to read the Tarot intuitively. If you have a Tarot deck that you would like to use please bring it.

Tarot Spreads and Readings: Stella Bennett. Learn individual spreads. Everyone will be practicing by doing a one-card reading. If you have a Tarot deck that you would like to use please bring it.

Fire Circle Participation for the Non-Musician: Morganne Baum. What if you don't own a drum, do not want to become a drummer, but want to engage in being part of the music making at the fire circle? What if you want to chant, or don't know how to sing in a way that works with a rhythm already being played?

The experience of being part of a group sound can be extraordinary! Each person feels in their small way that they are significant to the music. Unfortunately, some people who feel shy or uncertain may feel that they can't contribute to the music because of their inexperience. This workshop would explore the ways to become connected with and participate in the music making through voice, movement, and the use of supporting percussion, (shakers, claves, clapping, etc.) while teaching non-musicians how to listen for the beat and compliment their fellow drummers. We would also discuss the energetic flow and ritual components of the music

228

at an all-night fire circle, and how people can stay engaged and create their own transformative experience.

Making a Joyful Noise: Morganne Baum. Come learn the basics of rhythm and drum skills while playing with friends in a safe and sacred learning environment. We will focus on keeping time, listening to each other, learning hand drum and rhythm skills, and creating a group sound together. All levels of experience are welcome, as well as all drum types. We will have some percussion instruments to share.

2011

Fire Circle Orientation: *Lady Nytewind:* required for beginniers.

Past Lives; *Lady Nytewind:* Nytewind will lead a discussion of reincarnation, followed by a group past-life regression that incorporates the sounds of the crystal singing bowl. Please bring blankets and pillows as you will be laying on the floor.

Drumming Workshop – MMC members

Water Yoga, *Eryn Braida:* Water Yoga incorporates the flowing qualities of water into physical practice. We will be connecting with the element of water by linking poses with the breath and creating fluid movements from one pose to the next. While we do this practice, we will be focusing on aspects such as love and healing, which are traditionally associated with Water. Through Water Yoga, you will experience healing, rejuvination, and the love of the divine.

MMC: Seance' Since the West, or water, is the gate to the spirit world in many different cultures, we will also be conducting a seance' (held within a cast and sealed circle).

Dance to Awareness, *Madeline Martin:* Dance to Awareness is a movement meditation through the Chakras in two parts. It is designed as a tool to experience Awareness. When we are Aware, we are in our Power and who we truly ARE. We will be exploring each of the seven energy centers of the body in great detail through Dance, meditation, and, sound. No prior dance experience required, only willingness and a desire to move. There is no right way or wrong way to dance, surrender yourself to the beat, lend your ear to the music and your body will follow, have fun and feel great!

Quantum Physics: *Shannon Kennedy-Kahyler* will enlighten us on this subject.

Rune Readings

Installations for Water, 2007

Portal of Water: In a blue 10 x 10 gazebo with a blue tarp and rug on the floor, the walls were hung with blue satin. This was unmanned. A statue of Poseidon sat on a blue-covered table. Another table held a mermaid statue, a third, with a large wall hanging of a dragon hanging behind it, held a bowl of sand. The forth table held cowrie shells and mermaid/dolphin oracle cards. Other arrangements included:

Poseidon (There were little bottles of sea water and this sign)

In Greek mythology, Poseidon was the Supreme Lord of the inner and outer seas and of everything that swam in or on the water. Poseidon drove a chariot pulled by the Titans blowing conch horns. He was said to live in a golden palace in the depths of the ocean, and his ten sons were made the rulers of Atlantis. With Demeter, he fathered the wild winged horse, Arion.

He would use his trident to stir the seas into furious storms, and to pierce the clouds to release the rains. He was also responsible for earthquakes.

Accept a bottle of sea water and remember the Gods and Goddesses of the sea and our kinship with them and with the sea, the lifeblood of the planet.

Merfolk (Seahorse statue, mermaid incense holder, incense and lighter)

Merfolk are sentient creatures, humanoid above the waist, merging into a strong fish-tail below. Their hair comes in a wide range of naturally occurring oceanic colors; black, dark green through pale green, turquoise, blue, lavender, white, and silver.

Merfolk are said to come in male (mermen) female (mermaids) and neuter genders (mer) although only the females appear in public; that is, above water in view of other races. Thus most legends and sailors' tales speak only of mermaids.

The Freshwater Mermaid is said to have a talent for healing. The solitary males are totally marine, meeting the females only once a year when they descend into the rivers to mate at sea.

Great Water Dragon, Naelyn (A bowl held sand dollars, buried in sand, corals, and the sign)

Naelyan is the Elemental dragon of the West and thus, the element of Water. He oversees the Dragons of Seas, Springs, Lakes, Ponds, Rivers, etc. His coloring is mostly blue to help him blend well with his habitat.

He can be called upon to help with emotions, either calming them or breaking through a barrier built around them.

Sea dragons are basically shaped like Oriental Dragons. They are long and serpent-like, usually without legs or wings.

Take a sand dollar, shell of a sea creature who wears the five-pointed star; a gift for you from the creatures of the sea.

Oshun (with shells and cards for divination)

Oshun is the Yoruban Orisha (deity) of the sweet or fresh waters. She is widely loved, as She is known for healing the sick and bringing fertility and prosperity. She especially watches over the poor and brings them what they need.

As Orisha of love, Oshun is a beautiful, charming and coquettish young woman, but in some tales, a mermaid with the tail of a fish.

She is especially worshipped in river towns. During Her yearly festival, She chooses one or more women dancers to descend into. These women then take new names in honor of Oshun and are thereafter consulted as healers.

Oshun was taught divination with cowrie shells by Obatala, the first of the created gods. She brought the teaching to humans. Pose a question. Throw

3 cowrie shells. If the majority land face up, the answer is yes. Draw a card from the deck for a further divination.

Selkies *(Setting included conch shell, large and small shells)*

<u>Selkies</u> are sea folk known to the inhabitants of the Orkney Islands and the Hebrides. These enchanted creatures dwell in the depths of the sea, occasionally shedding their sealskins to pass on the land as humans. Legend has it they then find human partners, and some families on the islands trace their ancestry back to such alliances.

The great seal, gray seal, crested seal and others are called the Selkie folk because it is believed that their natural form is human. They live in an underwater world or on lonely skerries and put on the appearance of seals which enables them to pass through the waters from one region of air to another. The human-like quality of their cries and their human eyes reinforce this belief.

Underwater Panthers *(I don't remember the particulars – maybe it hung on a wall)*

These were powerful creatures in the mythological traditions of some Native American tribes; particularly tribes in the Great Lakes region. They were supreme and frightful, masters of all water creatures and snakes.

The underwater panther was an amalgam of features from many animals: the horns of deer or bison; snake scales; bird feathers; the body and tail of a mountain lion; and parts from other animals as well, depending on the particular myth.

They were a source of great wisdom and healing power, particularly with herbs. They could bestow blessings on humans, but they fought a constant battle with Thunders, other supernatural beings that flew in the sky. This opposition brought balance to the cosmos, but danger to humans in the path of their anger.

Purification Ritual: A 10 x 10 gazeebo was set up in the woods. As described earlier in the rituals, Death is encountered along the way, as people were taken from the fire circle in small groups. The gazeebo was draped in black. I used my painting again of three Egyptian Gods on the back wall, used my blow-up mummy and other Egyptian statues and things HPS wore an (attractive) mummy outfit, and HP wore a black robe.

Temple of Atlantis: This involved a 10x20 tent with a dividing curtain. The front part was decorated to resemble the sunken ancient city of Atlantis. I made wall coverings by using a blue, watery-looking taffeta fabric and attached a fabric that resembled sand a couple of feet from the floor. Décor included pillars, fish, seaweed, broken pillars, etc. and the seated King and Queen of Atlantis. The back half was an undersea environment, with florescent sea weed, lots of florescent fish and sea creatures on the walls, and populated with 2 mermaids and a mermaid queen. Black lights created the atmosphere!

It was supposed to have been a rental hot tub, but the day before camp when I was to get it delivered, I was told they had all been sold. I'm sure they found out we were Wiccan, since the town nearby had previously given us a bad time. SO – I had to find a kiddie swimming pool and a way to heat it. Unfortunately, the aquarium heaters didn't work very well, so it was too cold for comfort.

There were 2 mermaids in the second section of the tent that helped people in and out of the pool. (People had been warned they would be getting wet.)

2011

Removal of the Heart: For this pre-ritual ritual, I covered the interior of a 10 x 20 gazeebo with canvas cloth painted with Egyptian Gods and décor. Tarps on the floor were covered with mats, as the people would be lying down. See ritual.

Purification Ritual: We used the 2007 one again.

Portal of Water: This also was the same as 2007.

APPENDIX S

Mountain Moon Circle's Summerfest: Rituals from "Spirit – 2008"

I have to say that this might be my favorite of the nine events. It was very, very magickal! I regret that I was only able to present "Spirit" once due to circumstances beyond my control. Since the camp we had been using was primarily a youth camp, all youth groups had first dibs on scheduling, and there were no weekends left for our group. That made is hard for people to get time off from work to attend, so 2012 was the last Summerfest.

Also, unfortunately, I was preparing for *SummerFest 2013; Spirit,* and was replacing the 2008 information on the web page, which then was lost. This is all I can find.

Opening Ritual, 2008 – Honoring the Spirits of All

Needs: For all: Prayer Incense, (cauldron, lg charcoals, sand), flash paper or flame color, corn meal (bowl) or petals, silver into bowl of water, fairy, dragon, mermaid, gnome, altar cloths & tables, Gaia & green man, black altar cloth, scrolls, feather fan,

Cast & Seal Circle

HPS: *(join hands, saying 'from hand to hand this circle is cast'.)*
We swear by peace and love to stand,
Heart to heart, and hand to hand,
Hark, O Spirit, and hear us now,
Confirming this, our Sacred Vow.

East: Spirits of East! Spirits of Air!
Guardians of the Watchtower there!
Come gentle winds, around us blow,
Within and without, the air doth flow...

South:
Spirits of South! Spirits of Fire!
Guardians of the Watchtower spire!
Come warm flames all aglow
Within and without, your spark doth grow.
Fire of life, give us strength and will
Our purpose here we will fulfill...

West:
Spirits of West, Sprits of Water
Guardians of the West Watchtower
Come waves dancing in moonlight glow
Within and without, your love doth flow.
Cleanse us, heal us from our plight
As we dance the fire this night...

North:
Spirits of North, Spirits of Earth
Guardians of the Watchtower perch
Come earth's strength of rock and stone,
Within and without us, flesh and bone.
Ancient magicks, mysteries deep
Health and plenty, ours to reap...

HP: Statement of Purpose:

We come this night, to honor the many spirits that speak to us across the veil from their various realms or Summerland. Let us begin by honoring the spirits of this place—this land.

Oh spirits of the mountains, the forest, the air and the water in this place, we ask your permission to work our sacred magick these next few days. Accept this offering of sacred incense, given with our love and our respect. *(Throw into the fire)*. So mote it be!

> We call the All-Father,
> Sun King, benevolent protector...
> Be with us during this long night.
> Guard and guide us during our journey.

HPS:

> We call the All-Mother
> Moon Queen, loving care-giver...
> Be with us during this long night.
> Care for us and guide us during our journey...

East:

> O Ancestors and blood-kin many...
> We come before you this night
> With clean hands and pure hearts...
> *(Offerings of incense)*

South:

> O beloved heart-kin...
> Your lives to us are luminous, for
> You walked your ways in truth and wisdom...
> *(Offerings of flash paper or flame color)*

West:

> Soul-kin, Guardians and guides...
> Teachers of our souls, we call to you...
> Your stories are honored at our shrines,
> You struggles shaped our souls...
> *(Offerings of silver)*

Charlyn Scheffelman (Lady Nytewind)

North:

> Other-kin, beloved pets, and animal friends,
> Whose lives we've shared with love and joy...
> Your lives to us are luminous, for
> You walked your ways in truth and wisdom...
> *(Offerings of corn meal or petals)*

HP: *The Charge of the God* From: *Internet Book of Shadows*, (Various
Authors), [1999], at sacred-texts.com

> I am the fire within your heart,
> The yearning of your soul.
> I am the hunter of Knowledge
> And the seeker of the holy Quest
>
> I, who stand in the darkness of light,
> Am He whom you have called Death.
> I, the Consort and Mate of Her we adore,
> Call forth to thee.
>
> Heed my call beloved ones,
> Come unto me and learn the secrets of death and peace.
> I am the corn at harvest
> and the fruit on the trees.
> I am He who leads you home
> Scourge and Flame,
> Blade and Blood –
> These are mine and gifts to thee.
>
> Call unto me in the forest wild
> and on hilltop bare
> and seek me in the Darkness Bright
> I who have been called:
>
>> Pan,
>> Herne,
>> Osiris,
>> and Hades,

Speak to thee in thy search.
Come and dance and sing:
come live and smile, for behold:
this is my worship.
You are the children and I am thy Father
On swift night wings

It is I who lay you at the Mother's feet
to be reborn and return again.
Thou who thinks to seek me,
Know that I am the untamed wind,
the fury of storm and passion in your Soul.
Seek me with pride and humility,
but seek me best with love and strength.
for this is my path.
and I love not the weak and fearful.

Hear my call on long Winter nights
and we shall stand together guarding Her Earth
as She sleeps.

HPS: *(Same source)*
I am the harmonious tune of the songbird
And the laughter of a gleeful child.
I am the bubbling sound of the running brook
And the scent of the flowers wild.

I am the floating leaf upon the breeze
And the dancing fire in the forest glade.
I am the sweet smell of rains upon the soil
And the rapture of passion when love is made.

I am the germination of seed in the Spring
And the ripening of wheat in the Sun.
I am the peaceful depth of the twilight
That soothes the soul when day is done.
I am found in the twinkling of an aged eye...

And found in the birth of a newborn pup...
Yes...Birth and Growth and Death, am I
I am the gracious Earth on whom you sup.
I am your sister, your mother, the wise one.
I wrap you gently in the warmth of my love.
That which you seek you shill find within:
Not without...not below...not above.

Remember always, my children, be reverent.
Be gentle, loving and kind to each other.
And hold sacred the Earth and its creatures:
For I am the Lady: Creatrix and Mother!

HP & HPS:

We stand with you this night, guiding, warding, loving, supporting. We will show you the way to your highest good.   *(Move altar. Quarters come forth to light the central fire)*

Chant:

We are a circle moving
One with another we are
Moving together we are one.
We are a circle moving
One with another we are
Moving together we are one.

I am spirit and I flow in you.
You are spirit and you flow in me.
  Begin the fire circle...

At Dawn: (Best to have everyone memorize this before the event.)

Solar Salutation, by Katlyn Breene

HP: All-Father, Sun King, benevolent protector,
He who sustains us and provides for us,
We offer our gratitude for your guidance and protection...
We bid you Hail and Farewell.

HPS:

> All-Mother, Moon Queen, loving care-giver
> She who sustains us and provides for us,
> We offer our gratitude for your guidance and protection
> We bid you Hail and Farewell.

East:

> Portal of the Eastern Light,
> Begin the day anew
> Messages received this night
> The dark has brought us through...

North:

> Portal of Midnight
> Through the dark, we've come
> Wisdom gained through ancient rite
> And rhythm of the drum...

West:

> Portal of the Eventide,
> Presence of the One,
> Our soul's we've reexamined,
> Our work this night is done...

South:

> Portal of the Midday sun,
> Bring your strengthening rays
> That all we've done throughout the night
> Sustain us through the days...

Dismiss Circle:

> May the circle be open but unbroken
> May the Lord and the Lady be ever in your heart.
> Merry meet and merry part
> And merry meet again.

2nd Night, 2008 – Angle Ritual

Needs: flute, systrum, crystal singing bowl, drum, conch shell, chime, staff, 3 swords, chalice, platter, earth bowl, silver water bowl, oil lamp, Gabriel incense/sensor, 7 colors yarns, 4 scissors, CD: angel song, black lights. (No center altar)

Cast: *(in silence)*

Seal Circle: *(Quarters carry elements doesil, with instruments)*

(Use Lesser Banishing Ritual of the Pentagram, stopping at the mention of each angel for the quarter call). Available in Wikipedia <u>Creative Commons Attribution-ShareAlike License</u>
Also http://www.kheper.net/topics/Hermeticism/LBR.htm

HPS: Ah-**TAH**

East:

Raphael, staff bearer of the All-Holy,
Servant of the altar of life we call upon thee.
Come to the East, O praise-singer of the Eternal,
And fill this place with the breath of life,
And the powers of light!
Raphael, Healer, Angel of communication,
With the sound of the flute, we call thee!

HPS: Mahl-**KOOT**

South:

Mikhael, Sword bearer of the All-Holy
Servant of the altar of life, we call upon thee.
Come to the South, O angel of the solar rays,
And fill this place with the fire of creation,
And the powers of love!
Mikhael, Protector, Patron of true priests,
With the sound of the systrum, we call thee!

HPS: Vih-G'Boo-**RAH**

West:

Gabriel, cup bearer of the All-Holy,
Servant of the altar of life we call upon thee.
Come to the West, O angel of the Word
And fill this place with the waters of grace,
And the powers of life!
Gabriel, Herald of the High Self,
With the sound of the singing bowl, we call thee!

North:

Uriel, platter bearer of the All-Holy,
Servant of the altar of life we call upon thee.
Come to the North, O angel of the Throne,
And fill this place with the stability of Earth
And the powers of law.
Uriel, Transmitter of magickal force,
With the sound of the drum, we call thee!

HPS: Vih-G'Doo-**LAH**

HP: *(raise sword upright)*
Samael, ruler of the planet Mars,
Benevolent power, bringer of good fortune,
Come to this sacred circle, O Great protector.
And fill this place with the courage of the warrior
And the powers of perseverance
Samael, overcomer of obstacles,
With the sound of the horn, we call thee!

HPS: Lih-Oh-**Lahm,**

HPS: *(raise the sword, point down)*
Haniel, ruler of the planet Venus,
Compassionate one, bringer of mercy,
Come to this sacred circle, O creator of beauty,

And fill this place with peace and harmony
And the powers of love.
Haniel, overseer of the fairy world,
With the sound of the bell, we call thee!

Ah-MEN
Angels all, we call thee!

Angels: (Dance troupe to – *Bring in the Angles*, by Abigale McBride)

(Quarters light fire)
Chakra healing: *(passing hand to hand each of 7 colors of yarn with the appropriate chant which is call and response)*

HP:
The first energy center or charka lies at the base of the spine. It is our foundation, our earthly bodies, health, and survival. It is the ability to focus and manifest our needs—our security.

Root – *(red) stamp feet 1-2 after each phrase; raise cord at the end*
I am of the Earth; the earth is around, about and within me!
I am spirit living in a physical body
I claim healing for my insecurities
I claim the power of life, for I have chosen to exist!

HPS:
The second charka lies in the abdomen and makes us aware of a feeling of separateness. This leads us to join with another, to grow and change, to express our feelings of passion and emotion.

Spleen – *(orange)*
I am of the water; the water is around, about and within me!
I contain qualities both masculine and feminine
I claim healing of assaults to my gender
I claim the power of creativity
    (Complete yoga breath w/retention 4 4 4 4 hands palms up)

HP:

The third charka, located in the solar plexus, is the seat of our will. We take action, bringing together intention, emotion, and consciousness to fulfill our purpose.

Solar Plexus - *(yellow)*

I am of the fire; the fire is around, about and within me!
I am a child of the universe!
I claim healing of my ego self!
I am valued and valuable, calm and self-assured
('AHH' yoga breath, finger 1 & thumb)

HPS:

The heart charka opens us to the power of love; but to love another, we must first love and accept ourselves. Only then can we love others unconditionally. Through love, we connect to the divine.

Heart – *(green)*

I am of the air; the air is around, about and within me!
I am loved and lovable
I claim healing of my emotional self
I claim the perfect love of self and receive the love of my gods
('A' yoga breath, finger 2 & thumb)

HP:

The throat charka gives us the power to communicate, to sing, and to give voice to our thoughts and feelings. Sound is the means by which our consciousness extends itself from one place to another.

Throat – *(blue)*

I am sound; sound is around, about and within me!
I am capable of succinct communication
I claim healing so that I may speak for myself
I claim communication with other beings in love and peace
('O' yoga breath finger 3 & thumb)

HPS:

Though the eyes give us the ability to see the world around us, the charka referred to as the third eye gives us the ability for inner sight—the ability to see beyond the physical world. This ability increases as we heal the wounds harbored in our subconscious.

Third Eye – *(indigo)*
> I am light; light is around, about and within me!
> I am intelligent and wise
> I claim healing of all pain harbored in my subconscious
> I claim the ability to create my reality with my thoughts
> *('OO' yoga breath finger 4 & thumb)*

HP:
> The seventh charka, referred to as the thousand-petaled lotus, blooms from the top of the head. This charka connects us to divine intelligence and the source of all manifestation. We are one with the angels and the Gods.

Crown – *(violet)*
> I am universal consciousness; all around, about and within me!
> I am able to transcend the physical world
> I claim healing of all that prevents me from reaching my spiritual best.
> I claim my divine birthright here and now!
> *('E' yoga breath make fists release; cut cords, each ties their bunch in a knot)*

Chant: *(fire circle begins)*
> We are opening up to the sweet sensation
> Of the luminous love light of the One.
> We are opening up to the sweet sensation
> Of the luminous love light of the One.
> We are opening, we are opening
> We are opening, we are opening

At Dawn: *Solar Salutation*, by Katlyn Breene

HP: *(raise sword upright)*
> Samael, ruler of the planet Mars,
> Benevolent power, bringer of good fortune,
> We have felt your presence this night, O Great protector.
> You have given us the courage to do this work,

To persevere, to transform our lead into gold.
Samael, overcomer of obstacles,
Accept our gratitude as we bid you 'Hail and Farewell'.

HPS: *(raise the sword, point down)*

Haniel, ruler of the planet Venus,
Compassionate one, bringer of mercy,
We have felt your presence this night, O creator of beauty,
We have worked through the night and accept now
Peace, harmony and the powers of love.
Haniel, overseer of the fairy world,
Accept our gratitude as we bid you 'Hail and Farewell'.

East:

Raphael, staff bearer of the All-Holy,
Servant of the altar of life, you have been with us.
We have employed the power of our breath
And the powers of light this night to heal our wounds.
Raphael, Healer, Angel of communication,
Accept our gratitude as we bid you 'Hail and Farewell'.

North:

Uriel, platter bearer of the All-Holy,
Servant of the altar of life, you have been with us.
We have drawn from the strength and stability of earth
To steady and sustain us throughout the dark night
Uriel, Transmitter of magickal force,
Accept our gratitude as we bid you 'Hail and Farewell'.

West:

Gabriel, cup bearer of the All-Holy,
Servant of the altar of life you have been with us.
We have reveled in the power and ecstasy of life
And your transcendent grace this night.
Gabriel, Herald of the High Self,
Accept our gratitude as we bid you 'Hail and Farewell'.

South:

Mikhael, Sword bearer of the All-Holy
Servant of the altar of life, you have been with us.
The fire of creation and the power of love
Have been with us, aiding us in transforming our spirits.
Mikhael, Protector, Patron of true priests,
Accept our gratitude as we bid you 'Hail and Farewell'.

Open Circle

3rd Night 2008 – Spirit of Gaia

Needs: Anointing oil, bowls of water and earth, incense and flame, bubbles and sparklers for all, the gate is open for all magickal creatures, gong & drums, CD & player, fairy, dragon, mermaid, gnome, quarter capes,

Cast & seal circle *(Quarters to be at regular places but facing center)*

East: *(holding incense, face circle center)*
I am Air! I am everywhere. I fill the fleshy pouches of your lungs; I stir all things and bend them to my will, from the smallest blade of grass to the tallest tree. I cool you with my breezes and destroy you with my storms, but without me, you would die. Am I not holy and worthy of praise?
(Receives a blessing from HPS)

HPS: (anoint)
Thou art holy and worthy of the highest praise. Receive the blessings of Spirit!

East:
Oh Gwydion, Prince of the Powers of Air, bring forth your breath! Lend us your powers of magick to forge the first mighty link in this sacred circle of power! Call forth the inhabitants of your fairy worlds, and lend us your wisdom and knowledge as we open the first portal of this sacred space. So mote it be!

South: *(holding flame, face center)*
I am Fire! I live in the guarded embers of campfires and even the pilot lights of stoves. I spring from the lightning, erupt from deep within the earth and can be a tool in the hands of men. I keep you warm, and yet I destroy you in my flames, but without me, you would die. Am I not holy and worthy of praise?

HPS: (anoint)
Thou art holy and worthy of the highest praise. Receive the blessings of Spirit!

South:
Oh, Bridget, Goddess of fire and beauty cast your flames and powers of magick around us to forge the second mighty link in this circle of power! Call forth the salamanders, creatures of fire, and bring the strength of your

hearth, your knowledge, and wisdom to us as we open the second portal of this sacred space. So mote it be!

Water: *(holding bowl of water)*

I am Water! I rise from the moist crevices of the Earth. I beat on the shores of Her body. I fall from the skies in silver sheets and race toward the sea in rivers and streams. I revive you and yet I take your breath away, but without me, you would die. Am I not holy and worthy of praise?

HPS: *(anoint)*

Thou art holy and worthy of the highest praise. Receive the blessings of Spirit!

Water:

Oh Mannon Mac Lir, God of the Seas, God of water, circle us with the power of your oceans and rivers and form the third mighty link in this circle of power. Call forth your merfolk to protect us and shower us with your love as we open the third portal of this sacred space! So mote it be!

Earth: *(holding bowl of earth)*

I am Earth! I am your Mother. From my body comes the fruit, grain, and animals which feed you. I am your support, and my force on your bodies keeps you held firmly to me. I am also your destroyer, but without me, you would never have been. Am I not holy and worthy of praise?

HPS: *(anoint)*

Thou art holy and worthy of the highest praise. Receive the blessings of Spirit!

Earth:

Oh Oghma, Binder, Keeper of the secrets of this earth, Ruler of knowledge and bringer of wisdom to humankind, shape this last and final link in this circle of power. Bring forth your creatures of the earth, the wee folk, and give us your heart as we open the forth portal of this sacred space and raise power within it. So mote it be!

HP:

When we speak of spirit, we speak of the realm of the 5th dimension—that which is beyond the basic senses of sight, hearing, touch, smell, and taste.

Yet if our perceptions are heightened, our vibratory rate increased, we CAN perceive that which lies beyond the veil, at the edge of our ordinary senses.

HPS:

Spirit pervades all, is part of all, just as all is a part of it. It is the divine spark within us, and we week to connect with spirit in its many guises. We seek Spirit in the breeze, the Prana that gives us life. We seek Spirit in the fire of passion and the flame of courage. We seek spirit in the waters from which we sprang and in feelings of emotion and love. We seek Spirit in the glories of Earth as we revel in the beauty of all creation. We seek Spirit in the mysteries profound, glimpsed faintly through the darkling glass...

HP:

But most of all, we seek Spirit within ourselves as we follow that inner voice, the voice that calls us, whispers to us, says to us:

I am within you. I am within all mankind and I am in all life forms and manifestations around you. I reach beyond this planet into the vast reaches of space. Seek me. Follow me, and I will lead you home.

HPS: Gaia, Mother, embodiment of this blue-green planet! Come to our call!
All: Gaia, Gaia!

Gaia:

Look at me! I am not a separate woman! I am a continuance of the blue sky; my womb is the water of the deep ocean and the clear blue lake. I am the strength of the mountains and the passion of the molten lava at earth's core. The winds are my breath, sending chills up your spine...

Open the gates to the other-world! Let all creatures of spirit join with me in celebration!

Enter fairies - to DonaCreaTun (give bubbles to all, dance and play, then pass out sparklers)

Enter Dragon - to drum beats and gong, light sparklers

Enter Mermaids - to conch shell or rain stick

Charlyn Scheffelman (Lady Nytewind)

Enter Tree, *(this costume included (homemade) stilts, and a very proficient young man that could handle them, even on the uneven ground!!)*

Enter gnome, troll, Unicorn to Trees of Annwn *(all of the above were appropriately costumed)* All dance and celebrate as fire circle begins!

At Dawn: Solar Salutation, by Katlyn Breene

East:

Gwydion, Sweet Prince of Air, return now, if you must, to the brisk Autumn breezes which are brimming with the excitement of the year's climax. Take with you our gratitude for your presence in our sacred circle this night. But stay if you will, and join us in feast and celebration. We bid you Hail and Farewell.

North:

Oghma, Keeper of the Secrets of the Earth, return now, if you must, to the Earth where worms burrow deeper and seeds nestle awaiting the long sleep of Winter. Take with you our gratitude for your presence in our sacred circle this night. But stay if you will, and join us in feast and celebration. We bid you Hail and Farewell.

West:

Great Mannon Mac Lir, God of Water and the Sea, return now, if you must, to the Autumn rains which cool Earth's fevered brow, baked in the heat of Summer afternoons. Take with you our gratitude for your presence in our sacred circle this night. But stay if you will, and join us in feast and celebration. We bid you Hail and Farewell.

South:

Fair Bridget, Goddess of fire and beauty, return now, if you must, to the dying fires of Autumn's heat soon to give way to Winter's chill. Take with you our gratitude for your presence in our sacred circle this night. But stay if you will, and join us in feast and celebration. We bid you Hail and Farewell.

Dismiss Circle:

Closing Ritual - 2008

(Cast circle hand to hand, sing "behold")

East: **Cannot find the author – eliminate what you need to**

I live on a planet, the blue planet
My feet patter it every day
So do others'.
My lungs breathe its air
So do others'.
The creatures also share
But our breath can't explain it.
We can't live without it.

South:

I live on a planet, The blue planet
My feet patter it every day
So do others.
Fire in the sky warms the earth;
The mighty earth, churning along
In sunlight and darkness and shadow
A star, a rock, a vessel of life.
We can't live without it

West:

I live on a planet, The blue planet
my feet patter it every day
And so do others.
I gulp its cycled rain
And so do others.
We make fountains, lakes and drains
Our blueprints plan it.
We can't live without it

North:

> I live on a planet, The blue planet
> My feet patter it every day
> So do others'.
> We stir the dust and clay
> And make our marks upon it.
> Life is a Mystery

HP: To be of the Earth is to know of restlessness,
HPS: of being a seed

HP: The darkness of being planted
HPS: The struggle toward the light

HP: The pain of growth into the light
HPS: The joy of bursting and bearing fruit

HP: The love of being food for someone
HPS: The scattering of your seeds

HP: The decay of the seasons
HPS: The mystery of death and the miracle of birth.
> By John Soos

HPS:

We came to this place to honor the land upon which we dwell, and to honor the life within us and the life within all things created. We came to change ourselves and our lives for our better good, and now we prepare to take what we have been given here back into our mundane lives.

We came in perfect love and perfect trust, to build bridges between each other, to honor our similarities and our differences, and our various paths as Pagan People. We came to honor the Earth, the good, green Earth.

HP:

I'd like to offer special thanks to our guest teachers for their wonderful contribution to our work, and to all of you, who came and worked and played and made this event possible; who drummed and danced and opened your hearts; who explored the deep, sometimes dark, places within; who dared to come and grow and transform in the presence of the Gods.

HPS:

Thanks to you--all the MMC members who pitched in and helped me so much this year, enabling the preparation for this event to proceed quite smoothly.

And thanks to all of you first-timers, who are now also members of the FireTribe, as similar alchemical fire circles occur in Nevada, California, Georgia, West Virginia, Massachusetts, New York, Oregon, Belize, Holland, Hawaii and perhaps other places by now.

HP: Thanks also to those who have returned to share their magick with us all; accept our heartfelt thanks for your presence at this event. We hope to see you all again next year.

HPS: Last and not at all least, let's heard for Art, who willingly puts up with us each year and works hard to make this camp the wonderful place that it is. (Yell "We love you, Art")

Chant: (3x) **CIRCLE OF LIGHT**

There's a circle of light around you
There's a circle of love in your heart
There's a circle of family around you,
There's a circle of you inside me.

Oh, sisters we love you
Oh sisters you help us to grow
Oh sisters we love you
My sisters we want you to know, that....

There's a circle of light around you
There's a circle of love in your heart
There's a circle of family around you,
There's a circle of you inside me

Oh, brothers we love you
Oh, brothers you help us to grow

Charlyn Scheffelman (Lady Nytewind)

Oh brothers we love you
My brothers we want you to know, that....

East: Ancient ones of the East, Portal of Air,
We thank thee for your presence here!
For dancing winds and sylphs of air
Winged ones, and birds of flight,
For power of thought, and spoken word
Healing ways and golden light
With Her breath, out and in,
With new knowledge we'll begin.
Stay if you will, but go if you must
We bid you hail and Farewell!

North: Ancient ones of the North, Portal of Earth,
We thank thee for your presence here!
For Wee Folk, Elves and Gnomes
Earth below, and sky above,
Creatures large and creatures small,
Seeds that grow, and flowers that bloom
With Her Body beneath our feet,
We've gathered for this Merry Meet
Stay if you will, but go if you must
We bid you hail and Farewell!

West: Ancient ones of the West, Portal of Water,
We thank thee for your presence here!
For Merfolk and water sprites,
The Mother's love and Secrets deep,
For lovers, sisters, brothers, friends,
And compassion that never ends.
By her blood, circling round
Love unconditional we've found.
Stay if you will, but go if you must
We bid you hail and Farewell!

South: Ancient ones of the South, Portal of Fire,
We thank thee for your presence here!

For Salamanders, and spirits of fire
Sparks and flames that transform
For the love and passion of life's flame
And fulfillment of will and desire.
With her Spirit as the spark
From this place we now embark.
Stay if you will, but go if you must
We bid you hail and Farewell!

Circle is Open

Workshops & Activities Offered during Spirit 2008

Humanity's Extraterrestrial Origins: by Arthur & Lynette Horn

Through their vast research, the Horns have made many discoveries that disprove the current scientific theory of evolution, including the sudden appearance and existence of advanced civilizations existing on this planet thousands of years ago. Dr. Horn also makes the case that humanity's real origins come from the constellation Lyra; specifically from a star system called Vega. From there our ancestors branched out to other areas of the galaxy, including the Pleiades. Some of our ancestors made lesser choices and became aggressive and war-like. Others made higher choices and are more spiritually advanced and benevolent.

The Inner Magick of Spiritual Alchemy, Part 1 & 2, Dr. Bruce S. Fisher, Author of *Science of Spiritual Alchemy Through the Art of Inner Magic (Personal Transformation), St. Germain : The Great Enigma - A Study Of The Adept As An Expression Of The Ultimate In Human Potential,* and *The Dark Night : Statements Concerning The Trials And Rewards Of The Spiritual Path.*

As human beings, we serve as the connection between an animal and a god. Our assignment then is redemption--that is, the redemption of consciousness from its attatchment to form, unfettering spiritual sight. Freeing up the all-seeing eye allows us to perceive the REAL--the interconnectedness of everything. The achievement of this goal is the true aim of the Great Work of

Spiritual Alchemy. This is the magick of Theurgy--the attainment of divine consciousness by developing and invoking our own higher faculties of abstract thought and intuition, our own inner god, which can then commune with other kindred entities. This is the true Hermetic Art.

Fire Circle Alchemy: *Nytewind*

Ancient mysteries and modern magic blend together to create the community fire circle, which is, for us, the elixir of life. In this workshop, you will learn the techniques that go into creating a vessel in which you can transform your personal lead into gold. Our workshop focuses on practical tools for transformation and provides an outline for the magic that happens in our community. Together, we will explore the Mysteries of the Fire Circle, and how to create safe, sacred space in which to become our highest vision. Drink deeply of these sacred secrets and prepare to be trance-formed in this fun exploration of symbol, ritual, and metaphor.

Damanhur and the Temples of Humankind, *Nytewind.*

I had seen some pictures of this temple on the Internet and was convinced there was a lot more to the story. I felt that they were time traveling, and wanted to see for myself, so I went to Italy. The temple is incredible, as the video will show, and yes, I met someone who confirmed my suspicions about time travel.

Quantum Evolution: Shannon Kennedy-Kahler - At SummerFest, 2007, Shannon introduced us to some of the most recent discoveries in Quantum Physics. She is back by popular demand this year to expand and update that knowledge.

Shannon has always been fascinated with science and the unexplained. Her search for uncovering the mysteries in the universe led her down many scientific paths as well as spiritual paths. Finding inspiration in Christianity, Hinduism, Buddhism, Taoism, Energy Healing, Paganism and Shamanism, ancient mysteries, Quantum Physics and Cosmology, she has set up her own lecture series called Quantum Evolution.

Quantum Evolution is the next gigantic leap in human evolution, a profound evolving of the human spirit rather than the physical body. As well as developing her lecture series, Shannon hopes to have a companion book finished by end of 2008 and available next year.

Optional Craft Project – Tee Shirts

We purchased purple tee shirts and had our basic Mountain Moon Circle logo printed on them. They were to be decorated and personalized at the craft table, which contained all kinds of fabric paints and sparkles, and everything we could think of that one might like to use. I think this was a big success.

Installations for Spirit, 2008

Portal of Spirit;

After this one, I thought to myself "I'll never be able to top this one!" And I never did. People were taken in groups after dark, continuing into the night I used a 10 X 20 gazebo with a 10 x 10 attached. The first gazebo was totally covered with black, including black painted tarps for the floor. I used one of those "disco" lights that pulsed colors in time to music, and *Spirit Rap*, by Astarius, one of my favorites; a very trance inducing piece. Following this, *Medicine Woman*, also by Astarius. One at a time, dancers entered and danced around – Air, robed in yellow, carrying a butterfly net; Fire, in red, carrying a hand-held fire bowl, Water, robed in blue, sprinkeling holy water, Earth in green, carrying a small bowl shaped like a leaf and filled with sand, and Spirit robed in purple, dancing with light sticks.

We had created a very large pentagram out of black plastic sprinkler pipe and rope. It took six of us to handle it. The small groups would wait in the little gazebo. Each person was then escorted outside, where they stood at the pentagram center, which was laying on the ground. We lifted the pentagram over their head, then said something like "receive the blessing of the Goddess" as we lowered it. I was surprised by the amount of power this action generated! It was great! (People stumbled away from that installation in a daze…in a good way!)

The Great Beyond: In front of a large open-air cabin, I created a graveyard with black plastic fence pieces, spider webs, spiders, and tombstones to create a scary atmosphere. This cabin was kind of an open air space, so we set up a 10 x 10 gazebo. The ceiling and walls were draped with seven colors of fabric to simulate a rainbow. A large fluffy cloud was on the back wall with these words stuck on it.

"What lies beyond the grave is naught to fear, for the souls of your loved ones await you here. Ancestors, too, here you will find, and love, and joy, and peace of mind."

Just below the "cloud" was a large, white unicorn statue, lying on a table covered with artificial grass and flowers. A representative of the God was hung in one back corner and the Goddess in the other. For these, I used blank white masks, taped little mirrors behind the eye holes, gave them crowns and gowns using white sparkly fabric to simulate their bodies.

There were two tables; near the front corners. One held Angel divination cards and the other was to honor your dead family members or friends with incense. They could also write the departed ones a little note, which would be burned later in ceremony.

There may have been other installations that I have lost track of, as well as the closing ceremony. I hope that some of you will be inspired and use some of these ideas in your own groups and events. We had a marvelous time putting together these special events and activities to honor the Gods and Goddesses, and the elements. We feel that people learned a great deal about Wicca through them.

I know that many, many people were healed, clarified their lives, became inspired, and were forever changed by the alchemical fire circles that Jeff McBride created. I was proud and happy that I could share them with others.

I would be happy to answer any questions you might have about any of the things that we did and used.

Blessed Be,
Nytewind

BIBLIOGRAPHY

Eddy, Karen. *Ganesha Script* on (page 74 and 83).

Phoenix, (page 96-97) **The Poems of John Dryden: Volume One: 1649-1681 p. 128**

Breene, Katlyn. *Solar Salutation* on page 85-86. The sunrise closing used for all fire circles: written for the Alchemical Fire Circle/Vegas Vortex

Conway, D. J. Salt, Water, Charcoal and Incense (110-111 & 115) taken from *Dancing with Dragons,* Llewellyn Publications, (1998).

Ikhnaton Songs to Aton on page 122 from http://www.love-egypt.com/hymn-to-the-sun.html ancient Egyptian text.

Maria Kay Simms. *A Witches Circle: Rituals and Craft of the Cosmic Muse,* Llewellyn publications, 2000, page 191. *Farewell to the elements.* My pages, 126 & 135.

Polynesian history, on page 145, information from www.starseeds.net/group/sorcerous-beings-mixed-and-in.../polynesian-spirituality

Io & Uli referenced www.ancienthuna.com/gods (adapted from Leenani Melvile, 1969).

Cunningham, Scott. *Prayer for Lughnassadh* in *Wicca, a Guide for the Solitary Practicioner,* on my page 139-140.

Fire Circle Orientation: by **Jeff & Spinner McBride, Michael Wall, and Dr. Joshua Levin** *on page 143 - 147.*

Jamie Sams. Information from *Clan Mothers*. http://nativehealth.tripod.com/ ClanMothers.html

Lucius Apuleius. From *The Golden Ass, Soul of Isis and Soul of Osiris* adapted on page 211-213.

American Druid Foundation (A.D.F.) ritual, by Isaac Bonewits, pages 194 - 206.

Tree Meditation (C) 1990 by P.E.I. (Isaac Bonewits). Tree Meditation on my pages 198-200. *Internet Book of Shadows* at sacred-texts.com

Ilan Shamir. *Advice from a Tree, 1999 on page 163.*

Soos, John. Quote; *To be of the Earth....* My pages, 165, 183 and 281.

Jeff & Spinner McBride. *The Alchemical Process,* my pages 188 - 190

Claude McKay *Thirst,* 2003, on my page 229.

Referenced D. J. Conway: *Magick of the Gods & Goddesses,* Llewellyn Publications, 1997

Printed in the United States
By Bookmasters